The Healthy Settings Approach in Hong Kong

Healthy Settings
SERIES

The Healthy Settings Approach in Hong Kong
Sustainable Development for Population Health

Albert LEE

香港城市大學出版社
City University of Hong Kong Press

All royalties from this book go to the Hong Kong Health Education and Health Promotion Foundation.

ISBN: 978-962-937-415-0

Published by
        City University of Hong Kong Press
        Tat Chee Avenue
        Kowloon, Hong Kong
        Website: www.cityu.edu.hk/upress
        E-mail: upress@cityu.edu.hk

Printed in Hong Kong

This book is dedicated to

my beloved wife, Emma, for her staunch and everlasting support
of my lifelong journey

my beloved son, Alpha, for bringing joy to the family
and enlightening me with his wisdom

Table of Contents

List of Tables

List of Information Boxes

List of Figures

Abbreviations

AFHC	Alliance for Healthy Cities
ATASO	Assessment Tool for Affective and Social Outcomes
BMI	body-mass index
BRFSS	Behavioural Risk Factor Surveillance System
CESCR	Committee on Economic, Social and Cultural Rights
CHEHP	Centre for Health Education and Health Promotion, Chinese University of Hong Kong
CIA	Central Intelligence Agency
CIST	Critical Incident Support Team
COPD	chronic obstructive pulmonary disease
COVID-19	coronavirus disease of 2019
CSDH	Commission on Social Determinants of Health
CSHP	Comprehensive School Health Programme
CWD	Central and Western District, Hong Kong
DALYs	disability adjusted life years
DH	Department of Health
DM	diabetes mellitus
DSRS	Depression Self-rating Scale
EAP	Employee Assistance Programme
EEA	European Economic Area
EMR	Eastern Mediterranean Region
EU	European Union

FCAC	Framework Convention on Alcohol Control
FCTC	Framework Convention on Tobacco Control
GDP	gross domestic product
GEQ	General Evaluation Questionnaire
GOPC	general outpatient clinic
GP	general practitioner
HA	Hospital Authority
HCP	Healthy City Programme
HI	high income
HIV/AIDS	human immunodeficiency virus/acquired immunodeficiency syndrome
HKHSA	Hong Kong Healthy School Award
HMSC	Health Management and Social Care
HOHCS	The Haven of Hope Christian Service
HPH	Health-promoting Hospital
HPS	Health-promoting School
HRBA	Human Rights-based Approach
ICESCR	International Covenant on Economic, Social and Cultural Rights
IPH	Institute of Public Health
IT	information technology
IUHPE	International Union for Health Promotion and Education
iYCG	Investing in Young Children Globally
KHCP	Korea Healthy Cities Partnership
KNUS	Knowledge Network on Urban Settings
KTD	Kwai Tsing District, Hong Kong
KTSCHCA	Kwai Tsing Safe Community and Healthy City Association
LIFE	Satisfaction with Life Scale

LMI	low-middle income
LPHP	Logan Public Health Plan
NCDs	non-communicable diseases
ND	Northern District, Hong Kong
NGO	non-governmental organisation
NHS	National Health Services
NIH	National Institute of Health
NICE	National Institute for Health and Care Excellence
PDCA	Pingtung Healthy City Association
PMH	Princess Margaret Hospital, Hong Kong
PTA	Parent-Teacher Association
RCT	randomised controlled trial
RTHK	Radio Television Hong Kong
SAR	Special Administrative Region
SARS	severe acute respiratory syndrome
SDGs	Sustainable Development Goals
SING	Study on Impact of Nutrition and Growth
SPS	Signature Project Scheme
SRRH	Special Rapporteur on the Right to Health
STD	sexually transmitted disease
SWOT	strengths, weaknesses, opportunities, threats
TKO	Tseung Kwan O, Hong Kong
UHC	universal health coverage
UK	United Kingdom
UKDH	United Kingdom Department of Health
UN	United Nations
US	United States

VW	Volkswagen AG
WHO	World Health Organisation
WHOQOL	World Health Organisation Quality of Life
WHSA	Wessex Healthy School Award
WPRO	Western Pacific Region
YRBS	Youth Risk Behaviour Survey

Healthy Settings Series Foreword

The role of healthy settings in the overall health of a person can best be discussed in the context of the public health pyramid described by Frieden (2015). Each level of the pyramid highlights specific interventions that can be made to better the health of a person or community. At the base of the pyramid are interventions that focus on changing socio-economic factors, such as income, education, housing, social inclusion, and race. This includes increasing public health efforts (e.g., through health insurance coverage that reduces poverty or through the prevention of teen pregnancy to reduce the perpetuation of poverty) and enhancing health services (e.g., establishing a better primary healthcare system with accessible preventive health care and health promotion services to empower self-management and self-care). However, effective intervention to better a person's heath via socio-economic conditions requires actions beyond the health sector. At the next level of the public health pyramid are interventions that change the context to make healthy choices the default decision (e.g., improvement of health literacy, creating supportive environments conducive to healthy living, and establishing healthy public policy). The next level is long-lasting protective interventions (e.g., immunisations requiring intermittent action by the healthcare system). The next level is clinical interventions requiring long-term, daily care (e.g., diabetes control and care measures). The top level includes personalised individual counselling and education. While the interventions at each level are important, those at the pyramid's base will generally improve the health of more people at a lower unit cost than those at the top.

In a world that is constantly changing and evolving, so too must our understanding of health. The health pyramid for the future needs to address the complexity of public health problems resulting from social, economic, political, biological, genetic, and environmental causes. Intersectoral collaboration, community participation, innovation, and setting approaches are important instruments to initiate and promote change. The "Healthy Settings Approach" advocated in this series attempts to highlight areas for change to better personal, community, and global health in the context of their environments — where people live, work, study, and interact — and point out possible remedies for health issues. Investigating different settings allows the approach to achieve balanced and proportionate development at all levels based on the health needs of different sectors of the population. The Healthy Settings Approach provides an integrated and holistic framework to understand public health, thus allowing policy, environmental, social, behavioural, and biomedical interventions to be pursued side by side.

The importance of healthy and sustainable settings for personal and community health has been advocated by many. Marmot and Bell (2012), for instance, emphasise an approach termed "proportionate universalism" and stress a need for action across the whole of society, focusing on social factors that determine health outcomes. They identified six domains for action: giving every child the best start in life; enabling all children, young people, and adults to maximise their capabilities and have control over their lives; creating fair employment and good work for all; ensuring a healthy standard of living for all; creating and developing healthy and sustainable places and communities; and strengthening the role and impact of ill-health prevention. Thus, any policies to be implemented need to consider both the people at the bottom of the health gradient and the gradient as a whole, ensuring that their impact is proportionately greater at the bottom end of the gradient. The Healthy Settings Approach facilitates policy development along this direction in promoting health in a variety of settings, including schools, municipalities, villages, workplaces, and primary healthcare venues.

To address the needs of these different settings and to better explain the Healthy Settings Approach and how to apply it, myself and others in the field have organised a series of books that make use of the most recent research as well as our own experiences. Topics in this series include:

- Healthy settings theories and practice
- Health-promoting schools and school improvement
- Healthy cities, social inclusion, and connectedness

- Health-promoting workplaces and total quality management
- Promoting health in the delivery of primary health care
- Health promotion policy

It is our hope that the series will build the concept and mediate implementation of the Health Settings Approach into day-to-day operations across a broad range of environments, both in Hong Kong and globally. This collection of publications is one step towards a "health for all" concept that will not only help us achieve the United Nation Sustainable Development Goals for 2030 (UN, 2015) but will also help increase the health and happiness of people across society.

Albert Lee
Series Editor-in-Chief
Healthy Settings Series

References

Frieden, T. R. (2015). "The future of public health". *New England Journal of Medicine*, Vol. 373, No. 18, pp. 1748–1754.

Marmot, M., and Bell, R. (2012). "Fair society, healthy lives". *Public health*, Vol. 126, Supp. 1, pp. S4–S10.

United Nations [UN]. (2015). *Transforming our world: The 2030 Agenda for Sustainable Development* [online]. Available at: https://sustainabledevelopment.un.org/post2015/transformingourworld/publication.

Foreword

I congratulate Professor Albert Lee on his book, *The Healthy Settings Approach in Hong Kong: Sustainable Development for Population Health.* I am honoured to have been invited to write a Foreword. I worked with Albert during our time as World Health Organisation (WHO) advisors (at the WHO Kobe Centre for Health Development) for the Knowledge Network of Urban Health of the Commission for Social Determinants of Health in 2006. Our thematic paper, "Improving Health and Building Human Capital through an Effective Primary Care System and Healthy Setting Approach", has highlighted the shift of this approach away from specific health behaviour changes towards creating the conditions supportive of health and well-being. The focus has switched from risk factors and population groups to organisational change. Organisational change ensures sustainability of the system. In our report, we described a model of how a comprehensive and integrated primary health care and healthy settings can cut across different levels and interact with each other, showing the interconnectedness of the three levels of intervention (individuals, families, and peers). This book serves as a new model of health improvement and building up human capital. The COVID-19 pandemic has forced us to rethink the importance of strong community action for health protection and health promotion, leading to a greater emphasis on developing closer collaborations between different settings.

I have had several other opportunities to work with Albert, including a collaboration with the Institute of Medicine (now renamed the National Academy of Medicine), USA Forum on Investing in Young Children Globally (iYCG) from 2013–2016. In 2015, iYCG held a workshop "Using Existing Platforms to Integrate and Coordinate Investments for Children". The key objective at this workshop was to define and identify platforms and settings, such as schools, to scale up coordination. In my keynote address, I presented the Chilean experience of the national programme "Chile Grows with You", which targets children aged 0 to 4 (and plans to be extended to children 8 years of age), and highlighted the importance and lessons learned from implementing this intersectorial public policy on childhood and social protection. These findings were based on two important elements: making use of the available resources, including a health system with good primary health care; and working with general practitioners and other health professionals. We used a holistic, evidence-based and life-course approach.

It is very important to have more publications on healthy settings and, in particular, about how the approach integrates different sectors and how synergy between them is enhanced. In the face of the global pandemic and other crises, it is more relevant than ever to address the challenge of achieving sustainable development goals for a better and more sustainable future for all.

I would like to congratulate Albert and his contributing authors in their efforts to substantiate the implementation of the Healthy Settings Approach. This book is good resource for practitioners and policy makers, and I am sure it will contribute to and strengthen the current literature in the healthy settings field in addition to helping inform and enhance current policies and practices.

Dra Helia Molina Milan
Past Minister of Health
Dean of the Faculty of Medical Science
at The University of Santiago, Chile

Foreword

I am delighted to write a Foreword for the book *The Healthy Settings Approach in Hong Kong: Sustainable Development for Population Health* by Professor Albert Lee. Professor Lee and I are among the pioneers in healthy city development in the Western Pacific Region, both starting in the field in the early 1990s. Our efforts and those of our colleagues culminated in the establishment of the Alliance for Healthy Cities (AFHC) during the World Health Organisation (WHO) consultation meeting in Manila in 2003. The first AFHC Global Conference was held in Kuching in 2004, and Professor Lee was invited to be one of our plenary speakers. He outlined the evaluation of healthy cities and introduced the "SPIRIT" framework for accreditation of cities for AFHC Healthy City Awards. The SPIRIT framework is described in detail in Chapters 2 and 3 along with an evaluation framework covering input, process, and impact, which can be used to measure the success of a healthy city.

In 2001, Professor Lee also successfully developed the "Hong Kong Healthy School Award", further establishing him as one of the leading experts utilising the Healthy Settings Approach to improve population health. I also worked closely with him when we were WHO temporary advisors for the Knowledge Network of Urban Settings of the Commission for Social Determinants of Health in 2006 at the WHO Kobe Centre for Health Development. We wrote a thematic paper on "Improving Health and Building Human Capital through an Effective Primary Care System and Healthy Settings Approach". The intervention strategy recommended in this paper involves developing a comprehensive primary health care system to join up different settings for health promotion and integrating the efforts of different parties and stakeholders within and outside the health sector. Different components of the primary health care team would then work more closely with individuals and families as well as different healthy settings. Closer integration of primary health care and healthy settings would almost certainly help to solve the problem of essential services not being delivered to the population groups with the greatest needs. This model will help to improve accessibility of essential services to less advantaged group. The COVID-19 pandemic has shown us the importance of delivering essential services to vulnerable population groups. The Healthy Settings Approach facilitates the integration of different sectors and different disciplines.

Professor Lee was again invited to be a plenary speaker for the AFHC Global Conference in Kuching in 2018 on "Enhancing Sustainable Development Goals and Health Equity via Healthy Setting Approach". He mapped out the significant contribution of the Healthy Settings Approach to achieve health equity and sustainable development in line with UN's Sustainable Development Goals (SDGs) to be achieved by 2030.

Professor Lee, with his substantial experience as both a primary care and public health physician as well as his deep engagement in public and social services, shares his insights in this book and successfully puts health in the context of daily living in different settings. In these pages, he discusses not only the principles and concepts of different healthy settings, but also the broader framework for measuring the success of the strategies adopted. This multifaceted focus provides tools to help the schools, cities, workplaces, and healthcare organisations implementing the approach to be successful in their efforts to improve health. This book is a useful reference for professionals seeking to learn how to make use of different settings for health promotion and disease prevention as well as how to design appropriate measuring tools for monitoring and evaluation. Researchers will also find this book useful when generating new research ideas involving healthy settings. Lastly, Professor Lee's book will undoubtedly generate more intellectual exchange on healthy settings among healthcare professionals, academics, social scientists, public policy makers, government officials, and politicians.

Professor Dr Andrew Kiyu
Former Director of Sarawak State Health Department, Malaysia

Foreword

I am delighted to write a Foreword of the book *The Healthy Settings Approach in Hong Kong: Sustainable Development for Population Health* by Professor Albert Lee. I have known Albert for over two decades and we have worked closely in the development of Family Medicine and Primary Care. Albert has published a lot in the field of Family Medicine, Public Health, Health Promotion, and Primary Health Care. He is one of the pioneers in applying the Healthy Settings Approach to promote population health and synergy across settings, focusing on schools, municipal settings, workplaces, and primary healthcare settings.

Albert has supported various districts in Hong Kong as well as in overseas locations in their adoption of the Healthy Settings Approach. One of his greatest achievements is his success in facilitating the "Medical-Social-Community" model in Kwai Tsing District, Hong Kong, by linking various healthy settings, including Healthy Cities, Health-promoting Schools, Health-promoting Workplaces, Health-promoting Housing Estates, and Health-promoting Hospitals. This led to the establishment of the first District Health Centre in Kwai Tsing, a government funded primary healthcare initiative following the Policy Speech of Chief Executive of Hong Kong Special Administrative Region in 2017.

Integrated primary healthcare systems and comprehensive healthy settings models can be implemented and monitored to allow for the greatest level of interconnectedness between individuals, families, and peers. As Albert's research has shown, this would strengthen the primary healthcare delivery system, leading to better health improvement across diverse communities. The COVID-19 pandemic has only further highlighted how important it is to promote closer collaboration of different settings. The Healthy Settings Approach provides seamless cooperation across primary, secondary, tertiary, and quandary levels of care, particularly when applied with the active engagement of primary healthcare providers.

I would like to congratulate Albert and his contributing authors in their research and the publication of this book. In it they share their knowledge and experience in the implementation of the Healthy Settings Approach in a variety of settings. This book is undoubtedly a good resource for healthcare practitioners and policy makers searching for evidence underlying the success of the Healthy Settings Approach and for ways to incorporate the approach into policies and practice.

Dr Donald K. T. Li
President of World Organisation of Family Doctors (WONCA)

Foreword

It is my privilege to be asked to write one of the Forewords for this book. So that you, the reader, may know more about Professor Albert Lee and the Healthy Settings Approach, please allow me to tell you some of what he has accomplished.

Professor Takehito Takano from Tokyo, Professor Francis Baum from Adelaide, Professor Lee from Hong Kong, and I were among the academic collaborators involved in Healthy City development in the Western Pacific Region during the WHO consultation meeting in Manila in 2003, which led to the establishment of the Alliance for Healthy Cities (AFHC). Albert was one of the founding members of the Steering Committee of the AFHC and has been instrumental in promulgating Healthy City development. In his pioneering work on the assessment of healthy school initiatives, he developed the "SPIRIT" framework to evaluate the progress of healthy cities as they are being developed. This framework is used as an assessment tool for the AFHC Healthy City Award. Albert also chaired the Scientific Committee of the 2014 AFHC Global Conference and was as an awardee of the AFHC Pioneer Award in Research in October 2014.

AFHC is an international network aimed at protecting and enhancing the health of city dwellers. The group of cities and other organisations involved in the network try to achieve this goal by using the Healthy Cities Approach. The AFHC believes that international cooperation is an effective and efficient tool, and promotes the interaction of people who are in the front lines of health issues. The AFHC also advocates for linking up different settings to exert synergistic actions to improve population health. The "SPIRIT" framework puts strong emphasis on the Healthy Settings Approach. Presentations on different "healthy settings" have always been the highlight of AFHC Global Conferences. The theme of the 2014 Global Conference was "Health in All Policies", and the presentations and discussions focused on ways to assist policy makers in the systematic integration of health, well-being, and equity. The theme of the 2018 Global Conference was "Our Cities, Our

SDGs, Our Journey", which brought concerns about human development and health equity to the forefront. This theme complemented more traditional efforts that prioritise economic and environmental sustainability. Albert was invited to be plenary speaker at the 2018 conference on the theme of "Enhancing Sustainable Development Goals and Health Equity via the Healthy Setting Approach". In his presentation, he mapped out the significant contribution of the Healthy Settings Approach towards achieving health equity and sustainable development in line with the UN's Sustainable Development Goals (SDGs) for 2030. The role of Healthy City development to make cities and human settlements inclusive, safe, resilient, and sustainable (SDG 11) has only been further stressed by the COVID-19 pandemic. The Healthy Settings Approach is, thus, an important tool for strengthening the implementation and revitalisation of the Global Partnership for Sustainable Development (SDG Goal 17).

This book is full of useful guidance for policy makers, practitioners, and administrators of varying settings in their efforts to promote health and well-being of their communities and fellow citizens. The AFHC will also find helpful resource materials in this book to help in their collaborative effort to promote the Healthy City movement. I congratulate Albert and the contributing authors for their work in taking the Healthy Settings Approach to a higher level.

Professor Keiko Nakamura
Head of Secretariat of the Alliance for Healthy Cities;
Director of WHO Collaborating Centre for Healthy Cities
and Urban Policy Research;
and Professor and Chair of the Department of Global Health Entrepreneurship,
Graduate School of Medical and Dental Sciences,
Tokyo Medical and Dental University, Japan

Preface

The third Sustainable Development Goal (SDG) for 2030 established by the United Nations is to "ensure healthy lives and promote well-being for all at all ages". This goal refers to more than just the prevention of premature death, it is also about empowering individuals and communities to achieve optimal health. Health is more than the absence of disease or infirmity; it is a state of complete physical, mental, and social well-being. To improve their health, people must increase control over the determinant factors of their health (Ottawa Charter for Health Promotion, 1986). In particular, efforts should be made to promote equity in health, as emphasised in the World Health Organisation's "Health For All" principles. Health depends on the personal lifestyles and living conditions of individuals, as well as a host of complex physical, social, and economic determinants. These determinants go beyond healthcare; thus, a concerted effort of all sectors of the community is required to bring about sustained improvement in public health. At the time of this book's publication, the world is still reeling and recovering from the COVID-19 pandemic. The implementation of physical measures to interrupt or reduce the spread of respiratory viruses based on sustained physical distancing, restricted social gathering, and "shut down" measures, have a strong potential to reduce the magnitude of the epidemic peak of COVID-19. Successful implementation of those measures is largely dependent on precautionary behaviour of the population. It requires society to have an understanding of the boarder dimensions of health promotion in the context of everyday life.

Notwithstanding the increasing expenditures to healthcare services, we are still observing health inequalities within communities as well as inequities between high-income (HI) and low-middle-income (LMI) countries. Investments in healthcare systems have largely ignored social structure, especially when it comes to providing services to vulnerable populations. Like developed countries in the West, developing countries also struggle with the burden of chronic diseases but at an even faster pace. Meanwhile, communicable diseases still pose a big health burden in both HI and LMI countries, and the impact of globalisation on non-communicable diseases (NCDs) and mental health in LMI countries has been minimal.

Contemporary society exposes people to more health risk factors, and failure to recognise the importance of non-health-sector contributions to health improvement places a greater burden on conventional health care providers. Subsidised or free health services for LMI countries would only solve immediate concerns and ignore the local culture and social contexts that lead to inequitable distribution of health. Such efforts treat symptoms rather than the cause and may ultimately have a negative impact on the system of governance in the future.

There is a global aspiration for all citizens to enjoy the highest attainable standard of health. However, the standard varies in different parts of the world, and there is a need for a universal standard to be established. The Healthy Settings Approach provides social structures so people can participate in healthy activities in the context of their daily lives. This approach facilitates the "right to health" as it argues for investments that address multiple determinants of health at all levels of society.

This book reflects how the Healthy Settings Approach can ensure healthy living in different countries, with a particular focus on the Asia Pacific Region, as well as how health promotion in different settings can facilitate different SDGs. To help illustrate this, each chapter starts with a brief explanation of a fictitious example. In this hypothetical situation, "City-super", the superintendent of the city, embarks on a journey to learn more about the Healthy Settings Approach. He reflects on what he learns and provides advice to the City Mayor to enhance the health and well-being of his fellow citizens.

Why we need the Healthy Settings Approach and how it works are the focus of the **Preamble** and **Chapter 1**, while later chapters focus on particular settings. The concept of a Healthy City (described in **Chapter 2**) and several case studies (described in **Chapter 3**), illustrate how implementing this approach can make cities more inclusive, safe, resilient, and sustainable (SDG 11). Some of these case studies even report that Healthy City initiatives protect, restore, and promote sustainable use of terrestrial ecosystems, and can reverse land degradation and halt biodiversity loss (SDG 15). This is further exemplified in **Chapter 4**, which focuses on urban environments in Hong Kong and reveals both the detrimental and positive effects of urban development by assessing city health profiles for two districts.

Chapter 5 describes the evaluation and monitoring framework for Health-promoting Schools (HPSs), while **Chapter 6** reports the effectiveness of these tools. The Healthy Settings Approach applied in an educational context encourages the healthy development of children and adolescents from a much broader perspective than conventional approaches. This "Healthy School movement" can help to ensure inclusive and equitable quality education and promote lifelong learning opportunities for all (SDG 4).

Chapter 7 shifts to focus on healthy workplaces and how understanding the environment and individual wellness is essential to promote health within the workforce while enhancing productivity and economy. The measures described in this chapter are in line with SDG 8, which is to achieve sustained and inclusive economic growth, full and productive employment, and decent work for all.

The next chapter focuses on the health care system. Studies have shown that many households in HI countries have family members with chronic conditions, and they carry severe economic burdens as a result, even in communities with a well-developed health care system or universal health coverage. Therefore, universal health coverage is not a panacea if the resources for broader public health and preventive services are channelled towards covering clinical services at an individual level. It is important for healthcare organisations to collaborate with other sectors beyond health that have the capacity to control the determinants of communicable and NCDs. **Chapter 8** provides some success stories of how healthcare organisations have engaged with community organisations to improve the health of the population, while **Chapter 9** uses focus group interviews to zoom in how parents in Hong Kong and Scotland view the measures of and barriers to successfully prevent childhood obesity.

The right to health should ensure a healthy environment with minimal exposure to health risks, as well as enhanced opportunities for protective measures. **Chapter 10** revisits the Healthy Settings Approach and argues for its implementation to ensure the right to proper healthcare and living environments. The approach highlights tools which can be used to accomplish SDG 16, which promotes peaceful and inclusive societies for sustainable development, access to justice for all, and effective, accountable, and inclusive institutions at all levels. Lastly, **Chapter 11** provides some final insights about the Healthy Settings Approach and a conclusion to the City-super example narrative.

Taken together, this book aims to improve health and well-being as well as enhance urban governance, school effectiveness, productivity, and re-orientation of health services to meet the needs of the population. The Healthy Settings Approach can be an effective means to help poor, vulnerable, and marginalised groups access health-related services and improve the quality of life for all. It is also time for the community to start taking action to prepare for future health crises. A move towards healthier settings and environments across sectors, socio-economic divides, and locations will not only promote individual and collective health but will provide a platform for strengthening and revitalising global partnerships for sustainable development (SDG 17). With a focus on addressing the social determinants of health, this book provides a reference for professionals and practitioners in the fields of health and social care, education, community service, and public administration and policy, who are interested in improving population health and quality of life.

Albert Lee
June 2021

Preamble

Why We Need a Healthy Settings Approach

City-super (fictitious name) is working as a special assistant to the City Mayor. The Mayor received several reports concerning the level of physical fitness and sub-optimal functional health status of the residents of the city. The reports did not make explicit which particular aspect(s) of health was of great concern. The Mayor called City-super asking him or her (hereafter refer as "him") to contact the City Health Authority and City Public Health Bureau to improve the situation.

City-super had a meeting with senior representatives of the City Health Authority. They told City-super that they had reviewed the city's health statistics based on hospital activities. There was no major increase in hospital admissions or visits to outpatient clinics. They did not identify any changing disease patterns, but they said they would closely monitor the situation. To promote greater health in the city's population, they suggested seeking advice from the City Public Health Bureau.

Thus, City-super met with the City Public Health Bureau. The representatives mentioned that they did not detect any major changes in mortality or morbidity patterns for the city's residents. They suggested talking to the Sport and Recreation Bureau for improving the general fitness of the population. They also suggested contacting the Social Work Bureau because there may be psycho-social issues causing a sub-optimal health status.

Following their advice, City-super visited the Sport and Recreation Bureau. They agreed to provide more facilities for sports and exercise. They also started a programme for people diagnosed as "unfit" to help them improve their fitness. City-super asked how these individuals would be diagnosed. They told him that some schools would perform fitness tests for students and adults, and individuals could also be referred to the programme by their family physician. However, the number of referrals was low as not all schools or family physicians performed routine fitness assessments.

City-super then discussed with the Education Bureau whether every school should conduct an annual assessment of physical fitness for students. Their response was that individual schools would decide on the scale and time frame of fitness assessments through school-based management. City-super then met with a local group of family physicians to ask whether they would be willing to conduct periodic assessments of their patients' fitness. The physicians indicated that they would conduct the assessments based on need and refer any individuals for further training if necessary.

City-super finally visited the Social Work Bureau to request improving the psycho-social well-being of the city's population. The Bureau agreed to step up measures for cases referred to social workers. However, they could not commit additional manpower to work with individuals without known psycho-social problems.

Over the course of these various meetings, City-super had been in contact with colleagues from many different departments and disciplines, but he was not given any constructive advice to rectify the situation. Considering this, City-super reflected, asking himself: "Do we have a system to address health promotion within our city?" The answer seemed to be "Sorry, no."

The situation outlined above is a common one. In many countries, there is a well-structured health care system to address diseases and illnesses but there is no system addressing health, particularly the promotion of positive health. The United Nations has set Sustainable Development Goals (SDGs) to be achieved by 2030, called the "UN 2030 Agenda" (United Nations [UN], 2015). These goals are structured to enable our planet to not only be more peaceful and pleasant for those living on it, but they also seek to bring equality and equity to mankind irrespective of age, gender, ethnicity, or socio-economic background. SDG 3 — "Ensure healthy lives and promote well-being for all at all ages", for example, is referring to more than just the prevention of premature death but also includes the empowerment of individuals and communities to protect themselves from harm and enhance their capacity to achieve optimal health and well-being. Regarding the right to health, there is a global aspiration for all citizens to enjoy the highest attainable standard of health. However, this standard varies among different countries and locations, and it might not be justifiable or equitable to impose a fixed standard. Even so, a universal standard would still provide a benchmark for health. The Ottawa Charter for Health (WHO, 1986) asserts that "health is created and lived by people within the setting of their everyday life; where they learn, work, play, and love".

After three decades, the Ottawa Charter is still seen as a "gold standard" for health promotion practitioners worldwide wishing to improve health and enhance health equity. However, the opportunities to transfer these principles into the radical changes and practical solutions needed globally to improve health are still missing. Thompson et al. (2018), for instance, examined how the Ottawa Charter had influenced health care policies in the UK and found that the emphasis is still very much focused on personal responsibility and behavioural change, rather than tackling fundamental societal issues. While the Ottawa Charter itself may not fully address these issues, some of the concepts it inspired, including the Healthy Settings Approach, are making greater headway as they are implemented in more locations. It is only natural that the settings where people live, play, learn, and work are a part of the framework for building healthy public policy and re-orienting health services to promote and protect health. Using an approach that encompasses all of the environments an individual encounters will allow health to be viewed as more than just treatment. It will instead promote the strengthening of community actions for better health, building up of personal health skills to enhance health literacy, and the development of greater health advocacy.

The Healthy Settings Approach has a long history of being organised around settings such as schools, communities, and workplaces. It is an umbrella term for concepts such as Health-promoting Schools, Health-promoting Workplaces, Health-promoting Health Care Organisations, and Healthy Cities, and provides the social structures to reach the defined population and deliver health promotion activities in the context of people's daily lives. The Healthy Settings Approach has the ability to translate change into real terms that fit the context of each particular setting. This approach is an ecological model of health promotion in which health is determined by a complex interaction of environmental, organisational, and personal factors. It can be used to tackle the determinants of health at the downstream, midstream, and upstream levels, and reduce health inequities. The Healthy Settings Approach also facilitates the right to health for all as it argues for investment in social systems in which people spend their daily lives and addresses the multifactorial determinants of an individual's health at all levels of society.

Winslow (1920) defined public health as

> the science and the art of preventing disease, prolonging life, and promoting physical health and efficiency through organized community efforts for the sanitation of the environment, the control of community infections, the education of the individual in principles of personal hygiene, the organization of medical and nursing service for the early diagnosis and preventive treatment of disease, and the development of the social machinery which will ensure to every individual in the community a standard of living adequate for the maintenance of health. (p. 30)

Similarly, Mckeown and Lowe (1974) concluded that social advances in general living conditions, such as improved sanitation and nutrition, have been responsible for the decrease in mortality rate achieved during the last century. The contribution of medicine to this reduce mortality level has been minor compared with the contribution of improved environmental conditions. Promoting health is not just the business of health professionals within the healthcare industry, but is "everybody's business" (National Health Services [NHS] Providers, 2017). Viewed through the lens of the Healthy Settings Approach, public health is concerned with a health problem, based on the assumption that the social, physical, and political environments play major roles in the amelioration of the problem (Hanlon and Pickett, 1984), but it is distinguished from other approaches by its focus on comprehensively understanding the ways in which lifestyles and living conditions determine health status.

It is important to recognise the need to mobilise resources and make sound investments in policies, programmes, and services which create, maintain, and protect health by supporting healthy lifestyles and creating supportive environments for health. Tulchinsky and Varavikova (2014) described this concept of "New Public Health" as

> a cumulative philosophy of saving lives and improving health by a wide variety of professions and methods based on scientific achievements in the context of societal responsibility for the health and well-being of the population. The New

> Public Health is a composite of social policy, law, and ethics, with integration of social, behavioral, economic, management, and biological sciences. It is an intersectoral and interdisciplinary application of social policy, health promotion, preventive, and curative health services, all of which are vital to sustain and improve health for individuals and populations. (p. xxiii)

The Healthy Settings Approach can, therefore, be used to build the capacity of individuals, families, and communities to create strong human and social capital. There is a widespread myth that economic growth will improve health conditions. In fact, one should aim to improve population health conditions to enhance the economy. It will take years to build up the economy, but it only takes a short time to see the impact of poor population health and the burden it creates on society and community resources. The notion of human and social capital begins to offer explanations as to why certain communities are unable to achieve better health compared to other communities with similar demographics (Yamaguchi, 2014). Thus, the synergistic effects of different settings and how they can be used to improve population health and reduce health inequity require exploration.

Chapter 1

The Settings Approach for Health Promotion: How Does It Work?

Albert Lee

City-super, the special assistant to the City Mayor, suggested to the Mayor that the Healthy Settings Approach should be adopted to solve the community's health concerns. The Mayor responded, "Excellent idea! Please help us implement this approach." City-super then wondered, "How can we apply the Healthy Settings Approach? How does it work?" Although City-super had obtained post-graduate qualifications in public health as well as public policy, and had been appointed as the special assistant to the Mayor so he could research better public policies for the city (focusing on health and well-being of the residents), he was not familiar with the Healthy Settings Approach or how it would enhance health promotion.

Evolution of Health Promotion

We have been largely successful in improving the health of the population by minimising risk factors through education and regulation as well as through better disease management and preventive measures, such as immunisation, periodic screening, and better access to health services. This leads to the question: What added value would result from implementing the Healthy Settings Approach? To appreciate the changing needs of a population and the benefits of implementing the Healthy Settings Approach, it is important to first understand the evolution of health promotion.

Pre-modernisation

During the pre-modernisation period (19th century), the main health threat was life-threatening infectious diseases with acute onset. The goal of health promotion at that time was to protect people by minimising health hazards and promoting better hygiene. The measurement of success was based on the reduction of mortality and incidence of diseases. A biomedical approach was used to find out the aetiological agent(s) and remove them, leading to the rapid decline of the disease. While this benefits the community, it did not address the complexity of health promotion. It was during this period that Snow (1849) identified polluted water as the source of the cholera outbreak in the mid-19th century. This was the first published germ theory of disease.

Post-World War II

Although infectious diseases still constituted a major health burden in the late 1900s and early 2000s, chronic diseases accounted for a much greater portion of the global health burden (Horton and Sargent, 2018). The first major step towards addressing these issues was the Ottawa Charter for Health established in 1986 (WHO, 1986). Table 1.1 outlines the evolution of health promotion since the Ottawa Charter and includes various Declarations of Health Promotion and recommendations by leading scholars up to the early 21st century.

The health-risk behaviours contributing to the leading causes of mortality and morbidity later in life, such as cardiovascular disease, cerebrovascular disease, and malignant neoplasm, are often established during childhood and extend into adulthood. The Declaration of the High-level Meeting of the General Assembly on the Prevention and Control of Non-communicable Diseases (NCDs) was adopted by the United Nations General Assembly in September 2011 (UN, 2011). It set out a new international agenda on the prevention and control of key NCDs. The World Health Organisation (WHO) pointed out that, with the exception of sub-Saharan Africa, NCD-related mortality "exceeds that of communicable, maternal, perinatal, and nutritional conditions combined", accounting for 36 million

Table 1.1: Global Movement of Health Promotion

Sources	Key contents
Adelaide Recommendations on Healthy Public Policy: *Extracts from the Second International Conference on Health Promotion in Adelaide, Australia* (WHO, 1988)	• Healthy public policy is characterised by an explicit concern for health and equity in all areas of policy and by accountability for health impact. • The main aim of health-focused public policy is to create a supportive environment to enable people to lead healthy lives. Such a policy makes health choices possible or easier for citizens. • In the pursuit of healthy public policy, government sectors concerned with agriculture, trade, education, industry, and communications need to consider health as an essential factor when formulating policy. • These sectors should be accountable for the health consequences of their policy decisions. They should pay as much attention to health as to economic considerations.
The 3rd International Conference of Health Promotion was held in Sundsvall, Sweden, in 1991 and the focus was on creating supportive environments (WHO, 1991)	Key strategies at the community level are: • Strengthening advocacy through community action, particularly through groups organised by women. • Enabling communities and individuals to take control over their health and environment through education and empowerment. • Building alliances for health and supportive environments in order to strengthen the cooperation between health and environmental campaigns and strategies. • Mediating between conflicting interests in society in order to ensure equitable access to supportive environments for health.
Ten Vital Signs of Quality Health Promotion (Catford, 1993)	• Understanding and responding to people's needs fairly • Building on sound theoretical principles and understanding • Demonstrating a sense of direction and coherence • Collecting, analysing, and using information • Re-orienting key decision makers • Connecting with all sectors and settings • Using complementary approaches at both individual and environmental levels • Encouraging participation and ownership • Providing technical and managerial training and support • Undertaking specific actions and programmes
Jakarta Declaration on Health Promotion into the 21st Century (WHO, 1997)	• Promote social responsibility for health • Increase investments for health development • Consolidate and expand partnerships for health • Increase community capacity and empower the individual • Secure an infrastructure for health promotion

Mexico Ministerial Statement for the Promotion of Health: From Ideas to Action (WHO, 2000)	• To position the promotion of health as a fundamental priority in local, regional, national, and international policies and programmes.
	• To take the leading role in ensuring active participation of all sectors and civil society, in the implementation of health-promoting actions to strengthen and expand partnerships for health.
	• To support the preparation of country-wide plans of action for promoting health, if necessary drawing on the expertise in this area of WHO and its partners.
	• These plans will vary according to the national context, but will follow a basic framework agreed upon during the Fifth Global Conference on include among others:
	  – The identification of health priorities and the establishment of healthy public policies and programmes to address these.
	  – The support of research which advances knowledge on selected priorities.
	  – The mobilisation of financial and operational resources to build human and institutional capacity for the development, implementation, monitoring and evaluation of country-wide plans of action.

Table 1.1: Continued

Sources	Key contents
The Health Society: Importance of the New Policy Proposal by the EU Commission on Health and Consumer Affairs (Kickbusch, 2005)	• To protect citizens from risks and threats which are beyond the control of individuals and cannot be effectively tackled alone (e.g., unsafe commercial practice, unsafe products) • To enhance the ability of citizens to make better decisions about health • To mainstream health and consumer policy objectives, putting health on agenda
Bangkok Charter for Health (WHO, 2005)	• Advocacy • Invest in sustainable policies, actions, and infrastructure to address the determinants of health • Capacity building for policy development, leadership, health promotion practice, knowledge transfer and research, and health literacy • Regulate and legislate • Partner and build alliances with public, private, non-governmental, and international organisations and civil society to create sustainable actions
Nairobi conference closes with adoption of Call to Action (October 2009) (WHO, 2009a)	A consultation is under way with global health programmes, developing a practical package of evidence on health-promoting interventions that addresses the top health risks and the conditions with the highest disease burden. This product will be examined in the light of experience from various countries and emerge as consolidated, practical guidance for countries. *Call to action* • A political statement that calls for the inclusion of health promotion outcomes within the design of development programmes will be drafted through an expert- and Web-based consultation in the months leading up to the conference and will be adopted on the last day of the conference. • Advocacy for extending the international development goals to include non-communicable conditions will also proceed in parallel. The possibility of a launch of a Partnership Council on Non-communicable Diseases is being considered.
Shanghai Declaration on Promoting Health in the 2030 Agenda for Sustainable Development (9th Global Conference on Health Promotion) (WHO, 2016)	• We recognize that health and well-being are essential to achieving sustainable development. • We will promote health through action on all the SDGs • We will make bold political choices for health • Cities and communities are critical settings for health • Health literacy empowers and drives equity

deaths (63% of the global total), 80% of which occurred in low- and middle-income countries (WHO, 2011). The main areas of health concerns for healthcare systems and policy makers in the modern 21st century are:

- an ageing population;

- increasing health care expenditures;

- disrupted flow of health information, health products, and health services;

- increasing debate on rights and responsibilities; and

- changing views of the importance of health as major goal in life and a key component of a citizen's rights.

There is an overwhelming need to address the growing inequalities in access to resources for prevention and treatment of NCDs through improved regulations across jurisdictions to eliminate the legal and practical barriers for control of NCDs (Niessen et al., 2018). NCDs account for one-third of premature deaths so it is important to reduce the risk factors for NCDs early on in life (Norheim et al., 2015). Public health interventions should be re-oriented to minimise the exposure of citizens to high-risk health behaviours and to modify the lifestyle of the population, as these changes would substantially reduce the number of premature deaths and increase global health and life expectancy (WHO, 2011). According to Marmot et al. (2010) and Buck et al. (2018), the movement towards becoming a healthy society will need to:

- expand citizens' empowerment and choices as well as their rights and general health literacy;

- recognise the increasing presence of health in the marketplace and ensure consumer safety;

- address the problems of health inequalities; and

- recognise that the boundaries between different components of the health care delivery system, such as health promotion, disease prevention, treatment, and rehabilitation, are becoming increasingly blurred and need greater integration.

Furthermore, the UK Department of Health (DH) went on to indicate their new approach to the health of the public in 2004, specifying that the programme will need to

- respond to the needs and wishes of the citizens;

- reflect the realities of people's lives;

- respect the diversity of choices of individuals;

- realise the impact of consumer society;

- address the fact that some people and groups have been left behind; and

- reconnect with people by listening to their views, to get in touch with their real concerns; asking what *they* want, how *they* can be helped; and reshaping public health policy based on these responses.

The evolutionary change of health promotion has called for creating better health of citizens in their natural homes and working environments so health can be more connected to their daily lives. The Healthy Settings Approach provides the most logical route forward.

The New Millennium

In 1975, only five cities worldwide had 10 million or more residents (classified as "megacities") and three of these cities were in developing countries. The number of megacities increased to 23 by 2014 with more in developing countries (WHO Centre for Health Development, 2008), and this is expected to increase to 30 by 2025, with around 6.8 billion people living in these urban areas (Lineback and Lineback Gritzner, 2014). Urbanisation can be beneficial for health as urban areas can improve health via their various material, service provision, cultural, and aesthetic attributes. In fact, improvements in mortality and morbidity rates as well as increased health-promoting features of modern cities have been observed in highly urbanised countries, such as Japan, the Netherlands, and Singapore (Kirdar, 1997). Creating healthy urban living conditions is possible as long as a supportive political structure exists and financial resources are applied appropriately (Galea and Vlahov, 2005). Social systems based on democracy and strong equity policies have flourished with great social and health achievements observed in many developed countries — for example, Nordic countries and New Zealand (Vagerö, 2007) — and elected mayors and other city leaders can use their soft powers and formal responsibilities to drive pro-health policies (Naylor and Buck, 2018).

However, not all mainstream social and economic development in the 21st century has focused on social equity conducive to health (Vagerö, 2007). This is reflected by the development of health care systems that focus on the development of secondary and tertiary care while only operating insufficient community-based systems to alert neighbourhoods to high-risk health behaviours, which account for the majority of premature deaths and disease burden (Lee et al., 2007a; Lee, 2018a). Improving population health depends on coordinated action at multiple levels, and city leaders must ensure that decisions in areas such as housing, employment, and transport planning all have a positive impact on health. Furthermore, city-wide coordination requires effective leadership, robust governance, and adequate investment in central programme management (Naylor and Buck, 2018).

Over time, the context of health care has changed, and non-medical factors that affect health (but are beyond the health care sector) must be considered in a person's health choices and treatment (Marmot et al., 2008). Health promotion must focus on these key "social determinants of health". Indeed, the environments where people live, learn, work, or play on a daily basis have a profound influence on health as they can either promote or discourage behaviours associated with NCDs (Magnusson et al., 2011). There is a need for action across the whole of society, focusing on those social factors that determine health outcomes (Marmot and Bell, 2012). The Shattuck Lecture by Frieden (2015) on the future of public health has highlighted the role of the health pyramid, whereby improving health for more people at lower unit cost at the base of the pyramid (by tacking socio-economic factors such as income, education, housing, ethnic inequity, etc.) is necessary and will have a greater impact in the community than using intensive individual intervention at the top of the pyramid.

The opportunities offered by different settings for gaining entry to the lives of individuals and groups are of paramount importance for disease prevention and health promotion. A network of social pressure is needed to establish a normative system that can exert influence on an individual's intention to adopt or reject health actions (Tones and Green, 2004). When the factors in the heath sector and those in other settings are accounted for, it is obvious that effective health promotion intervention is needed to integrate the entire health ecosystem for health improvement (Hancock, 1985). Outcomes of this integration of health-promoting activities are highlighted in Figure 1.1. The application of these healthy activities in elemental settings is the premise of the Healthy Settings Approach. However, the success of this approach should not be measured by the end-point outcomes alone; it also requires evaluating the process of change in the social system, environment, and infrastructure that mediate health improvement.

Healthy Settings Intervention: How Does It Work?

Conceptualisation of Healthy Settings

The Healthy Settings Approach was born in the Ottawa Charter, which claimed that health is not created outside of contexts but within the settings of people's everyday life, and it offers a much richer and more powerful means of promoting

Figure 1.1: The Human Health Ecosystem and Intervention for Health Improvement

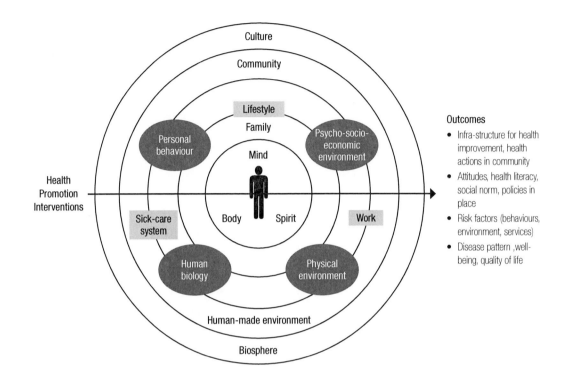

Source: Hancock (1985).

health and well-being (Dooris et al., 2014). The WHO defines a setting as "the place or social context in which people engage in daily activities in which environmental, organizational, and personal factors interact to affect health and wellbeing" (WHO, 2013a). It considers the multiple, interacting components that make up a whole system and adopts interventions that integrate these components to minimise risk factors and conditions that contribute to disease (Dooris, 2006; Poland et al., 2000; Whitelaw et al., 2001; WHO; 2013a). Green et al. (2000) expanded the meaning of "setting" to include the arena of sustained interaction, with pre-existing structures, policies, characteristics, institutional values, and both formal and informal social sanctions having an effect on behaviour. The Healthy Settings Approach addresses the social, cultural, and political determinants of health, and facilitates organisations and institutions to create a culture for health improvement. It is a value-based approach which has the ability to translate these factors to fit a particular setting (Dooris, 2004; Dooris et al., 2007).

Looking more closely, the key characteristics of a Healthy Settings project are that it should be integrated, comprehensive, multifaceted, participatory, part of an empowerment partnership, responsive, and tailored towards the needs of the population (Poland et al., 2000). There is good evidence that health promotion interventions focusing on changing lifestyle behaviours are more effective if they are conducted by targeting specific settings rather using a broad population-based approach alone (Verstraeten et al., 2012). This is supported by a systematic review by Jeet et al. (2018), which highlights the effectiveness of NCD control by promoting health in targeted settings.

There are some health-promoting activities that can be applied to multiple settings. For instance, developing personal competences, reshaping environments, building partnerships, promoting sustainable change by community participation, empowering yourself and others, and owning these changes have all been shown to improve health in various environments (Whitelaw et al., 2001). Evidence demonstrates that positive changes in these areas can lead to effective health improvements in a setting and for the individuals involved. If we use safe sex as an example, there is a solid theoretical framework to allow interventions at various stages along the proximal-distal chains. The most distal part is the decline of sexually transmitted diseases (STDs) and unplanned pregnancies, as reflected in the medical model. In the Healthy Settings model, we know that there are clusters of personal, psychological, social, environmental, and cultural issues that will influence the final outcomes. These include:

- Personal health skills in choosing protective sex measures
- Personal belief of benefits outweighing the possible disadvantages
- Self-confidence and self-efficacy
- Negotiation skills with partners
- Social and cultural norms
- Availability and accessibility of different types of contraceptive devices
- Affordability

Problems can arise if we only focus on the distal end as a measurement of success. Indeed, it is almost impossible to be certain which intervention leads to a decline in STD prevalence, unplanned pregnancies, or HIV-positive patients, as they all contribute, either synergistically or independently. Within one health condition, there can be many determinant factors, which makes controlling a potential confounder complicated and difficult. A very large sample size along with a long duration of intervention and study are needed to demonstrate a statistically significant effect if an outcome measure, such as the decline of STDs, unplanned pregnancies, and HIV-positive patients, is the main focus, and even then it may still not be possible to ascertain "why" or "how" the factor is mediating the change.

The Limitations of Conventional Methodologies

Epidemiological indicators might not fully capture all of the specified goals of programmes using the Healthy Settings Approach, especially those with indicators reflecting the process rather than outcome. In contrast, qualitative methods should be used to gain a better understanding of the complexity of health beliefs and intentions leading to behavioural changes. One such method is triangulation — the collecting of evidence from different sources (i.e., researcher triangulation, theory triangulation, and methodological triangulation; Denzin, 1978). This method has been shown to enhance the robustness of data using a pluralistic approach (Heale and Forbes, 2013). There are several types. *Investigator triangulation* enables the persons with the best skills to be closest to the data, thus mitigating bias because different investigators will be observing the same data and may offer different interpretations of it. *Theory triangulation* refers to the process of letting the raw data "speak" to the researcher to develop a new theory to expand one's knowledge of the known (Denzin, 2009). Lastly, *methodological triangulation* involves using data obtained from a combination of quantitative and qualitative techniques in a mixed-methods study. This form of triangulation can be further divided into between-method or across-method triangulation, which when used together can overcome the inherent flaws and deficiencies of each (Denzin, 2009). Triangulating a wide range of qualitative data can address completeness, convergence, and dissonance of the key themes (Farmer et al., 2006). Every study, whether qualitative or quantitative, can contribute to the body of knowledge, and triangulation of these collective data can enhance the validity of the study results to ensure that one's research becomes interwoven with the existing literature on the topic (Fusch et al., 2018).

A mixed-methods study will often begin with a qualitative method to identify and narrow down the problem, and then a quantitative method is then used to answer the research question. This process can be reversed as well. A pluralistic research method can also be referred to as a naive postpositivist assessment (Denzin, 2012). According to Janesick (1994), the rigour and validity of this method can be further enhanced by adding interdisciplinary triangulation. The term "judicial review" has been used to describe the process of assembling sufficient evidence leading to a confident decision even though absolute proof is not available (Tones, 1997). Similarly, triangulation is essentially a thorough review of all the accumulated evidence, and the final judgement is based on "the balance of probabilities" or "beyond a reasonable doubt". This is also similar to the use of a P-value in quantitative methodology, which reflects the size of a type 1 error (Green and Tones, 1999). Denzin and Lincoln (2011) have stated the obligation of qualitative research scholars to change the world by making a positive difference and confronting the facts of injustice opening up for change and transformation. The research methodology should encompass a family of approaches based on inductive reasoning, in-depth understanding of participants' points of view, data collection in natural settings, long-term immersion by researchers in the field, emphasis on process, non-random purposeful sampling, the researcher as the primary data collection instrument, and the use of multiple forms of data and perspectives (Denzin and Lincoln, 2018).

We need to modify our mindset in the evaluation of health promotion to avoid underestimating the effectiveness of the Healthy Settings Approach. Applying triangulation to the data would help to develop mixed-methods studies, ranging from case studies, focus groups, observational studies, surveys, and quasi-experimental designs to randomised controlled trials (RCTs), that can be used to evaluate the process and outcomes of the Healthy Settings Approach applied in a particular environment. The approach has several unique characteristics that make mixed-methods studies the ideal evaluation measure. For instance, the Healthy Settings Approach is regarded as an ecological model of health promotion that addresses the complex interactions of environmental, organisational, and personal factors (Dooris, 2009; Dooris et al., 2007) and is aimed at addressing the gaps in routine health services — namely, the over-reliance on RCTs. Since RCTs are designed to measure clinical intervention, these studies might not be a good evaluation tool for the majority of health-promoting interventions. In fact, imposing the criteria for intervention and control groups, essential aspects of an RCT, would mean putting the subjects into experimental conditions rather than their natural environment. Evidence-based practice focused on RCTs is equated with a reductionist approach that is not compatible with the holistic and empowerment approaches, which are the essence of health promotion (Green, 2000). Moreover, contamination is likely to increase over time, and the control groups would set up similar health-promotion initiatives, such as the Heartbeat Wales programme (Nutbeam et al., 1993). However, while conventional RCTs may not be the ideal means to assess the process and outcome of the Healthy Settings model, the principles of the other qualitative assessment methods, including case studies, focus groups, observational studies, surveys, and quasi-experimental designs, are suitable and can accommodate the unique aspects of this approach and the environment to which it is being applied. The approach also argues for investment in social systems in which people spend their daily lives, and there are many multifaceted components to be evaluated with different outcome measures.

Making healthy choices the easy choices is now a key aspect of the public health agenda (Buck et al., 2018; DH, 2004). This concept is also an important component of the Healthy Settings Approach, which stresses active participation by individuals and communities as being the key to success (WHO, 1986; WHO, 1997a; WHO, 2013a). The approach focuses on securing voluntary commitment of individuals rather than artificial manipulation, and the importance of choice and control to achieving outcomes is well recognised in the broader context of health promotion (Green and Tones, 1999). In an experimental condition, the healthy choice would become the easy choice, but this may not be the case in reality, especially with "hard to reach" groups. The true effectiveness of the approach, therefore, cannot be evaluated with a high degree of validity using such conditions. This is why the Healthy Settings Approach is about working with people within the setting rather than using a top-down experimental approach.

Green and Tones (1999) argued that to objectify human experience by researching *on* subjects, rather than *with* them, is to be consistent with the board ideology of health promotion. Type III errors occur if the programmes are developed on an ad hoc basis and are inadequate in terms of design and delivery (Green, 2000). Such errors reflect a failure in recognising changes that have actually occurred as a result of intervention. Choosing the wrong outcome measures, such as mortality and morbidity, for example, would lead to a type III error when assessing the Healthy Settings Approach, as such measures fail to reflect the success of the method in addressing the complexity of different factors involved in determining health, which could be behavioural, environmental, political, socio-economic, or a combination of these (Tones, 1998). The final outcomes would be clinically significant but statistically insignificant due to the large denominator in health-promotion intervention. The denominator for a clinical trial is the number of patients with the specified disease, which is smaller than the denominator for a health-promoting intervention in the population at risk. For example, reducing the number of students taking drugs in a school from ten students to five students would appear to have a clinically significant effect in a local school. However, if the student population of the school is 1,000, this means the reduction is from 1% to 0.5%, which is unlikely to be statistically significant. Therefore, we need to collect data capturing the process of change using qualitative methodologies, such as participant observation or in-depth case studies as well as a review of the school system and linkage to community resources, in order to get a complete picture of the effects of an intervention. In this example, it would be important to measure whether the intervention has created a school environment that is drug-free or discourages drug use. Other qualitative changes that could be assessed to evaluate effectiveness are if there is an increase in positive factors, including counselling and rehabilitative services. Although quantitative data can still be used to measure the changes, mixed-method studies are essential to evaluate the different components and analyse whether they are demonstrating positive changes as well as to determine their strength. It would then be possible for the researcher to conclude whether it is beyond a reasonable doubt that the observed effects are being mediated, at least in part, by that factor.

Success of the Healthy Settings Model

Dooris et al. (2007) have suggested that the Healthy Settings Approach is rooted in values such as participation, equity, partnership, empowerment, and sustainability, and is characterised by three interconnected dimensions: the ecological model of health promotion, systematic perspectives, and whole-system development and change. The ecological model reflects a paradigm shift from a reductionist approach focusing on a single health issue or risk factor towards holistic health determined by a complex interaction of personal, environmental, and organisational factors within the context of daily life. Dooris et al. (2014) have proposed a model that is a value-based approach underpinned by core principles of health promotion and public health which can be applied to fit the context of each particular setting.

By referencing the "Healthy Living and Working Model" by Paton et al. (2005), it is possible to draw on organisational theory to view the Healthy Settings Approach as a complex dynamic system with inputs, throughputs, and outputs that work in tandem to create a healthy living environment. Figure 1.2 illustrates the data collection (from input to process and impact, then to outcomes) that is necessary to get an accurate reflection of the effectiveness of the Health Settings Approach in a particular environment. Tackling health issues at different stages will help build up high levels of social, ecological, human, and economic "capital" (Box 1.1); this is collectively regarded as "community capital" (Hancock, 2001). This multi-levelled breakdown of community capital as well as the complexity of factors explains why certain communities are unable to overcome health challenges more effectively compared to other communities with similar demographics. The synergistic effects of different healthy settings combine the efforts of upstream, midstream, and downstream approaches to improve population health and reduce health inequity.

A New Paradigm for Health Promotion

Public health problems result from complex social, economic, political, biological, genetic, and environmental causes. Intersectoral collaboration, community participation, innovation, and implementation of the Healthy Settings Approach across various sectors are all important instruments to initiate and promote change. The complex interventions of these tools can provide a framework in which an integrated and holistic approach to public health can be pursued so policy, environment, social matters, behaviour, and biomedical interventions can take their rightful place side by side.

To successfully implement the Healthy Settings Approach, a health profile reflecting the state of the population's health is needed. This is required to determine how different components (such as policies, improvement of health literacy, re-orientation of health services, and building up social and human capital) would facilitate health improvement. The following chapters illustrate how to build up a health profile in various settings in order to mediate effective interventions.

Figure 1.2: Evaluating the Effectiveness of the Healthy Settings Approach

Process and Impact

Input

- Policies and Governance to Enhance Healthy Living
- Services to Protect and Promote Health
- Health Informatics
- Social Engagement and Mobilisation, Social Capital
- Infrastructure Planning, Putting Health High on Agenda
- Programmes for Healthy and Active Living

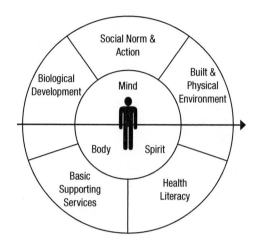

Outcomes

- Mortality and Morbidity
- Health Status (Physical, Psycho-Social)
- Quality of Life
- Health Behaviours
- Health Service Utilisation (fewer hospital admissions, higher uptake of preventive services)

Source: author.

Box 1.1: Community Capital
(Source: Hancock, 2001)

Human capital consists of healthy, well-educated, skilled, innovative, and creative people who are engaged in their communities and participate in governance.

Social capital constitutes the 'glue' that holds communities together formally (social development programme) and informally as a social network. The formal aspect also includes investment in social development so that citizens would have equitable access to basic determinants of health.

Natural capital includes high environmental quality, healthy ecosystems, sustainable resources, nature conservation, and biodiversity.

Economic capital refers to the level of prosperity that we need so we can feed, clothe, and house everyone; provide clean water and proper sanitation; ensure universal education; and provide accessible health and social services. It should also create healthy jobs and equitable distribution of resources.

Chapter 2

The Healthy City Concept and Evaluation Framework

Albert Lee

With a better understanding of how the Healthy Settings Approach works in general, City-super began his study of Healthy Cities. We can recall from the Preamble of this book that he did not manage to get support from the city government to help with improving the fitness and well-being of citizens. He hoped that understanding the history of the Healthy City concept would help explain the reasons for this difficulty. City-super also needed to develop healthy benchmarks for his city as well as choose appropriate outcomes for evaluation. This would allow for a more comprehensive needs assessment to be completed.

What is a "Healthy City"?

A city is a unique setting, in that it includes almost all the other settings. The greatest attraction of city life is the diversity of "push" and "pull" factors for urbanisation — pushing individuals, families, and communities out of rural areas, depriving them of opportunities for traditional ways of life, and pulling them to urban areas with new job opportunities and community development (de Leeuw, 2009). A city is a complex setting because the governance of the population has to accommodate numerous stakeholders from a wide variety of sectors, so city governments are often much less in control of their setting. This can lead to a failure in addressing the determinants of health, resulting in health inequities (Marmot et al., 2008). In fact, this phenomenon explains why very little has been published in the public domain about the Healthy City Programme (HCP), which was established and initially discussed in academic circles over two decades ago (de Leeuw and Skovgarard, 2005). Hierarchical evidence of effectiveness favours biomedical interventions rather than socio-political interventions, and proximal health determinants rather than distal determinants, which explains the scant evidence regarding the effectiveness of the HCP.

This complexity also makes it more challenging to create positive change and to measure and attribute that change to specific interventions. Furthermore, cities usually have a long history and do not change quickly or easily. The challenge of creating healthier cities is not for the faint of heart or those looking for immediate benefits or for personal credit; only rarely do exceptional individuals make significant changes in cities.

What, then, is a Healthy City?

> A Healthy City is one that is continually creating and improving those physical and social environments and expanding those community resources which enable people to support each other in performing all the functions of life and in developing themselves in their maximum potential. (Ashton, 1992)

The model should encompass a pathway linking prerequisites (leadership, vision and strategy, structures and processes, networks) using activities (policies, programmes, projects) which "make a difference" to the city's status in the areas of health determinants, lifestyle, and health outcomes. This chapter explains the history of the Healthy City model and describes past experiences to illustrate its evolution. It also describes the framework for evaluating a healthy city. This discussion leads directly into the case studies described in Chapters 3 and 4, which focus on the current state of the HCP in urbanised cities in the Asia Pacific Region.

Evolution of the Healthy City Concept

The history of the HCP begins after the rapid urbanisation accompanying the Industrial Revolution in the 19th century. The programme was developed to clean up the "mess" and unpleasant health consequences caused by unregulated industrialisation and urbanisation. The decline of city health around the world was profound, being exemplified by the poor health of citizens as well as the environment. Engels, for instance, described Manchester's River Irk in 1845 as

> a narrow, coal-black, foul-smelling stream ... in dry weather, a long string of the most disgusting, blackish-green slime pools are left standing ... from the depths of which bubbles of miasmatic gas constantly arise and give forth a stench unendurable even on the bridge 40 or 50 feet above the surface of the stream.

In the United Kingdom, the British government established the Health in Towns Commission in 1843, and Edwin Chadwick, the "father" of modern public health, was then named Secretary to the Commission. The installation of the Commission led directly to the "sanitary idea" and to the establishment of essential public health measures such as housing standards, sewer systems, hygiene regulations, and proper public water supplies. It was quickly realised that public health was deeply connected to the issues of town planning. In response, a Health of Towns Association was established in 1844, and branches quickly sprang up in cities throughout Britain. As Ashton (1992) noted:

> The work of the Health of Towns Association in pressing for the application of the sanitary idea and its insertion into policy making had a dramatic effect on public health in Britain in a comparatively short space of time.

By 1876, Sir Benjamin Ward Richardson presented a plausible vision of a Healthy City — Hygeia — that still resonates today. In Hygeia, he foresaw a city of 100,000 people at a density of five houses per acre with no buildings rising above 60 feet. In this imaginary city, railways ran beneath the major highways and there was a subway system. The side roads here were lined with trees, with parks and gardens everywhere, and the street drainage was managed via sewers. The houses in Hygeia were light and airy, brick built, smoke-free, and had roof gardens, running hot and cold water, garbage chutes, and main drains and sewers (Richardson, 1876). Richardson took this vision with him when he went to Canada, where he was instrumental in establishing town planning. His work further links urban planning with public health. The concept of a Healthy City was by then established throughout the industrialised world. However, the links between public health, urban planning, and governance were lost as a result of the increasing dominance of the medical model and marginalisation of public health.

However, all was not lost. These links were re-established as a result of work in Canada and Europe lead by Len Duhl, a professor of Public Health and City Planning at the University of California Berkeley in 1984. Much of this work was presented at the "Healthy Toronto 2000" Workshop (Duhl, 1986, 1996; Hancock, 1988; Toronto Health Department, 1988; Tsouros, 1993), which was part of the "Beyond Health Care" Conference in Toronto, the first international conference on healthy public policy (Last, 1985). This was led by Ilona Kickbusch, the then newly appointed Health Promotion Officer for WHO Europe, who launched the Healthy Cities project in early 1986 (Ashton and Kickbusch, 1986). That same year, the Healthy Settings Approach became an important part of the Ottawa Charter for Health Promotion (WHO, 1986), as described in Chapter 1. Mayors from a highly diverse group of cities pledged their commitment to developing Healthy Cities at the Ninth Global Conference on Health Promotion in Shanghai in November 2016 (WHO, 2017). The political commitment to health in cities expressed by its leaders in Shanghai and, even more prominently, in Quito at the launch of the *New Urban Agenda* (UN Habitat III, 2016), aligned well with the established value system for Healthy Cities (de Leeuw, 2017a; Tsouros, 2013). Thus, the contemporary history of the Healthy City concept has evolved since the 1980s (de Leeuw, 2017b; Hancock and Duhl, 1986), with new qualifications and key players being identified as the cities themselves evolve.

How to Qualify as a Healthy City?

To be considered a Healthy City, a city should strive to develop the "Eleven Qualities" (de Leeuw, 2017a), which build on established qualities and thresholds (WHO, 1997a; Tsouros, 1993) and reflect the United Nations 2020 agenda for Sustainable Development (UN, 2015). These include having

- a clean, safe, high-quality physical environment (including quality housing);

- an ecosystem which is stable now and sustainable in the long term;

- a strong, mutually supportive, and non-exploitative community;

- a high degree of public participation in and control over the decisions affecting one's life, health, and well-being;

- the ability to meet the basic needs (food, water, shelter, income, safety, work) for all the city's people;

- access to a wide variety of experiences and resources with the possibility of multiple contacts, interaction, and communication;

- a diverse, vital, and innovative city economy;

- connection with the past, with the cultural and biological heritage, and with other groups and individuals;

- a city form that is compatible with and enhances the above parameters and behaviour of citizens;

- an optimum level of public health and sick care services accessible to all; and

- a high-health status (both high positive health status and low-disease status).

Who are the Key Players?

The following is a list of those individuals and groups that play the most essential roles in a Healthy City:

- Community members

- Local, provincial, state, and national politicians

- Government service providers from a variety of sectors (e.g., health, welfare, transport, police, public housing authority)

- Community service providers

- Non-governmental organisations (NGOs)

- Community-based organisations

- Private enterprise interests

- Consumer groups

- Local government authorities

- Provincial and state government authorities

- Relevant national government authorities

- Ethnic groups

- Community media

- Educational institutions

Ongoing Development

Development in Europe

Although urbanisation in the 18th century caused ill health among much of the world's population, modern urbanisation has been shown to be associated with multiple health benefits if a healthy living environment is created. Indeed, in highly urbanised countries, including Japan, Singapore, the Netherlands, and Sweden, there have been notable improvements in mortality and morbidity over the last 50 years (Kirdar, 1997). Healthy urban living conditions are possible with a supportive political structure and when financial resources are being applied in an appropriate manner (Galea and Vlahov, 2005). Nordic countries have demonstrated great social and health achievements using social systems based on democracy and strong equity policies (Kirdar, 1997; Kjellstrom et al., 2007). Thus, since their inception in 1986, Healthy Cities as a European experiment (Tsouros, 1991; Wilding et al., 2017) have experienced periods of both glory and neglect (de Leeuw and Simos, 2017).

The HCP promoted by WHO Europe engages the local governments in health development through a process of political commitment, institutional change, capacity building, partnership-based planning, and innovative projects. It promotes comprehensive and systematic policy and planning with a special emphasis on health inequalities and urban poverty; the needs of vulnerable groups; participatory governance; and the social, economic, and environmental determinants of health. It also strives to include health considerations in economic, regeneration, and urban development efforts. Europe now has a strong network of over 1,200 cities and towns from over 30 countries in the process of developing Healthy Cities. This programme was initiated in 1987 and involves six phases, beginning with planning and the development of city policies and profiles in phases 1 and 2, and leading to innovation, sustainability, and thematic development in phase 3 (WHO, 1997e; Hall et al., 2009). In phase 4 (which was implemented in 2003–2008) (WHO, 2003), these cities worked on three core themes: healthy ageing, healthy urban planning, and health impact assessment. In addition, all participating cities focused on the topic of physical activity and active living. The overarching theme for phase 5 (2009–2013) (WHO, 2009b) was health and health equity in all local policies. The concept of "health in all policies" is based on the recognition that population health is not merely a product of health sector activities but is largely determined by policies and actions beyond the health sector. Phase 6 (2014–2018) will support cities in strengthening their efforts to bring key stakeholders together to work for health and well-being; to harness leadership, innovation, and change; and to enhance the potential to resolve local public health challenges (WHO, 2013b). The two strategic objectives of "Health 2020" (the new European health policy framework) are (1) to improve health for all and reduce health inequalities, and (2) to improve leadership and participatory governance for health. The concepts of the city health profile and the intersectoral city health development plan remain valid, and they will be adapted to reflect the wider scope of the WHO European Healthy Cities goals in phase 6.

European mayors and civic leaders, who are members of the Healthy Cities network, have pledged to promote health, prevent disease and disability, and take systematic action on inequality at the civic level (WHO, 2018). They will be advocates and custodians of their citizens' health.

Development in the Asia Pacific Region

Healthy City networks have expanded to all six WHO regions, including the Western Pacific Region (WPRO) and its many emerging megacities. The Alliance for Healthy Cities (AFHC) was established in 2003, and membership has expanded from 10 to over 160 cities at the time of writing. In 2010, the AFHC established the Gangnam Declaration for Ubiquitous Healthy Cities (Box 2.1). The Declaration emphasises the reduction of health inequity and a commitment to using the outcomes of a Healthy City to achieve the WHO's Millennium Development Goals. It also demonstrates the importance of city mayors as advocates for a Healthy City and their role in tackling the public health crises and health inequities, and also in the improvement of the health information system and more detailed measurements of health outcomes. Ubiquitous Healthy Cities reflect innovation and a readiness to change in the face of public health challenges, similar to Phases 5 and 6 of the European Healthy City movement.

In Korea, for example, the programme has grown rapidly, with 53 cities joining the AFHC in 2010. Healthy Cities in Korea are based on a project model led by municipalities and financed by the Health Promotion Fund (Nam and Engelhardt, 2007). The government is preparing to launch an evidence-based Healthy City programme by conducting a Health Impact Assessment (Yoo et al., 2007; Moon et al., 2014). The health-promotion capacity map in Korea highlights their intention to get started, but what is needed next is

Box 2.1: Gangnam Declaration for Ubiquitous Healthy Cities

The Fourth Global Conference of the Alliance for Healthy Cities (AFHC), held 26–29 October 2010 in Gangnam, Seoul, Republic of Korea, was attended by 2,700 people from 16 countries, including 50 mayors or representatives. The members of the AFHC shared their experiences and views on strategies for developing "Ubiquitous Healthy Cities" and declared the following:

- Creating "Ubiquitous Healthy Cities" does not mean the mere application of e-based health care but involves achieving the highest attainable accessibility to health information, activities, and basic health care services for all citizens.

- We hereby propose information and communication technology as a solution to resolve the emerging and traditional health issues in our society by:
  - Providing ubiquitous information on the social determinants of health to empower citizens to gain control and enhance capacity for health.
  - Improving access to a supportive environment and information for health to reduce health inequity and the digital divide.
  - Improving the quality of and access to health care services, particularly preventive health services to vulnerable groups and the aged population.
  - Establishing a systematic database for health data management including data reflecting the determinants of health and an effective emergency health care system.

- We will use the Healthy Cities framework to prepare cities to face the challenges of an emerging health crisis and share our mutual experiences and expand the Healthy Cities movement.

We, the leaders of cities, towns, communities, private companies, and NGOs as well as members of the academia, reaffirm our commitment towards building healthy cities and, by working in partnership, commit to:

- Expanding the use of information and communication technology and develop social, environmental, and economic programmes, and local infrastructure to build healthier cities.

- Developing effective and affordable healthcare technology to reduce health inequity.

- Encouraging mutual learning by exchanging experiences in creating ubiquitous healthy cities.

- Supporting the outcomes of healthy cities to contribute to achieving the Millennium Development Goals.

- Promoting environmentally sustainable transport measures and options to minimise pollution and public health impacts.

- Comprehensively evaluating the HCP using the SPIRIT framework.

a plan that looks behind the façade and shows the challenges and areas requiring attention, essentially the "speed bumps", "construction sites", "radar traps", and "one-way streets". A combination of methodologies is needed to produce such a map.

In the Gangnam Declaration, the members state their plan to use the SPIRIT framework to evaluate their Healthy Cities and the programmes they are using to develop them (Lee, 2010a). The SPIRIT framework was initially developed by the AFHC in their accreditation scheme for cities and for the Healthy City Award (Lee, 2004a), and it has been used in various studies to assess HCPs. For instance, Nam et al. (2010) used the SPIRIT framework to evaluate the Wonju Healthy City project and identified various problems and challenges, as well as improvements that could be made based on the Healthy City project philosophy and strategies. The SPIRIT framework serves as a means to create a more detailed map to show the efforts necessary to become a Healthy City. For the Wonju Healthy City project and many others, this involved increasing the engagement of key stakeholders, among other things (Nam et al., 2010; Lee, 2010b; Lee, 2019a). The SPIRIT framework and how it can be used as an evaluation tool will be discussed in detail in the next chapter.

Linking e-based health care with Healthy City development is a good example of how urbanisation can bring benefits to the residents, as it not only facilitates their access to health care services but also to information about the social determinants of health. A robust system of information technology can reduce health inequities, thus enhancing the capacity to tackle unexpected health crises and emergency conditions and leading to a more rapid response from various sectors to address the health needs of the population. E-health also allows surveillance of not only the health status of the population but also on the determinant factors for health in that community. Taken together, these advances and the information gained from them will provide a more comprehensive evaluation of a city's health. Data and evidence, and technological advances in e-health, ultimately provide the glue that holds the complex urban health system together (Elsey et al., 2019).

The Sixth Global AFHC Conference was held in Hong Kong in 2014 and had the overarching theme of "Health in All Policies". The conference was attended by over 800 delegates from 18 countries. It received an overwhelming response, with 273 abstracts submitted, signifying the staunch support within the region for the sustainable development of Healthy Cities to build up community resilience for future challenges and to preserve and better the health and well-being of citizens. Health in equity, social justice, social inclusion, strengthening of social capital, ecological sustainability, creating supportive environments, integrated health services, and health skill development for citizens have emerged as key issues for the sustainable development of Health Cities. The Hong Kong Declaration for Healthy Cities (Box 2.2) supported good city governance based on the concept of a Healthy City so that citizens have easy access to the necessities of city life, such as adequate shelter, security of tenure, safe water and food, a safe and hygienic environment, services for health promotion and health protection, education, balanced nutrition, social security, and free mobility.

The Hong Kong Declaration highlights the importance of tackling the issues of the ageing population, emerging epidemics of NCDs, re-emergence of communicable diseases, and natural disasters. This sets the scene for good city governance by adopting the "Health in All Policies" concept. It also encourages development of other healthy settings with the Healthy City Model being used as the overarching framework.

Using the Healthy City Model to Tackle the Challenges of Urbanisation

People now live in a society that has increasing ecological and socio-economic risks and increasing individualisation (Kjellstrom et al., 2007). Health disparities still exist even in economically well-developed societies in Asia (Lee et al., 2015a). The challenge of maintaining quality urban health in low- and middle-income countries, and especially the challenge of addressing the health concerns of the 1 billion people living in slums and informal settlements, has been clearly highlighted in the report of the WHO Commission on the Social Determinants of Health (Kjellstrom et al., 2007). This was reiterated in the report of the Commission of the Knowledge Network on Urban Settlements (Kjellstrom et al., 2007). Urbanisation poses specific risks to citizens that policy makers and Healthy Settings advocates must be aware of. The key recommendations made in the Commission's report on the Knowledge Network were to:

- build social cohesion;
- improve environments for health;
- adopt accessible primary health care for all;
- utilise healthy settings as vehicles; and
- proactively coordinate urban planning and good urban governance.

Box 2.2: Hong Kong Declaration for Healthy Cities: Health in All Policies

At the Sixth Global AFHC Conference held from 29 October–1 November 2014, in Sai Kung District, Hong Kong, members gathered to commemorate the 10-year journey of the AFHC and reflected on the vision of building cities and communities of peace where all citizens live in harmony reaching for the highest possible quality of life and equity of health by promoting and protecting health in all settings. Participants shared their experiences in promulgating further development of Healthy Cities under the overarching framework of "Health in All Policies". With an ageing population, emerging epidemics of non-communicable diseases (NCDs), and increasing challenges in tackling the re-emergence of communicable diseases and public health crises, the keynote and sub-plenary presentations as well as oral and poster presentations created a dynamic and vibrant platform to formulate strategies in achieving optimal health of citizens through city development and governance while meeting the health needs of the local population.

We, the leaders of cities, communities, NGOs, academic institutions, professional organisations, industries, and community support groups make a strong pledge to the Healthy Cities Approach in sustaining city development and the advancement of health and well-being of citizens. At the conclusion of the Conference, we resolve and commit our actions through participatory and partnership approaches across sectors, disciplines, cultures, boundaries, and ideologies, and call for action to be taken on the following top priorities:

- Enhancement of city development strategies by incorporating the concept of "Health in All Policies" and "Health in Equity" as key elements of city governance.

- Prevention of early origins of diseases by tackling the determinant factors and promoting uptake of preventive measures through the Healthy Settings Approach.

- Development of age-friendly cities so that all citizens can benefit from the changes.

- Building community resilience in preparedness and responsiveness for public health emergencies adopting the Healthy Settings Approach.

- Re-orientation of health services towards preventive care and a community-based model to reduce health inequity and enhance accessibility.

- Putting the concept of Healthy Cities as a core value of city development to uphold social justice, build social capital, and enable social inclusion.

We also resolve to continue to advance the development of Healthy Cities by sustaining the pledges made by Declarations of previous Conferences and continue efforts towards the following:

- Creating a city with an environment supportive of sustainable ecology and with a high level of safety and security as well as barrier-free access for all citizens.

> - Investment in research to develop an evidence-based practice for Healthy City development and valid indicators for outcome measurement.
>
> - To use Healthy Cities development as an overarching framework for other healthy settings initiatives, such as Health-promoting Schools, Health-promoting Workplaces, Healthy Villages, Health-promoting Hospitals, Health-promoting Health Care Organisations, and Health-promoting Universities to create synergy in health.
>
> - Incorporating the concept of Healthy Cities beyond the health and social sectors into other disciplines involved in city planning and development.
>
> We all believe that good city governance and policy-making should be based on the Healthy City concept.

A document by the WHO/WPRO (2011), titled "Healthy urbanisation: Regional framework for scaling up and expanding Healthy Cities in the Western Pacific 2011–2015", was based on several working group meetings held in 2009 and 2010, and laid down the following key domains for achieving healthy urbanisation:

- Empowerment of individuals and communities

- Engagement of all sectors

- Environmental sustainability

- Energy efficiency

- Equity-based health system

- Elimination of extreme urban poverty

- Expression of cultural diversity and spiritual values

- Enforcement of safety and security

Thus, the global Healthy City movement is a driving force for mainstream social and economic development in the 21st century, focusing on social equity. HCPs provide a means to address health inequalities that arise not only from poverty in economic terms but also poverty of opportunity, of capability, and of security. Elsey et al. (2019) discuss the key challenges of urbanisation particularly in low-income countries, including the response to the rising tide of NCDs and to the wider determinants of health, and suggest strengthening urban health governance to enable multisectoral responses as well as to provide accessible, quality primary healthcare and prevention from a plurality of providers. They also propose implementing an urban health system model focusing on a multisectoral approach to look beyond the health sector and engage urban residents through participatory decision-making.

Evaluation Framework of a Healthy City

Critically Analysing the Effectiveness of an HCP

The approach underlying an HCP is largely based on the assumption that health can be enhanced through improvements in certain social, cultural, and economic conditions which alter human attitudes. The approach involves initiatives in improving personal and environmental health, and regards health as an integral part of development in the community. Critical analysis of the current literature has highlighted the importance of political commitment and policy development; engagement of stakeholders from wider sectors; linking urban environment and urban development; empowerment of community development; addressing inequity, poverty, security, and safety; interaction between stakeholders; strong networking; and preservation and efficient utilisation of community resources in building a sustainable and healthy city (Baum, 2003; Capello, 2000; de Leeuw, 1993, 1999, 2000, 2017c; de Leeuw and Skovgaard, 2005; de Leeuw and Simos, 2017; Frank et al., 2003; Goumans and Springett, 1997; Hall et al., 2009; Smedley and Syme, 2000; Takano et al., 2002a; Tokano et al., 2002b; Tsouros and Draper, 1993; Tsouros, 2000). Access to green areas has also been found to have a direct impact on senior citizens' health in Asian megacities such as Shanghai and Tokyo (Takano et al., 2000a, 2000b).

In measuring the success of the HCP in a particular city, the most important consideration is whether the city is politically committed to improving the health of the residents and willing to create policies, organisational structures, and collaborative processes to reach their goals (de Leeuw et al., 2015; de Leeuw, 2017c; Baum, 2014; Lee, 2019a). The Healthy City concept is about a process rather than an outcome. Therefore, a Healthy City is not necessarily the one that has achieved a particular level of health but is conscious of health and is striving to *improve* it. Table 2.1 illustrates different types of evaluation tools utilised by different cities.

The complexity of cities, and the layers and domains of their governance, is further complicated by the divergence of socio-political conditions and

Table 2.1: Methods of Healthy City Evaluation

Authors	Summary of the Projects	Types of Evaluation
Werna and Harpham (1996)	Process evaluation using both local and international indicators for the HCP in Chittagong, Bangladesh	1. A series of in-depth, open-ended interviews carried out with 47 key actors 2. Observation of different actors during visits and meetings 3. Informal conversations with actors and citizens
Boonekamp et al. (1999)	Process evaluation of 13 out of 98 cities in the Valencian Community Health Cities Network, Spain	Semi-structured interviews which included questions about the following issues: 1. The health concept 2. Perception of the role of the local government to promote the citizens' health and possible ways of doing so 3. Role of the community in the municipal policies related to health 4. Strategic opportunities and difficulties for inter-departmental collaboration between different local government departments
Burton (1999)	Stakeholder analysis for two HCPs in Bangladesh	1. Review of project and evaluation documents 2. Semi-structured interviews with 21 stakeholders 3. Structured interviews (in the form of a questionnaire) of 62 participants 4. Two focus group meetings
Donchin et al. (2006)	Process evaluation on Israeli HCP network	A questionnaire with open- and closed-ended questions on six areas: 1. Health promotion programmes and activities in the city 2. City policy for reducing inequalities 3. Management of the HCP 4. Community participation 5. Intersectoral partnerships 6. Environmental protection Each dimension has several components and measures with rank score systems.
Webster and McCarthy (1997)	Review of international HCP indicators from WHO, Europe	Used 32 indicators in the following domains: 1. Health Indicators 2. Health Services Indicators 3. Environmental Indicators 4. Socio-economic Indicators

Baum and Cooke (1992); Baum (1993) Baum et al. (2006)	Progress and outcome evaluation of Noarlunga HCP pilot in Australia	1. Key informant interviews (face-to-face interviews)
		2. Audit of attendance at meetings of committee members
		3. Questionnaire surveys of key groups
		   • Management and reference committee members
		   • Local health and education workers
		   • Local community
		4. Analysis of local media
		5. Documentation of additional resources attracted to the projects
		6. Ongoing monitoring of the project by members of the research team

governance arrangements, which has profound roots in social, cultural and political history (Kickbusch and Gleicher, 2014). Thus, a corresponding evaluation method is required to understand the context and impact of the HCP (de Leeuw, 2015). Apart from using indicators reflecting performance, the evaluation methods must also determine how the community is engaged, how different stakeholders collaborate, and how the HCP is managed. Indeed, the evaluation methods have moved beyond using quantitative data, and instead make better use of qualitative data captured from focus groups, interviews, observations, and documentary reviews.

Table 2.1 outlines various evaluation methodology. These methods have been shown to help enable the cities to act upon the needs of key stakeholders and make changes to policies and services at the community level to meet the needs of the population. The process evaluation method used by Werna and Harpham (1996), Boonekamp et al. (1999), Burton (1999), and Donchin et al. (2006) focuses on qualitative data from key stakeholders obtained during interviews, focus group meetings, observations, informal conservations, and open-ended survey questions. These studies also investigated the perception of the local government in promoting citizens' health, community participation, and intersectorial partnerships in addition to reviewing the city's policies on Healthy City management. The progress and outcome evaluation of the Australian pilot project in Noarlunga used questionnaire surveys, documentary reviews, and interviews, and assessed the associated policies changes and the perception of key stakeholders, including local public services, intersectoral collaboration, and community involvement (Baum, 1993). International indicators from WHO Europe also include socio-economic indicators (Webster and McCarthy, 1997).

The efforts to implement an HCP in Noarlunga, Australia, have been documented for their success in starting from an environmental health needs assessment and orienting infrastructure towards becoming a safer community (Baum, 2003). If we adopt the approach of Eriksson (2000), which differentiates the four generations of "prevention projects" (I. clinical, II. bio-epidemiological, III. socio-epidemiological, IV. environment and policy-oriented) based on different theoretical framework, then we would measure the impact of intervention on determinants of health moving beyond individuals to the community, with a greater focus on social and environmental factors. The theory-based evaluation by Birckmayer and Weiss (2000) asks researchers to explain the outcomes rather than just producing the evidence fitting Eriksson's approach, focusing on the socio-epidemiology, environment, and policy. It is widely agreed that comprehensive health promotion interventions have a more sustainable effect on health indicators that reflect the determinants of health, health belief, and attitudes as well as the social norms, organisational capacity for health, and policies on health (Smedley and Syme, 2000; IUHPE, 2000a; IUHPE, 2000b).

For a better understanding of Healthy City development, there is a need to think beyond the conventional box of evaluation to explore the roots of socio-political and cultural perspectives of the cities involved. Although each HCP should decide its own short, intermediate, and long-term needs for evaluation and how to reach consensus among the various stakeholders (O'Neill and Simard, 2006), a universal list of indicators is possible if the evaluation framework focuses on factors driving the process of Healthy City development.

"Logan City" Cases Studies

The diverse needs of a city can always be linked to tackling the determinants of health from socio-political, environmental, and political perspectives. The phase 4 study in Brighton and Hove, for example, has demonstrated the merits of using a comprehensive monitoring and evaluation system with appropriate indicators so the key drivers and barriers for the HCP can be identified (Hall et al., 2009). The paper is commended as being a good start in the evaluation of the complexity of HCP and yields some important findings reflecting the needs of stakeholders (de Leeuw, 2009). The HCP in Logan, Australia, has also adopted an evaluation method using wider outcome indicators (Box 2.3) (Davey, 2010).

The evaluation of the Logan City Health Plan included an analysis of health service gaps, urban renewal initiatives, and community capacity (such as local event support, networks for social justice, and implementation of various projects). Their evaluation framework adopts a mixed method with interviews and focus groups, documentary analysis, and analysis of action status. They also take into account the capacity building and Logan's increased profile as leader in public health both nationally and internationally. Logan City is ideally positioned to prepare a "Community Plan" integrating strategic planning across different departments, a mandatory requirement under the Queensland Local Government Act. Logan's HCP has equipped the city to enhance city governance and management.

Box 2.3: Evaluation of the Logan Public Health Plan 2003–2008
(Source: Davey, 2010)

The Logan Public Health Plan (LPHP) 2003–2008 was a five-year strategic community-wide health action plan, and the evaluation results contributed to a new Healthy City Plan 2010–2020.

Mixed methods for evaluation

- An analysis of LPHP development, implementation process, and governance;
- A preliminary focus group workshop held in conjunction with an LPHP Advisory and Implementation (A&I) Committee meeting;
- LPHP-related document analysis;
- One-on-one interviews with key LPHP A&I Committee members;
- Analysis of LPHP action status; and
- Comparison with other health planning models.

Key issues and outcomes

- Public health and lifestyle outcomes

  Health service delivery outcomes: review framework for prevention and management of chronic disease, analysis of health service gap and consolidation of GPs, multicultural health, refugee, youth, self-management, allied health, natural health, oral health, asthma, diabetes, and other health-related support services.

  Affordable and appropriate housing outcomes: urban renewal initiatives, emergency housing needs assessment, installation of insect screens in all public housing stock.

  Community capacity outcomes: local event support such as multicultural and Indigenous Health expo, distribution network established for social justice and health inequity e-news, disaster management education and awareness initiatives.

- Acquisition of funding for and roll out of the Eat, Play, Live Well Logan Program
- Community Sharps Management Plan
- Water Fluoridation Group established and water fluoridation introduced
- Development of "Immunisation Blueprint" in collaboration with Queensland Health
- Integrated mosquito, animal, waste, and nuisance management initiatives
- Logan Healthy Living Program
- Social infrastructure initiatives
- School health screening and education strategies and other healthy school projects (e.g., oral health, nutrition, exercise)

- Community and industry focus on food safety management initiatives
- Communicable diseases prevention initiatives (e.g., hepatitis C)
- Youth support programmes
- Proactive advocacy for and contributions to environmental health-based legislative reforms

Implementation process and achievements

Through LPHP, substantial funding was granted to various projects such as Eat Well be Active; community renewal; Eat, Play, Live Well Logan Program; and Sharp Management. The achievements of this implementation included a framework for conceptualising public health planning and delivery of practical public health support, greater capacity building, increased Logan City's profile as a leader in public health, locally, nationally, and internationally with awards from the WHO and AFHC, leverage for funding into the city for public health initiatives, enhanced network with stakeholders, a reporting framework for documenting practical actions, and strategic planning which impacts stakeholder communication.

Significance and recommendations

The LPHP provided a secure platform to enhance Logan's health and well-being, and the commitment to Healthy City planning remains among the key stakeholders. The Logan City Council remains suitably placed to advance public health outcomes through the development of a new Healthy City plan — one which is a long-term strategic 10-year visionary that identifies current and future initiatives, and recognises the contributions and capacities of all relevant stakeholders. As the inherent relationships between the natural environment and sustainability issues, public health, and environmental health continue to evolve, the future Healthy City plan should adapt to emerging key issues. The Council is now integrating strategic planning across several departments to develop a Community Engagement Strategy with a "Community Plan", now mandatory in Queensland.

Future Monitoring and Evaluation of Healthy Cities

The challenge for the Healthy Cities movement in the coming years is two-fold: how to assert its own unique stance and contribution; and how to work in collaboration with other movements and networks that address other related aspects of urban life that affect the health of residents. There is a considerable body of

Figure 2.1: Scheme for Developing a City Health Profile and Outcomes Measures based on the Precede-Proceed Model

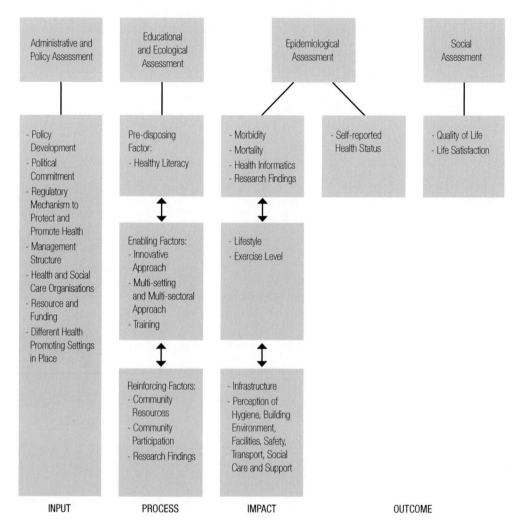

Sources: Green and Kreuter, 2005; author.

literature, both academic and professional, providing support for the concept as well as useful practical advice and tools, and some evidence of effectiveness. Figure 2.1 shows a model of developing a city health profile and measuring outcomes based on the Precede-Proceed model (Green and Kreuter, 2005). This model enables continuous monitoring and evaluation of Healthy City planning and development, and the data can be used by key stakeholders involved in urban development and improvement. This would facilitate continuous quality improvement from the public health and urban planning perspectives. The model also reflects the framework of the SPIRIT model in measuring the input, process, and certain components of impact which will be discussed in Chapter 3.

Chapter 3

SPIRIT Framework and City Health Profile: Concepts and Case Studies

Albert Lee

After learning the history and requirements to become a Healthy City, City-super recommended that the City Mayor establish a framework for the city to become a Healthy City in order to resolve the concerns about fitness and general well-being of the local population as well as future health issues requiring intersectoral collaboration. Using the documented experiences in Europe and the Asia Pacific Region, City-super also advised the City Mayor to adopt the Healthy City concept and lead other civic leaders as champions to reduce health inequalities and push different stakeholders to be more engaged in "health governance". While City-super now has a better understanding of the theoretical aspects of a Healthy City, it is essential that he understand how these are translated into practice. This specifically means understanding more about the application of the SPIRIT model in the Asia Pacific Region and how to create a city health profile.

The SPIRIT Framework

The concept of a Healthy City is based on a philosophy focused on enhancing health through improvements in certain social, cultural, and economic conditions through changes in human attitudes, implementing initiatives for improving personal and environmental health, and promoting the idea of health being an integral part of the community's structure. Taking into account the diverse needs of a Healthy City, the SPIRIT framework was proposed as an evaluation tool for the Healthy Cities Award (given out by the Alliance for Healthy Cities, AFHC). It was adopted by the General Assembly of the Alliance in October 2004 and put into use (Lee, 2004a, 2010a, 2010b). SPIRIT is an acronym, and positive outcomes from each component reflect the success of the Health City.

Settings Approach, Sustainability

The integration of activities at elemental settings can serve as entry points to develop a comprehensive Healthy City project. The Healthy Settings Approach can be an effective way to create supportive environments as it can facilitate complex interventions to suit particular settings. Mechanisms to secure political commitment, healthy public policy, intersectoral collaboration, community participation, information sharing, and resources are important to assure sustainability. Bloch et al. (2014) introduced the concept of the "Super-setting Approach", which optimises the use of diverse and valuable resources embedded in the local community and strengthens social interactions and local ownership as drivers of change.

Political Commitment, Policy, Partnership

There should be a written policy statement and health should always be on the agenda for public policies. It is important to note that health has no place on the political agenda, unlike health care policy which is usually accorded higher priority (Goumans and Springett, 1997). A Healthy City Programme (HCP) should not be regarded as something additional to mainstream activities and should instead be integrated into the mainstream structure. Healthy public policies, when effective, can be a threat to some established interests and existing groups, which are often powerful, so the balance should not only be based on political goodwill and commitment of local politicians and administrators but also on that of the community (Delaney, 1994; Boonekamp et al., 1999; Naylor and Buck, 2018). For example, equity in health and human-centred sustainable development are core values for the new European Health Policy Framework and Strategy, and cities have a significant influence on the wider determinants of health, with political commitment being one important mode of action (Tsouros, 2013). The Public

Health England report (2015) highlights communities as building blocks for health, and the National Institute for Health and Care Excellence (NICE) endorses community engagement as strategy for health improvement.

Information, Innovation

A Healthy City will naturally need to measure the "health" of the city. The many factors that interact to influence the health of citizens can be grouped into four main categories (Crown, 2003):

- health promotion activities (e.g., programmes that aid citizens in their lifestyle choices);
- health services (e.g., preventive treatments, screening, and rehabilitation services);
- social care efforts (e.g., increased social inclusion, reduced discrimination, and promotion of inter-generation solidarity and respect); and
- environmental factors (both physical and social).

The health determinants in each of the above categories can predict the health of a community. Quantitative and qualitative information should be utilised to assess the determinants of health. Such information includes general demography, household education, income and family expenses, employment and occupation, local economy and industry, infrastructure, living environment and sanitation, housing environment, environmental quality, land use, urbanisation, community activities, lifestyles and health behaviours, disease prevention activities, health care and welfare services, cultural values, and leisure and recreational services (Rydin et al., 2012; Sirgy et al., 2000; Lee, 2009a). A health profile should be created to highlight these determinants of health, and the HCPs should be innovative in meeting the public's needs and promote a climate to support changes. There should be a mechanism for sharing ideas with others and publicise best practices. Programmes should evolve in accordance with the local traditions of civil society and the experience and skills of government officials and the local community.

Resources, Research

A foundation of evidence is essential to develop a Healthy City as it forms the basis of policy-making, rational decision-making, effective planning, efficient allocation of resources, visible evaluation of outcomes, and fruitful exchange of experiences with other cities (Takano, 2003). As Healthy City projects encourage community participation and people's perception of health is an important factor for successful implementation of an HCP, research into health-risk perceptions and the best ways of conducting community consultations is needed (Ogawa, 2002). The city also needs to commit resources to support the HCP. However, it is important to be cautious whether cross-cutting health initiatives, including HCPs, justify a need for higher-end development and achievement. In some cases, the initiative might not appropriately address the needs of marginalised groups in the population and could ultimately exacerbate inequalities (Cole et al., 2017). Therefore, research guiding allocation of resources is essential for Healthy City development.

Infrastructure, Intersectoral

Effective implementation of an HCP requires the city to develop formal structures that see health as part of the mainstream activities of all key organisations and departments (Goumans and Springett, 1997; WHO, 2002). Intersectoral collaboration is important in a Healthy City due to the complexity of determinants of health making it difficult for any single institution to restore all issues. This was beautifully highlighted by Kang (2016), which uses the promotion of physical activity in Korean Healthy Cities as an example. Furthermore, Elsey et al. (2019) has proposed an urban health systems model focusing on multisectoral approaches to look beyond the health sector to tackle the determinants of health and recognise the plurality of health service providers.

Training

When developing and evaluating a Healthy City, it is crucial to observe the spirit of capacity building in the community. Thus, training is essential for the successful implementation of an HCP.

The SPIRIT model can provide a framework in which an integrated and holistic approach to public health can be pursued so policy, environment, social matters, behaviour, and biomedical interventions can take their rightful place side by side (Ashton, 1992; Kang, 2016; Naylor and Buck, 2018; Tsouros, 2013; WHO, 2016; WHO, 2018). Table 3.1 outlines the requirements for each domain.

Table 3.1: The SPIRIT Model

Settings approach, Sustainability	The city should put a strong emphasis on developing activities in different settings such as schools, workplaces, and marketplaces to promote and influence health. *Questions for assessment:* Has the city developed a strategic plan to ensure sustainable development? Is the programme engaging in strategic partnerships with city management and planning processes? Are all the stakeholders in agreement on the main health and environment problems in the city? Does the city secure the ownership of the programme to the community?
Political commitment, Policy, Partnership	The political leaders of the city should make a public commitment that they will move their city towards becoming a Healthy City. There should be a written policy statement. *Questions for assessment:* Are health issues accorded high priority in public policy? Has the city involved all stakeholders, professionals, and academics with expertise in the Healthy City process to formulate healthy public policies? Is there a mechanism for wide consultation and regular review of the policies? Is the city encouraging communities to participate in urban development for better health and quality of life?
Information, Innovation	Information should be available concerning (1) the important health problems and health issues in the city, (2) any analyses of the economic and social determinants of health for the city, (3) the concerns of the health care delivery system of the city, (4) the special population groups at risk, (5) the existing health promotion programmes organised by different parties, (6) the community's perception of health, and (7) the level and standards of primary health care in the city. *Questions for assessment:* Is information in each of these areas available? Is there enough research to draw valuable conclusions? Does the city have a comprehensive health profile based on this information and a city health plan that incorporates it? Has the city implemented programmes meeting the public's needs? Does the city share and incorporate the best practices?
Resources, Research	The city should have a full understanding of their current and future resources and how they will be utilised in the process of becoming a Healthy City. *Questions for assessment:* Is an adequate level of resources earmarked for the programme? Has a research framework been developed for needs assessment and measurement of outcomes? Has the city engaged experts in research?
Infrastructure, Intersectoral	There should be a steering committee responsible for the overall management and coordination of the programme. There should be a technical committee or working committee with members from different sectors to address specific projects. *Questions for assessment:* Does the steering committee include representatives from all sectors and local stakeholders? Does the committee have enough professional input?
Training	Training should target professionals, administrators, policy makers, politicians, and lay people. The city should identify institutions that can provide this training. *Questions for assessment:* Are there training courses at different levels in health education and health promotion? Are these training courses available in all sectors? Do interested parties know how to access such training? Is the training meaningful?

Source: author.

Case Studies of Alliance for Healthy Cities Award Winners

Levels of Achievement

The AFHC launched the Healthy City Awards, not only as an accreditation scheme for Healthy Cities but also as a way to foster the sharing of good practices. The criteria for award accreditation are based on the SPIRIT framework. There are three levels of achievement for good infrastructure, good dynamics, and strong action. The steps for each award build on from each level.

Healthy City with Good Infrastructure (Level 1)

To obtain this award, the city will need to have established the ground work for becoming a Healthy City. The city will need to:

(1) demonstrate initiatives in multiple settings to promote population health with strategic planning;

(2) establish political commitment to healthy public policy and involvement of different stakeholders;

(3) create a city health profile with resources earmarked to address the health needs of the city, including training at different levels;

(4) have the basic layout of good infrastructure and support established in different sectors;

(5) have laid down a good foundation of processes to help the city become a Healthy City;

(6) launch various health-promotion activities to improve the health knowledge of local citizens; and

(7) strengthen health services.

These steps establish the foundation and infrastructure of a Healthy City and are essential to engage and empower the community to build up a healthy environment and implement more health-promotion activities to promote wellness.

Healthy City with Good Dynamics (Level 2)

The steps for Level 2 accreditation focus more on enhancing city health. The city will already have a good infrastructure and adequate resources for support. For this award level, the city needs to:

(8) demonstrate action in linking healthy settings to promote better health;

(9) demonstrate how policies are being translated into practice and how the city makes use of its city health profile;

(10)   demonstrate how local leaders and stakeholders are placed in the city's infrastructure to push the Healthy City movement forward;

(11)   launch new initiatives to involve community members and establish a programme to assist "disadvantaged" groups (e.g., new citizens);

(12)   hold seminars on a wide range of topics to empower citizens to lead a healthy life and establish policies and community actions to sustain the effects;

(13)   develop a comprehensive set of indicators to measure the health of the population;

(14)   have made progress to support a healthy environment; and

(15)   hold local and international forums to promote the Healthy City concept.

Cities that follow through with these steps will be dynamic and full of energy. There will be a multitude of new initiatives to create a supportive environment for better health and well-being. The established infrastructure and enhanced dynamics of the city will support the next steps for strong action.

Healthy City with Strong Action (Level 3)

The top and final tier of steps for the award concerns the implementation and follow through to become an accredited Healthy City and the advancement of the Healthy City concept city-wide. The city will need to:

(16)   use the Healthy City concept as a well-embedded and integral part of city planning and development;

(17)   have resources allocated for research and development, including networking with other cities nationally and internationally, taking the city into the international arena;

(18)   ensure that local politicians and leaders are aware of the importance of a Healthy City to the livelihood of the local residents;

(19)   promote active participation from professional groups in both the academic and private sectors;

(20)   measure and take steps to preserve its natural capital and sustainable ecological system as well as invest in substantial environment improvement and ecological protections (e.g., move industrial enterprises out and move

tertiary industries in, stop or refuse projects with detrimental effects on the environment, group industries in certain areas to avoid scattering); and

(21) initiate the construction of rural concentrated living quarters, promote the concept of cycle economy, and connect economic recycling resources.

Box 3.1 provides a brief description of three cities that have received Level 3 AFHC Awards for being a "Healthy City with Strong Action". Each of these cities has started to include health in all policies and conducts research on Healthy City development. The cities also engage stakeholders across different sectors and have an effective administrative structure in place. These cities were assessed with the SPIRIT framework.

Creative Development

Building on the Healthy City Awards for different levels of achievement, the AFHC has further streamlined some of the factors of the SPIRIT framework to establish awards for "Creative Development" to cultivate creative and innovative approaches for Healthy City development. The criteria are increased levels of:

(1) relevance (i.e., how the city's specific needs are handled);

(2) originality and innovation (i.e., how the implementation of the Healthy City is facilitated); and

(3) influence (i.e., how the process and work impacts that in other cities).

Outstanding Awards are given to the Healthy City projects that demonstrate a high degree of innovation in addressing the specific needs of the population. The projects will need to have induced changes in people's mindset. The work will also need to have an impact on other cities and will need to have shown positive outcomes. Merit Awards in this category are also given to projects with innovative ideas and good potential for further development. However, the impact of these projects may only be at an early stage. Table 3.2 highlights some of the Creative Development Awards given in recent years. The awardee cities have demonstrated the impact of the Healthy City concept and include some of the components of epidemiological assessment featured in the Precede-Proceed Model explained in Chapter 2.

**Box 3.1: AFHC 2016 Achievement Awards for Healthy City with Strong Action
(Source: AFHC)**

Gangnam City, Seoul, Republic of Korea

- Barrier-free for physical activities and well-being is emphasised in city policies
- Promotion of bicycle use and green growth as well as a Health Impact assessment on the carbon mileage programme
- Many local ordinances have been enacted recognising health as an important determinant in developing local policies
- Initiatives are in place for community participation in budget planning
- World leader in e-government
- Various well-designed research studies have been conducted on population health and social indicators reflecting the well-being of citizens are used
- Involvement of private sectors and health professionals
- Active engagement in international Healthy Cities development, hosting two recent international conferences and the 2010 AFHC conference
- A Healthy City team is embedded in the city's administrative structure

Jinju City, Republic of Korea

- The city has a detailed budget plan for various types of city health programmes
- Various well-designed instruments have been developed to collect detailed information reflecting the city's health profile and improvement after programme initiation. Long-term sustainable development has taken place
- The city promoted business with local organisations to set competence of various standards
- Substantial investment has been put into training and further development of the Healthy City programme

Owarisashi City, Japan

- Under each item of SPIRIT, the city has illustrated at least one case study showing how the Healthy City programme has flourished
- Stakeholders are engaged and plans for research, development of a city health profile, training, and international development are established
- The city has demonstrated putting policies into practice
- The city has stressed the prevention of lifestyle-related diseases, safety (including child abuse), citizens' views on city development (by annual questionnaire), and wider intersectoral collaboration
- An environmental assessment has been conducted

Table 3.2: AFHC Creative Development Award

City, Year Awarded	Main Focus and Brief Description
Kwai Tsing District, Hong Kong SAR: Enhancement of Community Health Care** 2016	Good Health System The Medical-Welfare-Community Model not only filled in the gaps of mainstream services, but it also facilitated synergy between different healthy settings to promote health in the Kwai Tsing District. The model has made a significant impact to tackle the triple health burden of communicable and non-communicable diseases, mental health, and injuries. It also covered people of all ages by integrating the programme in different settings. The Kwai Tsing District was later selected as first pilot District Health development programme based on its success.
Kaohsiung Healthy Harbour City Association, Taiwan: Plan for Fall Prevention for the Elderly** 2016	Good Health System This programme focused on preventing elderly community members from falling. It is important to establish a good system to improve walkability with the assistance of new technology. This is an emerging area for Healthy Cities to focus on.
Pingtung Healthy City Association (PDCA), Taiwan* 2012	Evaluation The PDCA enabled the city to meet its quantitative and qualitative improvement goals. The model used could be a good learning and evaluation model, and the city should further discuss how its conceptual planning model led them to success. Clear links should be observed between the Total Quality Management and PDAC programmes and the improved health indicators.
City of Owariasahi, Japan* 2012	Prevention of Non-communicable Diseases The Healthy Asahi Plan encouraged health assessments and cancer screenings. The programme was structured well. The project managed to conduct a preliminary analysis of cost-effectiveness to show medical savings. The results would enable other cities to implement a similar NCD prevention strategy.
Tainan Healthy City Association* 2012	Prevention of Non-communicable Diseases The combination of hardware and software initiatives in this programme were innovative, meeting the needs of the 21st century. The establishment of a fitness database, "Sport and Health Map", and physical fitness volunteers is a good lesson for other cities/organisations. The project has shown improved outcome indicators (i.e., hardware construction, software construction) as well as increased physical activities and volunteer movements.
Yanggu Country, Gangwon Province, Republic of Korea* 2012	Prevention of Non-communicable Diseases The concept of an "Atopic Dermatitis Village" has clearly demonstrated a breakthrough in the management of difficult and highly prevalent chronic conditions that significantly impact daily life. Their results were promising and encouraging.
Miaoli Healthy City Association** 2012	Prevention of Non-communicable Diseases The association coordinated across different sectors and integrated the different domains of the Ottawa Charter for Health into different settings. The programme was planned well, with very encouraging results.
Zhangjiagang, China* 2012	Health Equity The city should be honoured for its "National Disabled People Rehabilitation Model". The city has widened its range of services to close the health inequity gaps for disabled persons.
Busanjngu, Busan, Republic of Korea* 2012	Health Equity The city has targeted the health issues of the under-privileged Gaegeum-3-dong with an innovative health improvement programme. The programme was based on community diagnosis and local partnerships, and makes use of local resources. Indicators reflected impressive improvements.
Gangnam, Republic of Korea* 2012	Ubiquitous City The city has enhanced its strengths in IT to further develop tele-health, with significant improvements in physical activities, drinking, weight management, and mental health.

Table 3.2: Continued

City, Year Awarded	Main Focus and Brief Description
Gwangmyeong City, Korea* 2012	Ubiquitous City This city is a good model for other cities to create safe and healthy settings with the U-Integrated Control Centre, which can be expanded to prevent various crimes.
Guangdong-gu Public Health Centre, Korea* 2012	Good Health System (Integrative Model) This project has demonstrated the importance and significant impact of integrated primary health care. It has led to both health improvement and better utilisation of services.
Logan, Australia* 2012	Disaster Preparedness This programme implemented an Aged Care Disaster Management Plan to ease the burden of existing services and highlighted the importance of such a plan for community health.
Owariasahi City, Japan** 2012	Disaster Preparedness A Mutual Support Agreement between this and other cities helped increase survival of citizens following big disasters, like earthquakes, in Japan. The citizens felt more secure.
City of Casey, Victoria, Australia* 2012	Healthy Urban Planning Healthy planning included enhancing the physical environment and social environment, with a focus on infrastructure to promote social connectedness.
Miaoli Healthy City Association, Taiwan** 2012	Healthy Urban Planning Upgraded infrastructure in both urban and rural areas using multi-sectoral action to address the determinants of health. The plan reduced travel time and increased energy savings.
Yeongdeungpoa-gu, Seoul Metropolitan City** 2010	Master Plan for Health Protection against Climate Change The project involved analysis and forecasting of problems related to climate change up to 2080. It dissected out the size of the population that would be harmed as a result of climate change for different types of diseases. The intervention strategies were planned systematically and comprehensively covered management and operation, capacity building, and health protection, as well as wider settings including schools and the local community, and different population groups such as children and the elderly. The outcome evaluation was based on process evaluation but indicated that a solid infrastructure was in place.

*Merit; **Outstanding

Source: AFHC.

The AFHC Creative Development Awards for different cities have highlighted a wide range of innovative approaches to address the health needs of the population. Each approach can bring closer integration of services from different disciplines and can be used as models for other locations and programmes. For example, the Medical-Welfare-Community Model in Kwai Tsing District, Hong Kong, evolved to become the first pilot District Health Centre commissioned by the Government in 2019 (Lee, 2019b). Similar cross-sector improvements were observed for programmes in non-communicable disease (NCD) prevention in Maoli, in health equity in Busan, and in primary care integration in Gangdong-gu. There are numerous projects making use of new systematic approaches for evaluation as well as advanced information technology (hardware and software), including,

Gangnam's tele-health project, Kaoshing City's technology-assisted walkability project, Tainan City's "Sport and Health Map" fitness database, and Gwangmyeong City's U-Integrated Control Centre to prevent crime. Healthy City development aims to enable the population to influence their health and emphasises the inputs for making changes and the impact at a societal level. A successful example of such a programme is the "Master Plan for Health Protection against Climate Change" in Yeongdeungpoa-gu, Korea. Similarly, programmes addressing the societal response to natural disaster have also been granted awards: Logan, Australia (for flooding preparedness), and Owariasahi City, Japan (for earthquake preparedness). Considering the various Creative Development Awards granted over the years, it is obvious that creative and innovative ideas should be gathered from wider sectors, and efforts should not be restricted to a purely biomedical approach. In fact, the experiences of different successful cases has created a learning platform for Healthy City development. These cases provide practical tips that other cities can learn from and put into practice in the context of their own localities.

Award for Pioneers in Healthy Cities

Healthy Cities continuously need pioneering spirits and efforts to make things happen in the real world. This award recognises individuals and groups (including AFHC members and non-members) who have more than 10 years of experience directly related to Healthy Cities and have contributed to the international development of HCPs. This award recognises pioneering work in research; national, regional, and international networking; political advocacy; capacity building; community-based activities; media advocacy and journalism; legislation and institutions; mentoring; arts; cooperate social responsibility in the business sector; and other areas.

Table 3.3 provides a brief description of the awardees for the Pioneers in Healthy Cities Award in 2016. The projects include pioneering work in knowledge transfer, enhanced setting synergy and community-based care, space and architectural vitality, and increased administrative support and financial investment for sustainable Healthy City development nationally and internationally. The experiences in these cities and the work done by these groups and individuals should be used to enlighten other cities and city leaders to be more creative in developing their cities in their Healthy City journey.

Table 3.3: Awards for Pioneers in Healthy Cities 2016

Miaoli Healthy City Association: Pioneer Study on the Health Promotion Model of the Government in Two Hierarchies	The association has focused on translating the Healthy City framework to develop a "Healthy Village" and empower the local community to develop expertise in building healthy villages. Preliminary data has shown success in health improvement.
Kwai Tsing Safe Community and Healthy City Association: Linking Health and Safety Together	The district has been a pioneer in involving many different stakeholders and joining up different healthy settings. This has been accomplished by making use of Geographic Information Systems to conduct injury surveillance identifying high-risk groups and planning effective improvement programmes. The group also joined up different healthy settings including schools, housing estates, workplaces, and elderly homes to evolve a multi-faceted Healthy City movement, in addition to collaborating with clinical settings to develop community health programmes for primary (CPR campaign), secondary (medical and health record, family practitioner services), and tertiary prevention (diabetic retinopathy).
Nakpyo Hong, Muju County, Korea	The county conducted impressive work to make use of abandoned space for revitalisation to engage the public. They also made use of public spaces, such as bus stops and rural parks, for social gatherings and festivals. This work utilised public architecture for more community-focused uses, leading to ecological improvements and increased vitality.
KIM Gi-Yeol, Former Mayor of Wonju City	A man of vision for health promotion, Kim used the entire revenue from tobacco tax to promote health in the community and as an investment for Healthy City programmes. He designated World Healthy Day as Wonju Citizen's Health Day and honoured local residents who follow good health practices. He secured a pathway to becoming a Healthy City with his plan within the city administration, committed to a robust evaluation method through a collaboration with an academic institution, facilitated infrastructure development, engaged the private sectors, and played an active role in international Healthy City development by fostering strong partnerships with other Healthy Cities in the region and also WHO.

Source: AFHC.

Healthy City Programmes Lead to Healthy Urban Governance

Before the turn of the 20th century, there were only a few megacities in the Asia Pacific Region. However, with the rapid increase in economic development came a rapid expansion of megacities (WHO/WPRO, 2011). The sudden influx of people into cities, both here and elsewhere in the world, led to a deficit in material conditions, psycho-social resources, and political engagement, resulting in poverty of empowerment at the individual, community, and national levels. Although the term is often only thought of in economic terms, poverty can also be observed in terms of social conditions, sometimes expressed as "relative marginality", and contributes to chronic stress, depression, and feelings of bitterness, hopelessness, and desperation (Corburn, 2017; Polit, 2005; Naylor and Buck, 2018). The levels of basic necessities are generally higher in urban areas, and a higher average income in urban areas creates an affluent minority. It is often rural poverty that leads to migration from rural to urban areas. In the poorest settings, urban populations are experiencing adverse, "obesogenic" shifts in dietary composition, which are taking place at a much faster rate than the potential benefits of living in an urban centre. In fact, recent studies have shown that obesity epidemics tend to hit medium-sized cities undergoing rapid economic development, such as Macao (Lee et al., 2011), and these epidemics are continuously occurring around the world as economies expand (Lee et al., 2015b). The residential density, neighbourhood safety (e.g., with regard to crime, traffic, and injuries), and increasing reliance on motor cars are all factors that are shifting citizens towards physical inactivity in both developed and developing countries (Kjellstrom and Hinde, 2006). The health of children in the community is also affected indirectly by globalisation and urbanisation as a result of ignored care and parents working longer hours.

Thus, it is important to study how the cultural, social, and political conditions enhance or diminish opportunities for the population to be healthy. The determinants of healthy actions at the macro-level focus on social change and are primarily related to the adoption of innovations within the social system (Rogers, 1995). The determinants of healthy actions at the micro-level involve the factors affecting individuals. It is individual people who make decisions, and the sum total of their decision-making ultimately determines the social action in the community. The WHO Commission on Social Determinants of Health (CSDH, 2008) recognised the importance of the urban setting as a social determinant of health. It is, therefore, important that HCPs address the individual as well as the wider social determinants of health, and see to not only improve population health but also mediate sustainable urban development. Developing a Healthy City is a solution to tackle many emerging issues of rapid development of urbanisation so residents can have the benefits of healthy governance of their living community. A Healthy City can also be a means to achieve harmonisation and revitalisation of the society.

Urban governance is an overarching concept that ties together three concepts: urban planning, urban sustainability, and urban social conditions. It is the process through which a balance is sought, ensuring compatibility between the need for social equity, environmental sustainability, and healthy built environments. Healthy urban governance involves putting people's health and human development at the centre of all decisions. The governance of an urban community needs to be healthy, and it needs to "enable people to increase control over and improve their health" (WHO, 1986). Elsey et al. (2019) have proposed an urban health systems model focusing on multisectoral approaches to look beyond the health sector to improve factors affecting health. The model seeks to engage urban residents through participatory decision-making and recognises the plurality of health service providers. There are four key elements of healthy urban governance:

- A *whole government* approach, which brings together various government departments to find ways to improve the health of the city with collective action and includes conducting health impact assessments of public policies beyond the health sectors.

- *Intersectoral action*, which brings together the public and private sectors, including statutory bodies, non-profit organisations, civic associations, religious bodies, and academic institutions, to improve health and human development in an equitable and sustainable manner.

- *Vertical coordination* of different levels of government along with non-governmental organisations (NGOs) and international donors, if applicable, including those involved in the development and implementation of urban policies and programmes.

- *Community engagement*, which refers to people's engagement in local actions to improve health and their participation in the democratic governance of the city and their own neighbourhoods.

These key elements are essential for healthy governance of a community. These elements can be incorporated into an HCP by first analysing how the cultural, social, and political conditions enhance or diminish opportunities for well-being by establishing a city health profile. The programme will then need to capture the local needs so residents can have equitable access to different services and be involved in decision-making. An HCP incorporating these element of healthy governance will be citizen-friendly for all ages, so all residents will be beneficiaries of city development. This will also help to build up community resilience for responding to crisis conditions.

Hong Kong as a Case Study

A "Family Letter to Hong Kong" was published on 10 December 2016 and focused on health care reform and raised the idea of a District Health System in Hong Kong (RTHK, 2016). Similar concepts (including the Healthy City model) should be adopted to empower different districts (mini-cities) to become smart, green, and resilient, as highlighted in the recent "Hong Kong 2030+" document. However, a Healthy City is more than just being green and hygienic. Apart from a stable ecosystem for sustainable development, a Healthy City also needs to emphasise a diverse and innovative local economy.

The AFHC Global Conference was held in Hong Kong in 2014. The conference focused on the key issues of health in equity, social justice, social inclusion, strengthening social capital, ecological sustainability, creating supportive environments, integrated health services, and health skills for citizens. The AFHC Hong Kong Declaration 2014 called upon governments to put the development of Healthy Cities as a core value of city development so that the citizens have easy access to the necessities of city life, such as adequate shelter, security of tenure, safe water and food, safe and hygienic environment, services for health promotion and health protection, education, balanced nutrition, social security, and free mobility. If all 18 districts of Hong Kong would adopt the Healthy City concept, this would create synergy to the 2030+ plan in addition to promoting revitalisation and harmonisation of society. Disappointingly, the government of the Hong Kong Special Administrative Region (SAR) has not taken some of the key steps to develop Hong Kong into a Healthy City. This is necessary to facilitate sustainable development and to develop visionary trajectory planning. The passion and enthusiasm of NGOs, academic organisations, and professional bodies alone cannot sustain a sustainable Healthy City movement. For Hong Kong, and other cities like it, the first step is to create a city health profile.

Creating Hong Kong's Health Profile

A city health profile should be established by community diagnosis and include indicators for the determinant of health in that local area. It is important to have a full picture of these determinant factors rather than just simple data on health in order for a more comprehensive plan to be created. This big picture plan should include both quantitative and qualitative data. Cities are complex environments and their layers and domains of governance require a correspondingly detailed method to understand the context and impact of the Healthy City Approach (de Leeuw et al., 2015). Besides taking into account the indicators developed based on European Healthy

Cities (WHO, 1998; Nakamura, 2003), city health profiles of districts in Hong Kong were created by collecting information on the residents' health status, health care services utilisation and satisfaction, lifestyles, personal safety, exercise level, quality of life based on the WHO Quality of Life (QOL)-BREF (Hong Kong Project Team, 1997; WHOQOL Group, 1994), and also the citizens' perception of the hygienic environment, security, fire safety, estate/building management, park and amusement facilities, and culture and leisure facilities with reference to the Community Quality of Life Questionnaire (Sirgy et al., 2000; Siu et al., 2004). This city health profile ultimately reflects each individual's perception of their position in life in the context of the culture and value systems where they live and in relation to their goals, expectation, standards, and concerns (Sirgy et al., 2000; Lee, 2009a).

Different means have been suggested for assessing public health interventions, and the most useful of these do not rely solely on technical exercises conducted by external experts but also incorporate dialogue, deliberation, and discussion between key stakeholders and consider the insights and experience of local communities. This kind of multifaceted assessment is discussed in a paper by the UCL Lancet Commission on urban environment (Rydin et al., 2012). Further, in phase 5 of the European Healthy City project, the General Evaluation Questionnaire (GEQ) also incorporated a self-assessment of the city's status (WHO, 2009c). In Hong Kong, the tools adopted for establishing city health profiles in different districts have taken into account the views of local communities, and focus groups were conducted in some districts to gain further insights.

Revitalisation and Harmonisation in Practice

Sai Kung was the first district in the Hong Kong SAR to advocate the Healthy City movement. According to the Hong Kong 2001 Population Census, Sai Kung had the highest growth rate over the previous decade among all 18 districts in Hong Kong, reaching 150%. This growth was mainly concentrated in the Tseung Kwan O (TKO) New Town. The population of Sai Kung was around 400,000, with more than 80% concentrated in TKO. Furthermore, the population is expected to approach half a million in less than a decade. Strategic development to adopt the Healthy City Approach is essential for local people living and working in the area to enhance their health and quality of life as well as to cultivate a sense of belonging in the community, particularly during stages of rapid development.

The Haven of Hope Christian Service (HOHCS), a local NGO, was founded more than 40 years ago and has committed itself to the betterment of the local community. In 1997, HOHCS initiated the development of TKO New Town as the first Healthy City in Hong Kong. This group was later incorporated into the Sai Kung District Council in 2002, and this change represented the transfer of programme ownership to the community. This bottom-up approach, while in stark contrast with most of the Healthy Cities in other parts of the world, bears the strategic advantage of building up an intersectoral partnership with different stakeholders in the community. These stakeholders include the district council, government departments, corporations, NGOs, schools, housing estates, commercial enterprises, community bodies, and local people. These various groups were engaged first through publicity events, the HOHCS/District Council website, and regular newsletters. Then, different programmes addressing the health needs identified through community diagnosis were implemented, promoting even more participation from these stakeholders. Together, these measures allowed individuals and groups to collaborate in the planning, implementation, and evaluation of health-promoting campaigns, further solidifying the feeling of shared ownership. Only through these measures could the momentum towards becoming a Healthy City be sustained in the long run.

Box 3.2 provides a summary of diagnosis, interventions, and achievements in the Sai Kung HCP. As the pioneering HCP in Hong Kong, this project can be used as a model for the development of Healthy Cities in other districts as well as other megacities in the Asia Pacific Region. The HCPs in two other areas (Central Western District and Northern District) are assessed in depth in Chapter 4.

Another Case Study: The Republic of Korea

Another country worth of study that has multiple locations implementing the Healthy City model is Korea. Healthy Cities in Korea use programmes that are based on a project model led by municipalities and financed by the Health Promotion Fund (Nam and Engelhardt, 2007). In 2004, four Korean cities joined the AFHC as founding members, and as of December 2010, there are a total of 53 cities among the 264 municipalities in Korea that have joined. Of these, 49 are also members of the Korea Healthy Cities Partnership (KHCP) and engage in related networking activities. One reason for this widespread implementation of HCPs

**Box 3.2: The Healthy City Programme in Hong Kong
(Source: Kjellstrom et al., 2007, Appendix 7, Case Study 1-D17).**

A community diagnosis was conducted in 2000 to identify the health needs and set the priorities for action. A follow-up community health survey was then conducted in 2006 to assess the impact of interventions under the Healthy City programme and shed light on the way forward.

Health Determinant(s): Social, economic, environmental

Health effect(s) included: Self-reported health status; health-enhancing and compromising behaviours; emotional well-being; family, neighbourhood, and community relationships

Issues of concern: Lack of physical activities; unhealthy eating; diminishing neighbourhood relationships; few public facilities such as transport, health services, leisure, and recreation

Solution: Establishing a Healthy City based on the WHO Model

Intervention(s):

1. Promoted physical activity for all by:

    - Encouraging local people to walk more in daily life and educated them about healthy choices using a multifaceted approach with behavioural, educational, and environmental aspects.

    - Encouraging people to adopt and sustain their habits of physical activity through peer support by forming different physical activity groups.

    - Collaborating with general practitioners to encourage their patients to start and maintain their physical activity for health reasons during consultations.

2. Established Healthy Schools through the collaboration of an interdisciplinary team of social workers, dieticians, nurses, and school heads to provide tailored programmes and activities to promote the health of students, teachers, and parents.

3. Organised the Sai Kung Elderly Service Coordinating Committee, a district-wide platform with representatives from most if not all elderly service providers in the community which seeks to promote physical activity, emotional health, flu prevention, fall prevention, home safety, and drug safety among the elderly and their caregivers.

4. Organised programmes to promote neighbourhood relationships (including the "Healthy and Safe Estates", "Hello, My Neighbours!", and "Health Everywhere, Blessings Every Year" campaigns) as well as to encourage estate management to perform daily exercises to improve physical fitness and reduce work-related injuries (the "Workplace Exercise" programme).

5. Under the three-year "TKO Is My Home" Community Health and Inclusion Project, a "Good Cooking Ideas" mutual help group was established where citizens were trained to cook healthy meals in addition to promoting mutual care and support in the community.

Evaluation and intervention outcomes:

- Over 65% of citizens perceived the city's health status as very good or quite good.
- Significantly increased physical activity and exercise level of the residents.
- Over 80% of citizens perceived family relationships as very good or quite good.
- Significant improvement in neighbourhood relationship: 61% of citizens rated relationships as very good or quite good in 2006 (compared with 51% in 2000).
- More people showed concern for local affairs (24% in 2006 vs 19% in 2000) and participated in volunteer services (42% in 2006 vs 30% in 2000).
- Significant rise (19% to 35%) in citizens knowing about the Healthy City model.
- Improvement in various types of facilities in the district as reflected by a significant lowering of dissatisfaction scores.
- Healthy Food Stall established to improve healthy eating.

Lessons and future prospects: A bottom-up approach can be used to facilitate flexibility in building intersectoral partnerships and encourage innovation in implementing local solutions to address local problems by pooling local resources among stakeholders. While efforts had been made previously to make the local environment more conducive to better physical health, interventions to enhance the psycho-social dimensions of health should follow so that the holistic health of the community can be realised in the long run.

is that the Korean government plays an active role in helping local communities diagnose issues and establish interventions, in part by conducting Health Impact Assessments (Yoo et al., 2007). These Korean cities have made full use of research facilities of academic institutions and information exchange within the nation and with international partners. The political commitment from the heads of municipalities has been consistently strong, particular under the guidance of the former mayor of the capital city Seoul who later became president and established a strong model for ecological restoration of the city to enhance healthy living for residents. The rate at which the Healthy City model was scaled up across Korea highlights an unprecedented ability to mobilise and motivate individuals and communities to adopt healthy behaviours in multiple aspects of their lives. Box 3.3 summarises some of the developmental milestones of Korea's HCPs and how this scaling up has been successful.

Building Social and Human Capital in Healthy Cities

The case studies outlined here as well as many others illustrate how HCPs can act at the macro, meso, and micro levels of health improvement. Healthy Cities should aim to address the determinants of health, particularly the social, cultural, and political aspects, and facilitate health for individuals and the community. They should collaborate with organisations and institutions to create synergy and place health on the wider political agenda. A Healthy City can empower the community to develop a positive culture for health, and this can further facilitate a higher level of health literacy and collective understanding of the social, environmental, organisational, and political factors that impact health. Improvements in health literacy can also help individuals tackle the determinants of their own personal health better as they build up the interpersonal, cognitive, and social skills that allow individuals to gain access to, understand, and use information to promote and maintain good health (Nutbeam, 2000). Community members are likely to be more empowered to engage in debates around local health issues and better able to collaborate with others in advocating for change at the community and government levels, thus supporting the original intent of the Ottawa Charter. Targeting health communication and education intervention at decision makers rather than just at individuals can provide impetus to challenge existing policies.

Taken together, the Healthy City Approach can build the capacity of individuals, families, and communities to create strong human and social capital. This social capital can also influence the health behaviours of neighbourhood residents by promoting more rapid diffusion of health information, increasing the likelihood that healthy norms of behaviour are adopted, and exerting social control over deviant health-related behaviour (Lee, 2011a). The city health profile and SPIRIT framework in particular provide a means of diagnosing issues and assessing outcomes. While this chapter has discussed broad case studies and pioneering examples, the use of these tools and the kind of full analysis available for post-modern urbanised cities is the focus of the next chapter.

Box 3.3: Scaling Up Healthy City Programmes in Korea
(Sources: Nam and Engelhardt, 2007; Yoo et al., 2007)

Why did the number of Korean Healthy Cities soar? Why has this scaling up been so successful? The following reasons are the underlying cause of this phenomenon:

- Korea raises funds for health promotion from the tobacco tax. It has also allocated a portion of this tax to the HCPs in each municipality.

- The government strongly supports HCPs across the country. These efforts are managed by the Office for Health Care Policy at the Ministry of Health and Welfare. The Korea Health Promotion Foundation has also supported the development and operation of HCPs. The Health Ministry hosted the first Healthy City Forum in six sessions from 2005 to 2006 to solicit opinions, and in 2009 it held the second forum in five sessions to propel discussion about the development of Healthy Cities. Since then, the Korean government has collected opinions from municipalities and awarded prizes to municipalities that had the best-performing health-promotion projects.

- The HCPs in Korea have made full use of the research facilities in local universities, with 41 medical schools and 20 public health schools offering their research capabilities. There is also widespread cooperation between adjacent cities to managing research and development projects (e.g., the Healthy City Research Center at Yonsei University is working in partnership with 13 adjacent municipalities to serve as an adviser for the development of municipality-specific HCPs) and to promote broad policy efforts and public health enhancements.

- Promotion of HCPs is a key agenda item for local political leaders. An example of this is President/Mayor Lee's initiatives for the restoration of Cheongyecheon, the building of new bicycle paths, and a ban on smoking in Seoul.

- Korean Healthy Cities encourage information exchange through network activities. Many Healthy Cities are now members of the KHCP and AFHC. The chair city (Wonju) is in charge of these efforts and acts as a liaison between the government, AFHC, and WHO to support the establishment of Healthy Cities.

Chapter 4

Using a City's Health Profile to Conduct a Post-Modern Analysis of Health and Urbanisation: A Tale of Two Hong Kong Districts in Different Phases of Urban Development

Amelia Lo and Albert Lee

City-super was introduced to the post-modern analysis of health and urbanisation by a study investigating two districts in Hong Kong. Each has a unique historical background: one district reflects early European settlement in the 19th century and is now one of the world's major financial centres, while the other district reflects local settlement (original population) in the 19th century and is evolving from rural to urban. This post-modern analysis provides insight for City-super about how to use a city health profile to assess urban development.

City Health Profiles in Urban Environments

While improvements in mortality and morbidity rates have been noted in various urbanised countries over the last 50 years (Kirdar, 1997; Kjellstrom et al., 2007), a WHO report in 2009, titled "City and Public Health Crisis", pointed out that urbanisation also increases the spread of disease (WHO, 2009d). The report states:

"Poorly managed urban settings can lead to increased exposure to unhealthy and risky conditions which can foster infectious diseases, violence and injuries, pollution-related health problems, and obesity."

Although public health emergencies pose a real threat in large cities, understanding the specific issues posed by urban settings and the appropriate preparation from municipal and national stakeholders would mitigate these threats (WHO, 2009d). Thus, it is essential to consider the different features of the urban environment that influence health (Ompad et al., 2007). Vlahov et al. (2007) outlines four broad categories of urban living conditions that affect health: population composition, physical environment, social environment, and availability of and access to health and social services. Each of these categories can be further divided into their various components. For instance, social environment includes social networks, social capital, and social support (Ompad et al., 2007), which can all affect health by enhancing or buffering stressors and improving access to goods and services influencing health (Vlahov et al., 2007). Ecological analysis, which can identify features of the urban environment associated with health, and multi-level analysis, which integrates individual level variables with variables at the macro-level allowing assessment of multiple levels of influence, are two methodological tools that can be used to examine the relationship between the social determinants of health and health outcomes (WHO, 2009d). Multi-level analysis also provides information about how specific features of cities contribute to individual health (Diez Roux, 2001). At the Urban Age Hong Kong Conference in 2011, researchers shared information confirming the potential power of health and well-being as a point around which to re-think city development, develop new approaches and methods of research, and identify more sensitive and inclusive ways of intervening in cities (Taylor, 2012).

In a report on reconnecting urban planning with health, Giles-Corti et al. (2014) state that liveable communities create the conditions to optimise health and well-being outcomes in residents by influencing multiple social determinants of health (e.g., neighbourhood walkability and access to public transport, public open space, local amenities, and social and community facilities). It is, therefore, essential that a city health profile include indicators of these determinant factors for health. Indeed, a comprehensive plan relies on having a full picture of these determinant factors rather than just simple health data. Chapter 3 describes how city health profiles are created by collecting information on the residents' health status and perception of their position in life in relation to their environment, as well as information gained from discussion between key stakeholders in the community.

A Tale of Two Districts: Data Collection

Hong Kong is a highly urbanised region, with a population density of 6,457 people per km² (7.071 million in mid-2011 in 1,096 km²), a gross domestic product (GDP) per capita of US$34,457 (UK$38,188) (World Bank, 2015), and a widening Gini coefficient (from 0.525 in 2001 to 0.537 in 2011). It is ranked the highest among other well-developed countries in Asia for household income (Hong Kong Census and Statistics Department, 2006b; CIA, 2015).

Hong Kong is sub-divided into 18 districts which have varying characteristics in terms of population demography, social environment, and access to services. Creating a city health profile for individual districts will, therefore, provide insight about how different levels of urbanisation impact on health. The Central and Western District (CWD), with a population of 250,064 (Hong Kong Census and Statistics Department, 2006a), is an affluent district supported by the financial industry and was the first European settlement in the 19th century. This area is located along Victoria Harbour and is regarded as the heart of Hong Kong. In contrast, the Northern District (ND), with a population of 280,730 (Hong Kong Census and Statistics Department, 2006a), was originally a village area with a large indigenous population (i.e., ancestors who settled a few centuries before the British administration arrived) and has undergone rapid urbanisation over the last two decades. It is the northern-most district of Hong Kong and shares a border with mainland China. Examining the city health profiles of these two different districts will provide further insight into post-modern urbanisation and health.

Thus, community diagnosis was conducted by cross-sectional study in 2008 and 2009 in CWD and ND, respectively. The study tools adopted were survey questionnaire on demographic data, chronic illnesses, lifestyle (including risk behaviours, exercise, sedentary activities, diet, mental well-being, interpersonal relationship, satisfaction level of services provided by the Government, voluntary bodies, or private entities), and health and safety. With reference to the WHOQOL-BREF (Hong Kong Project Team, 1997; WHOQOL Group, 1994) as described in Chapter 3, the subjective quality of life of the respondents was assessed in terms of overall quality of life, physical health, mental health, interpersonal relationships, and quality of the environment.

To further investigate the city health in CWD and ND, each district was geographically divided into different zones. Proportional sampling was used to select residents to be interviewed from each zone based on population size to make up a sample size of 800 to 900. The margin of error of the estimated proportion can be guaranteed to be less than 3.5% with a sample size of 800 or more. Thus, although interviews were conducted by random sampling at designated spots, the distribution of the housing types of the respondents was carefully matched with the general population of the specific district based on the 2006 Population By-census (Hong Kong Census and Statistics Department, 2006a). Post-stratification survey weights on age and gender are applied to all analyses in order to adjust for any sample bias.

Focus group interviews were also conducted among residents of CWD. Six focus group sessions were held with 47 interviewees. These interviewees were selected from the transient population working in CWD, community leaders, and established residents, and included men, women, elderly, working population, and students. The topics discussed included environmental hygiene, safety, security, fire services, transportation, and management, as well as civic, recreational, and community services of the district.

City Health Profiles for CWD and ND: Data and Discussion

Demographics and General Quality of Life

In CWD, 808 residents were successfully interviewed. Figure 4.1 shows their demographic characteristics in terms of distribution of age, types of housing, education level, and occupation in comparison to the total Hong Kong population. In ND, 917 residents were successfully interviewed. Figure 4.2 shows their demographic characteristics in comparison to the total Hong Kong population. The study populations of both districts had a higher proportion of elderly and professional residents compared with the general Hong Kong population. In CWD, the distribution of education level and types of housing of respondents were not markedly different from the Hong Kong population. In ND, a higher proportion of respondents lived in public housing and had received education up to the level of secondary 4 to 5, but had a lower proportion with a university education in comparison to the Hong Kong population.

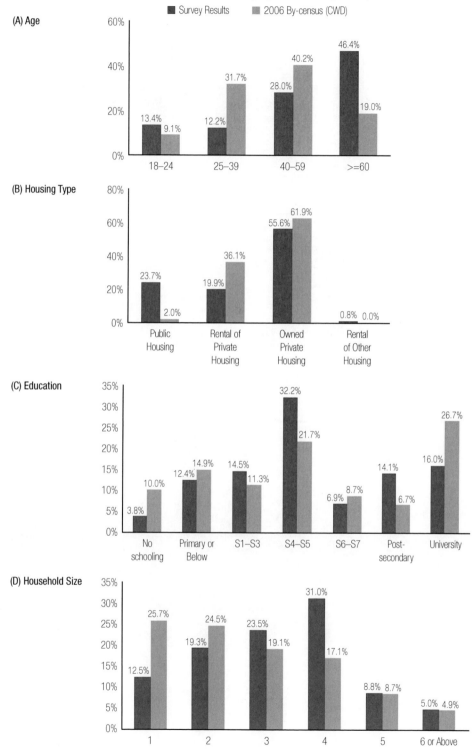

Figure 4.1: Respondent Demographics in CWD (n = 808)

■ Survey Results ■ 2006 By-census (CWD)

(A) Age

18–24: 13.4%, 9.1%
25–39: 12.2%, 31.7%
40–59: 28.0%, 40.2%
>=60: 46.4%, 19.0%

(B) Housing Type

Public Housing: 23.7%, 2.0%
Rental of Private Housing: 19.9%, 36.1%
Owned Private Housing: 55.6%, 61.9%
Rental of Other Housing: 0.8%, 0.0%

(C) Education

No schooling: 3.8%, 10.0%
Primary or Below: 12.4%, 14.9%
S1–S3: 14.5%, 11.3%
S4–S5: 32.2%, 21.7%
S6–S7: 6.9%, 8.7%
Post-secondary: 14.1%, 6.7%
University: 16.0%, 26.7%

(D) Household Size

1: 12.5%, 25.7%
2: 19.3%, 24.5%
3: 23.5%, 19.1%
4: 31.0%, 17.1%
5: 8.8%, 8.7%
6 or Above: 5.0%, 4.9%

Source: CHEHP, CUHK.

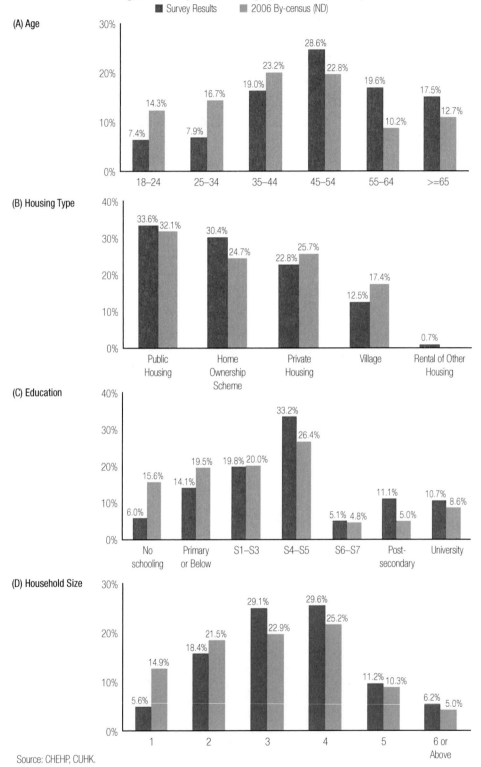

Figure 4.2: Respondent Demographics in ND (n = 917)

■ Survey Results ■ 2006 By-census (ND)

(A) Age

18–24	25–34	35–44	45–54	55–64	>=65
7.4% / 14.3%	7.9% / 16.7%	19.0% / 23.2%	28.6% / 22.8%	19.6% / 10.2%	17.5% / 12.7%

(B) Housing Type

Public Housing	Home Ownership Scheme	Private Housing	Village	Rental of Other Housing
33.6% / 32.1%	30.4% / 24.7%	22.8% / 25.7%	12.5% / 17.4%	0.7%

(C) Education

No schooling	Primary or Below	S1–S3	S4–S5	S6–S7	Post-secondary	University
6.0% / 15.6%	14.1% / 19.5%	19.8% / 20.0%	33.2% / 26.4%	5.1% / 4.8%	11.1% / 5.0%	10.7% / 8.6%

(D) Household Size

1	2	3	4	5	6 or Above
5.6% / 14.9%	18.4% / 21.5%	29.1% / 22.9%	29.6% / 25.2%	11.2% / 10.3%	6.2% / 5.0%

Source: CHEHP, CUHK.

Based on the WHOQOL-BREF, the average quality of life score was higher in ND (14.76 out of 20) compared to CWD (14.51). Concepts such as quality of life, liveability, living environment, residential perception and satisfaction, and evaluation of the residual and living environment all overlap and are often used synonymously. Van Kamp et al. (2003) summarised the literature defining liveability, environmental quality, and quality of life, and they define liveability as the resident's evaluation of the living environment, stressing that it is tied to the area's well-being and social network. Liveable communities rank high in terms of safety, attractiveness, affordability, social cohesiveness, access to public open space, resident education and employment, public services, effective public transport and walking infrastructure, and environmental and economic sustainability (Badland et al., 2014). In the present study, four quality of life variables were assessed: physical health, mental health, interpersonal relationships, and quality of the environment.

Factors Affecting Quality of Life

Figures 4.3 and 4.4 show the scores for the four quality of life factors assessed for three specific subsets of the population: youngsters, housewives, and the elderly. These groups were selected as they spend a significant proportion of their time within the community being assessed and will be the most impacted by the facilities and services offered there, as opposed to those in the working population. Of the lifestyle factors assessed, the quality of the environment was ranked poorest by respondents in both districts. It is probable that the high-density living in Hong Kong is the cause of this poor perception of the physical and psycho-social environment. The population density was 20,102 per km^2 in CWD and 2,055 per km^2 in ND in 2006 (Hong Kong Census and Statistics Department, 2006a). Migration from rural to urban areas often results in "poverty of empowerment" at the individual and community levels because of deficits in material conditions, psycho-social resources, and political engagement, or "relative marginality", as discussed in Chapter 3. This would undoubtedly contribute to chronic stress, depression, and feelings of bitterness, hopelessness, and desperation (Polit, 2005).

In CWD, the youngster age group ranked all of the variables low compared to the general district sample population, especially regarding physical health and interpersonal relationships. The elderly also ranked physical health lower than the general population. In contrast, the district's housewives and elderly ranked interpersonal relationships, mental health, and the quality of the environment

Figure 4.3: Comparison of Scores Given by Respondents of Different Background for Four Aspects of Subjective Quality of Life in CWD (Full score: 20)

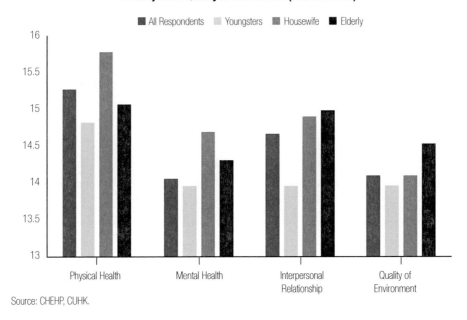

Source: CHEHP, CUHK.

Figure 4.4: Comparison of Scores Given by Respondents of Different Background for Four Aspects of Subjective Quality of Life in ND (Full score: 20)

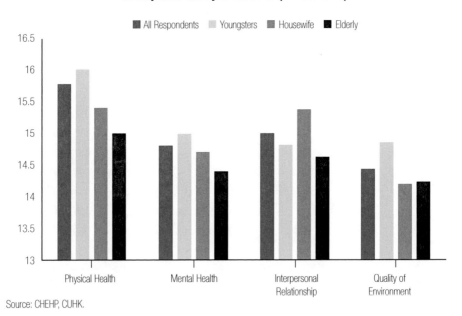

Source: CHEHP, CUHK.

higher than the general population. In ND, it was the elderly sample population who ranked all four variables the lowest, while the youngster age group ranked physical health, mental health, and the quality of the environment variables the highest. This trend in ND is most likely related to a shift in liveability for older residents. To them, the old fabric of life might feel eroded, leaving them deprived of social support and services. There is often less age-friendly infrastructure with increasing urbanisation. Liveable communities also tend to include walkable neighbourhoods and local amenities (Macintyre and Ellaway, 2003), and these components are more vulnerable during rapid urbanisation, such as that in ND, having a greater impact on the daily lives of older residents. However, these changes create an environment more favourable for young people, providing them more opportunities in terms of education and employment, and modernised facilities and better public transport. Yeh (2011) highlighted the advantages of living in high-density areas, specifically highlighting the benefits of more efficient public services, facilities, and transportation. These advantages would be of significant importance for young people. There will always be some gains and losses with urban development, so the possible detrimental effects on certain population groups while other groups are flourishing should not be ignored.

Regarding physical health, ND was found to have a higher proportion of people eating healthy foods and exercising (Table 4.1), with a marked difference in exercise level among students, retirees, housewives, and full-time workers, compared to CWD. In terms of having lunch at home, less than half of the sample population reported having lunch at home in ND (37.2%) and CWD (42.4%). There is evidence showing that objective measures and perceived features of the built environment are associated with positive physical health outcomes (Rydin et al., 2012). The objective and subjective perception of the physical features of the area and perception of residents of the benefits associated with walking and safety are, therefore, significant factors when determining whether the area is more conducive for physical activity or not (Amorim et al., 2010; Panter and Jones, 2010). It has been reported in both developed and developing countries that a pleasing aesthetic as well as spaces for recreation and play encourage outdoor activity and individual physical activity, but increasing reliance on transport systems shifts residents towards physical inactivity (Kjellstrom and Hinde, 2006). CWD is situated on Hong Kong Island, a mountainous landscape. Because of the natural features of the area, urban planning is primarily focused on the slope and narrow

Table 4.1: Comparison of Eating Habits and Level of Exercise of the Two Districts

District/ Lifestyle	Fresh Fruit at Least Once Daily	Vegetable at Least Once Daily	Exercise at Least 3 Days per Weeks of 30 Minutes (overall)	Students Exercising at Least 3 Days per Week of 30 Minutes	Housewife Exercising at Least 3 Days per Week of 30 Minutes	Retired Exercising at Least 3 Days per Week of 30 Minutes	At Least 60 Minutes of Exercise, Moderate Intensity or Above (overall)	Students at Least 60 Minutes of Exercise, Moderate Intensity or Above	Full-time Job at Least 60 Minutes of Exercise, Moderate Intensity or Above
CWD	48.0%	59.7%	40.2%	24.2%	39.2%	55.0%	20.7%	39.9%	19.8%
ND	80.3%	64.3%	50.9%	52.3%	58.3%	69.5%	26.3%	52.3%	29.1%

Source: CHEHP, CUHK.

Table 4.2: Level of Satisfaction with Health, Community, and Public Services by Residents of the Two Districts (Full score: 10)

District/ Services	Inpatient Services	Specialist Outpatient	General Outpatient	Accident and Emergency	Community Health Promotion	Security and Safety	Youth Services	Child Care Services	Elderly Services	Family and Crisis Management	Rehabilitative Services
CWD	6.10	5.75	5.80	5.57	5.95	7.31	6.31	6.26	6.46	5.82	6.04
ND	5.73	5.23	5.27	5.30	5.40	6.47	5.89	5.98	6.01	5.57	5.66

Source: CHEHP, CUHK.

strip of land near the harbour front. The physical features of high-rise buildings as well as the perception of congestion make the environment (physical and social) less conducive for physical mobility and exercise. The availability of fresh and healthy foods also differs based on the area. Mendez and Popkin (2004) observed that in areas shifting from rural to urban, there is increased consumption of foods from animal sources, foods with added sugar and caloric sweeteners, and foods processed with edible oil over a short period of time, while the supply level of fruit and vegetables changes very little. This transition is caused by the increased access to non-traditional foods as a result of low prices, changing production and processing practices, and the rise in supermarkets and hypermarkets (Dixon et al., 2007). Thus, the eating habits of CWD residents appears to be affected by this transition. However, although ND has a higher proportion of residents eating healthy compared to CWD, this district is also vulnerable to these changes, particularly as the transition from rural to urban takes place very quickly.

Other physical health factors assessed included smoking and time on the Internet. A higher proportion of residents reported no smokers at home in CWD compared to ND (79.3% vs 71.4%). Moreover, a higher proportion of residents in ND reported spending more than 2 hours of their leisure time on the Internet compared to those in CWD (23.9% vs 13.9%). These factors may reflect differences in access to other entertainment between the two districts.

Place of residence is an important determinant of health in urban areas, as the particular social environment can substantial impact health, not just with regard to exposure to risk factors but access to care (Ompad et. al., 2007). For instance, substantial differences in access to prenatal clinics were noted based on the resident's country of origin in New York City (McLafferty and Grady, 2005). In the present study, satisfaction with health services, community services run by non-governmental organisations (NGOs), and public services was higher in CWD compared to ND (Table 4.2). These results may be related to ND's shift from having an "original" population in a rural environment to a mixed population in a more urban environment, while that in CWD has not changed dramatically. More and more people have moved into ND from different parts of Hong Kong. With the changing features in urban and rural areas over time, some factors might be added or removed because of changing socio-demographic characteristics and nature of the neighbourhood. The business operating model of the area also affects these features, including if the district businesses are agricultural versus industrial (light or heavy); small, medium, or large enterprises; and commercial, residential, or mixed. Local politics (driven by local population or external agents) also play a significant role in the quality of services in an area. Improvements in health outcomes cannot be assumed to be correlated with economic growth or demographic changes (Rydin et al., 2012). Satisfaction with health services was also a main discussion point in the focus groups in CWD.

CWD Focus Groups

Most of the focus group interviewees reported that neighbourhood relationships were harmonious in CWD and that the neighbourhood was friendly and helpful in general. Traffic jams were considered the most serious issues by the interviewees, as underground transport to the western parts of the district was not in use at that time. Most interviewees felt that air pollution was also serious. The hygiene in the older areas of the district was also noted as being poor, with many of the interviewees linking this to the improper disposal of residential waste as a result of poor management of the estates/buildings in the area.

Regarding primary health care services, most interviewees felt that the services did not meet the needs of residents. The telephone appointment system for general outpatient appointments in the public sector caused great inconvenience to local residents, particularly the elderly, and the waiting times at the public hospitals were extremely long. Recreational and cultural facilities were reported to be inadequate by most interviewees. At the time data was collected, there was no indoor swimming pool for the district, minimising the opportunity for exercise during winter. The interviewees also expressed disappointment at the lack of large shopping malls and cinemas in the area. Some interviewees felt that resources were lacking for community services for different age groups and were also not fully aware of the types of services available. They suggested that there should be better promotion of these services so their use can be efficiently maximised.

Other issues were also expressed by younger residents of the focus groups, including concern over the strong social class gradient, community centres being too scattered, lack of green space and sports facilities, insufficient cultural and leisure facilities, traffic congestion, and poor hygiene of backyards of buildings. It has been shown that younger age groups in well-developed areas expect wider approaches to urban health and the development of the city environment, including the moral and ethical perspectives in dealing with the complexity of urban living (Pacione, 2003). Young people living in affluent areas would also include wider attributes as components of their quality of life, such as visual perception and scenic quality, individual development through recreation and leisure, economic security and living standards, goods and services, and social infrastructure and group relationships (Mitchell, 2000).

Using City Health Profiles to Understand Urbanisation and Health

The variables and quality of life measurements assessed in the city health profiles for CWD and ND are inherently linked to urbanisation and health, as well as to the ultimate goal of becoming Healthy Cities. A paper by Tsouros (2015) reviewing 27 years of the European Healthy Cities movement has recapped that becoming a Healthy City is not just a matter of achieving a particular health status, it involves the community becoming more conscious of health and health equity and a greater emphasis being placed on the importance of local action in all aspects of health. The built environment is one way to connect urban planning and public health (Giles-Corti et al., 2014). A paper on the conceptual framework and methodology of European Healthy Cities (de Leeuw et al., 2015) highlighted ways to synthesise evidence and explore how things would work under different conditions, elaborating on the "formula" by Pawson and Tilley (1997) that "context + mechanism = outcome". The Healthy Cities movement in the Western Pacific Region has been going on for over a decade, but efforts in synergising the ultimate goals of the movement as well as a conceptual framework are still in the early stages. Creating city health profiles will help cities to understand the way in which the urban environment influences population health and provide relevant information for policy makers and the public (Webster and Sanderson, 2012).

The findings of this study reflect how districts in Hong Kong can become more conscious of health and health equity, as well as how residents can become more aware of local actions and have a better understanding the unique context of their district. Furthermore, a Healthy City should offer a physical and built environment that supports health, recreation, and well-being, in addition to offering high levels of safety, social interaction, mobility, and accessibility. These characteristics, as well as promoting a sense of pride and cultural identity, are described by Grant (2015), which focuses on healthy urban planning in the European Healthy City Network. The city health profiles of CWD and ND have captured some of those features.

However, there are some limitations to these findings. First, the study uses cluster purposive sampling. In comparison with the general population of the districts, the study population is not markedly different in various demographic characteristics, except that the study includes a higher proportion of older residents. Age adjustment has, therefore, been performed in this analysis. Second, comparison of the two districts is based on descriptive statistics with no statistical analysis. However, this limitation does not diminish the impact of these data. The main purpose of this study is to review the general patterns in the two districts rather than quantitatively analyse their difference. Healthy City development should be more focused on community participation, empowerment, and creating a supportive environment rather than on experimental interventions. The outcomes should be more focused on a broader description of different factors affecting the quality of life, health behaviours, and perception of important services in the district. Third, the outcome measurements do not consist of health data such as mortality and morbidity rates. While this will be seen as a limitation by some, it is essential to look past these basic parameters and investigate the processes. Indeed, becoming a Healthy City requires complex interventions at various levels, and urban environments are influenced by numerous factors, making it difficult to ascertain which interventions have a direct impact on the final health outcomes of residents. Therefore, it is more appropriate to assess the "intermediate process indicators" as parameters in a city health profile, as they measure processes or actions rather than outcomes.

Assessing intermediate process indicators allows cities to demonstrate that they are moving forward towards long-term aspirations and goals (Webster and Sanderson, 2012). For instance, data collection focused on intermediate indicators plays a major role in helping areas determine the optimal level of public health and sick care services and making these services accessible to all, both of which are essential in a Healthy City (de Leeuw, 2011; Hancock and Duhl, 1998). Intermediate indicator assessment was even been specified as an important aspect of evaluation during phase 4 of the European Healthy Cities movement (de Leeuw, 2011). Change in city ethos and mindset is slow, but the intermediate parameters adopted in the present study can help enlighten local districts in terms of how Healthy Cities can act as catalysts for developing a caring and supportive environment with greater equity in health (Green et al., 2015).

Apart from objective measures, there is also compelling evidence that perceived features of the built environment are associated with health outcomes (Rydin et al., 2012; Giles-Corti et al., 2014). Understanding how people feel about individual life concerns can be used to evaluate their quality of life, identify problems meriting special attention and action, and aid policy makers in addressing the distribution of satisfaction and dissatisfaction across society (Mitchell, 2000).

Taken together, this assessment of two unique districts in Hong Kong has provided insight into post-modern urbanisation and health in the Asia Pacific Region. The data presented here indicate that urbanisation of traditional rural areas might have had a detrimental effect on the local population, especially older residents. However, these findings also suggest that younger residents may thrive in more urban environments. Although living in a high-density urban environment may result in the adoption of unhealthy lifestyles, and in some cases a lower quality of life, there are also added benefits in terms of land use, transport, and public services. Urbanisation is both a joy and sorrow for certain age groups and those in certain life circumstances. Thus, it is essential that a city health profile be created to aid local policy makers and to make them more aware of the feelings of local residents. Doing so will enable city development to be undertaken in a complementary way that maximises the advantages of urbanisation and mitigates the negative effects.

Chapter 5

Health-promoting Schools: Key Elements and the Framework for Monitoring and Evaluation

Albert Lee, Vera Keung, Amelia Lo, and Amy Kwong

City-super now has a full understanding of the complexity of a city and of the merits of developing a Healthy City using the Healthy Settings Approach. He has identified key stakeholders and engaged them in the planning process. City-super also realises the importance of conducting needs assessments and community diagnosis, which not only reflects the health status of the population but also the determinants of health through the evaluation of lifestyles of residents and their perception of the environment, health services, safety, and utilities of the cities. City-super can now advise the City Mayor to strengthen city governance by adopting the Healthy City concept and also strengthen the social and human capital for sustainable city development.

During City-super's research on Healthy Cities, one aspect he took particular interest in was the health status and determinants of health for students and young people. He specifically noticed an increasing prevalence of obesity, unhealthy eating, physical inactivity, and high levels of emotional stress. In a discussion with the City Mayor, City-super recommended that they should also consider a Health-promoting School approach, focusing on the health and well-being of students. The success of a Health-

promoting School would also synergise with creating a Healthy City, and vice versa. Thus, City-super was entrusted with another mission — to learn more about making healthy changes in the school setting by adopting the Healthy Settings Approach.

A Healthy School or Health-promoting School (HPS) seeks to ensure better health for younger generations by creating a healthy environment (physical and social) for students, enhancing their action competencies for healthy living, fostering a community link for health promotion, and developing school policies conducive for health. The health-promotion actions adopted by an HPS focus on changing the attitudes and behaviours of students using positive, life-enhancing activities to improve health and well-being as well as encourage social inclusion and social justice. The HPS framework is, therefore, an effective means to help children enjoy healthy growth and optimal development so their rights, interests, and well-being are respected and safeguarded. It is a school-based initiative for school improvement. It is *not* a top-down approach, nor does it operate as a conventional public health model. In Hong Kong, the Centre for Health Education and Health Promotion (CHEHP) at the Chinese University of Hong Kong has cultivated the interests of key stakeholders and expertise from different disciplines to map the pathway for the positive and healthy development of children, recognising the importance of culture, environment, and socio-economic determinant factors. The Hong Kong Healthy School Award (HKHSA) Scheme is still ongoing. There are numerous published assessments of the data from the award scheme, which is used as a comprehensive system to monitor and evaluate HPS performance (Joyce et al., 2017; Macnab et al., 2014a, 2014b; Moynihan et al., 2016).

The Health-promoting School Framework as an Effective Strategy to Promote the Positive Development of Children

The United Nations Agenda on Sustainable Development Goals 2030 (UN Agenda 2030) has stipulated two important goals for healthy and positive childhood development:

1. Ensure healthy lives and promote well-being for all at all ages (Goal 3); and

2. Ensure inclusive and equitable quality education and promote lifelong learning opportunities for all (Goal 4) (UN, 2015).

With the fast-growing economy and the rapid pace of urbanisation, we are exposing younger generations to increasing ecological and socio-economic risks, including health inequalities, as well as increasing individualisation in society. The factors accounting for substantial morbidity and mortality for children in developed countries are highly interrelated with socio-economic, behavioural, and biological characteristics (Sidebotham, 2017). The World Health Organisation (WHO) Commission on Social Determinants of Health (CSDH) examined the inequitable access to health and education as well as the factors constituting the social determinants of health (CSDH, 2008). The CSDH emphasised the importance of early life investment in health by risk minimisation of obesity, malnutrition, mental health, and non-communicable diseases (NCDs) as well as enhancement of physical and cognitive development (Marmot et al., 2008).

A strong link between education and health is needed to tackle the social determinants of children's health and effective intervention needs to consider the diverse conditions and locations where children spent most of their time — that is, school (Lee and Cheung, 2017). There have been many published evaluations of school health initiatives in the last 20 years suggesting that health-protection and reduced risk-taking behaviour is built through partnerships between how a school is led and managed; the experiences students have to participate and take responsibility for shaping policies, practices, and procedures; how teachers relate to and treat students; and how the school engages with its local community (including parents) (Patton et al., 2006; Steward Brown, 2006; Stewart-Brown et al., 2009). Many of these gains have occurred without a specific health "intervention", and a whole-school approach applied within a caring school social environment is the most effective way of achieving both health and educational outcomes (Blum et al., 2002; Symons et al., 1997). The Social Development Model hypothesises that children learn behavioural patterns, social or anti-social, largely from their environment, and when socialising processes are consistent with the development of a social bond of attachment, behaviours inconsistent with the beliefs held are inhibited (Catalano et al., 2004).

However, improvement of student behaviour and well-being would not naturally occur without a specific "intentional intervention". Child and adolescent health promotion should focus on improving health literacy, advocating healthy behavioural changes, mediating changes in the environment (physical and social) to be more conducive for health, improving public policies for healthy youth development, engaging stakeholders, and enhancing services — in particular, the accessibility and acceptability of these services. The health-promotion framework ought to be complex, multifactorial, and innovative in many domains (curriculum, school environment, and community), and implemented with a long-term commitment to be effective (Stewart-Brown, 2006).

Evolution of the Health-promoting School Movement

In the 1980s, the WHO initiated the HPS movement, shifting the focus beyond individual behaviour changes to organisational structure changes for health improvement (WHO, 2009e; WHO, 1996). This includes improving physical and social environments in schools, actively promoting student self-esteem by demonstrating that everyone can make a contribution to school governance, developing the education potential of the school's health services beyond routine screening, and strengthening the links between the school, homes, and the community. The HPS movement is intended to empower students, staff, and parents to actively influence their lives and living conditions. The revision of the HPS framework in 2008 refined the six key areas, now identified as Healthy School Policies, School's Physical Environment, School's Social Environment, Community Links, Action Competencies for Healthy Living, and School Health Care and Promotion Services. However, this framework only provides a rough outline, and work still needs to be done by key stakeholders to develop a robust model to fit their school.

In a paper on school health, Lee (2018b) discusses how the American Academy of Paediatrics (2004) has further recommended a shift in focus from urgent care and illness management towards more primary and secondary prevention as well as comprehensive school health education, stressing the link between the school environment and school policies and a child's health and performance in school. Allensworth (1997) highlights eight key elements of a Comprehensive School Health Programme (CSHP):

(1) Health services — A CSHP should be a coordinated system to ensure a continuum of care from school to home to community health care provider, ranging from a health aide's office in the school to a school-based clinic;

(2) Health education — A CSHP should strive to empower students with the knowledge and skills necessary to maintain and improve their health, adopt

healthy behaviours, and avoid health-threatening behaviours, thus allowing them to become health-literate consumers and decision makers;

(3) Biophysical and psycho-social environments — The school environment ought to be safe and mediate health. The building design should ensure adequate ventilation, lighting, noise abatement, heating, and cooling. Regarding the psycho-social environment, a CSHP should ensure that students and staff function in a supportive atmosphere that encourages open communication, respects individual differences, and promotes each student's full academic and social potential as well as addresses the diverse needs of students.

(4) Psychological, counselling, and social services — The services offered in a school with a CSHP should aim to promote the mental, emotional, and social health of students and deal with any problems interfering with teaching and learning;

(5) Physical education and other physical activities — A CSHP should include criteria regarding the physical health of students at school, at home, and in the community focused on increasing awareness of healthy activities;

(6) Food services — While it is essential to provide nutritious and appealing meals, a CSHP should also help students develop lifelong healthy eating habits;

(7) Employee health policies and programmes — In a CSHP, the policies for the staff should establish rules and regulations to promote the physical, psychological, and social health of students; and

(8) Integrated efforts of schools, families, and communities — The essential foundation for any successful CSHP is built from the involvement of a wide range of community stakeholders — parents, students, educators, health and social service personnel, insurers, and business and political leaders.

Modern school health programmes have also been outlined by Kolbe (2005). These programmes should address the health and education context in which they evolve, with the goal of improving health literacy, healthy behaviours, and outcomes as well as improving educational achievement and social outcomes. The school organisation itself should enable relevant education, while health and social services agencies could work to help schools attain specific goals and enhance links with the community. Within the school administration, there should be a school health coordinator and designated school health team.

The principles of school health promotion outlined by St Leger (2005) share a similar philosophy. Indicating that an HPS

- promotes the health and well-being of students;
- upholds the concepts of social justice and equity;
- involves student participation and empowerment;
- provides a safe and supportive environment;
- links health and education issues and systems;
- addresses the health and well-being of staff;
- collaborates with the local community;
- integrates health promotion into the school's ongoing activities;
- sets realistic goals; and
- engages parents and families in health promotion.

St Leger goes on to discuss issues inhibiting HPS development and sustainability. These issues include the following:

- Many school health initiatives are only funded over the short-term, while HPS outcomes occur in the medium- to long-term.
- Evaluation is difficult and complex.
- Health sector funding often focuses exclusively on morbidity and mortality reduction approaches.
- The education sector uses certain language and concepts which have different meanings to those in other sectors, leading to communication barriers caused by the lack of a shared understanding.
- The education sector often needs to be convinced of the advantages an HPS can offer schools to improve educational outcomes, creating delays in implementation.

However, there are several strategies that can be used to help a school transition towards becoming a sustainable HPS. These include:

- Developing partnerships between education and health sector policy makers.
- Ensuring students feel a sense of ownership in school governance.
- Ensuring diversity of teaching and learning strategies.

- Allowing for adequate time for class-based activities, organisation and coordination, and out-of-class activities.

- Establishing all the elements and actions as core components to the working of the school.

- Exploring health issues within the context of the students' lives and community.

- Seeking and maintaining credibility for HPS programmes and actions both within and outside the school.

- Having an active expectation within the community that their schools will promote the health of their children.

- Ensuring there is time and resources for appropriate staff development.

- Maintaining a coordinating group to oversee and drive the HPS with continuity of some personnel and the addition of new personnel.

- Ensuring that most of the new and ongoing initiatives involve most of the staff, students, and families in consultation and implementation.

- Monitoring services in the education sector to promote health promotion as an integral part of school life and using appropriate monitoring indicators.

The HPS concept should ultimately focus on improving the school's physical and social environment, curricula, and teaching and learning methods (Lee, 2002; WHO, 1997b). For effective implementation of the HPS approach, stakeholders need to identify the missing elements in their school's overall health so remedial actions can be put into place.

What Is Missing in School Health? How Can the Success of an HPS be Measured?

Using a traditional medical approach, which evaluates a narrow set of pre-determined outcomes, to evaluate an HPS would miss out on the richness of school health activities. Langford et al. (2014) conducted the Cochrane Review of the WHO HPS framework. The review was based on 67 cluster randomised controlled trials (RCTs) conducted at the level of school, district, or other geographical area. Unfortunately, RCT design does not lend itself to assessing outcomes involving organisational or structural change as the statistical assumptions underpinning this type of analysis do not reflect these changes, thus limiting the practical applications of the results of the study. In addition to assessing standard outcomes for school health promotion intervention, it is important to find out what constitutes a successful outcome and what outcomes reflect increased input from students, teachers, and parents. Inchley et al. (2006), for example, argues that such potential markers of success need to be identified in the early stages of the process as a means of supporting schools and teachers. These indicators should highlight the ways in which schools are able to adopt HPS principles successfully and the conditions necessary for the HPS concept to flourish.

The Healthy School Award Scheme as a Framework for Evaluation

The Wessex Healthy School Award (WHSA) Scheme in England and the HKHSA Scheme in Hong Kong use detailed systems to analyse whether each individual school has reached the standards of a model HPS, thus reflecting a more holistic appreciation and understanding of all the effects of school-based health promotion (Moon et al., 1999a; Lee et al., 2006). The audit-style evidence collected for these awards provides a comprehensive map showing what initiatives are being taken and their effects based on how they rank compared to other HPSs, which can help guide school administrators as well as health and education authorities. These data can help stakeholders concentrate on the gaps and missing elements hindering them from obtaining an award (Moon et al., 1999b; Lee et al., 2007b).

The CHEHP has developed a comprehensive HPS framework that includes specific indicators for monitoring and evaluating success (Lee et al., 2005a). The system was built on data derived from several different sources and makes use of both qualitative and quantitative information, which allows it to more comprehensively reflect success in health promotion and guide actions for improvement (Baum, 1995; Steckler et al., 1992). Furthermore, triangulation using multiple methods should be used to improve confidence in research findings (Denzin and Lincoln, 2011, 2018; Gifford, 1996). Box 5.1 describes the four primary types of indicators — health and social outcomes, intermediate health outcomes, health promotion outcomes, and health promotion actions — as based on model by Nutbeam (1996). This model forms the basis of outcomes reflecting whole-school activities as well as the health and well-being of students (Table 5.1). Lee et al. (2014a) provides the details of the six key areas of the HKHSA. The assessment of these areas allows a school health profile to be created, as demonstrated by the CHEHP (2012, appendix). This approach can be regarded

---

Box 5.1: Four Different Types of Outcomes for Health Promotion
(Source: Nutbeam, 1996)

Health and social outcomes represent the end-point of health and medical interventions, and are usually expressed in terms of mortality and morbidity; disability and dysfunction; health status; and social outcomes, such as quality of life, life satisfaction, and equity.

Intermediate health outcomes represent the determinants of health and social outcomes such as healthy lifestyles, healthy environments (the physical environment as well as the economic and social conditions that have a direct impact on health and support healthy lifestyle), and effective health services.

Health promotion outcomes represent modifiable personal, social, and environmental factors to change the determinants of health, such as health literacy, social actions (an organised effort to influence lifestyles and environment), and healthy public policy and organisational practices.

Health promotion actions include three domains: education (opportunities for learning to improve health), facilitation (actions taken in partnership or groups to mobilise human and material resources for health), and advocacy (actions taken on behalf of individuals or communities to overcome structural barriers to achieve positive health.

Table 5.1: Indicators and Measuring Instruments for the Different Types of Outcomes for Health Promotion in a School Setting

Types of outcomes	Indicators to be measured	Measuring instrument
Health and social outcomes	Depressive symptoms, life satisfaction, perceived health status, perceived academic achievement	Validated questionnaires: Satisfaction with Life scale (LIFE), Depression Self-Rating Scale (DSRS), Youth Risk Behaviour Survey (YRBS)
Intermediate outcomes	i. Attitudes, lifestyles, and risk behaviours ii. School environment and school ethos iii. School health services	Questionnaires to students and schools, school observation, documentary review, interviews
Health promotion outcomes	i. Health skills and knowledge, and self-efficacy ii. School health policies iii. Networking with parents, local community, and other schools to launch health programmes	Questionnaires to students and schools, curriculum review, documentary review, individual or focus group interviews, participant observation
Health promotion actions	i. School timetable for health education activities (formal and extra-curricular) ii. PTA and community involvement	Documentary review

Source: Lee et al., 2005a.

as an ecological model for health improvement as the complex interactions of environmental, organisational, and personal factors are addressed (Figure 5.1). The resulting school health profile allows components to be identified for each area and specifies subsets of checkpoints and targets for schools to achieve (Lee et al., 2014a, appendix). An overall score for each key area can then be calculated, and points can be given for each checkpoint achieved.

The assessment tool used for the HKHSA that schools utilise to evaluate their performance against the HPS indicators is a questionnaire. This questionnaire is based on the CSHP components of an effective school-based intervention (Box 5.2) as explained by Allensworth (1994; 1997) as well as on the principles of health promotion described by St Leger (2005), the school health programme outlined by Kolbe (2005), and the WHSA Scheme (Moon et al., 1999a; 1999b). For the HKHSA, questionnaires are sent to schools in advance of visits by the evaluation team. The questionnaire template was designed to include both qualitative and quantitative data. During the visit by the evaluation team, the questionnaire can be expanded based on their review of school documents, examination of the school curriculum, observations of the school's physical environment, interviews with teachers and principals, and focus groups with students and parents. The questionnaire is then used to calculate a final overall score based on the accreditation system, which is converted into a percentage for each of the six key areas.

Validation of the School Health Profile

The evaluation system and school health profiling described above is subsequently validated using multiple approaches as follows:

- Face validation: Pilot testing is performed in some schools with principals and teachers that have a basic understanding of HPS.

- Content validation: Local and international HPS experts comment on the content of the system and school health profile.

- Criterion validation: HPS experts with experience in applying similar Healthy School Award schemes or other health promotion evaluation tools compare the process of accreditation and benchmarking with international standards within the local context (Moon et al., 1999a, 1999b; St Leger and Nutbeam, 2000a; Tones and Tilford, 2001; Kolbe, 2005).

**Figure 5.1: Conceptual Framework to Enhance School Capacity
to Implement the Health-promoting Schools Approach**

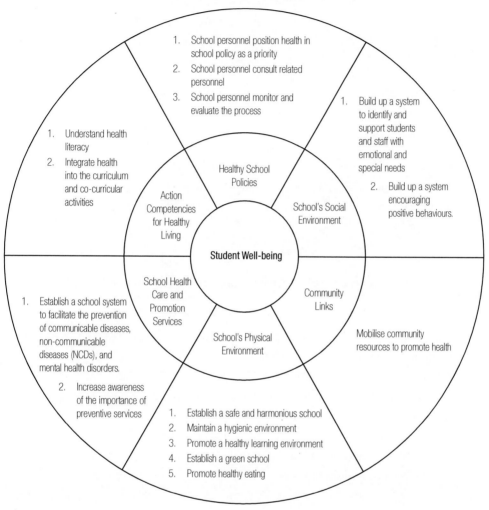

Source: Lee, 2019c.

- Construct validation: An ongoing, thorough analysis of the correlation of school performance in and between the different indicators: element, component, and HPS key areas and overall performance of the school (Lee et al., 2014a).

These processes allow each school health profile to be validated and compared to the performance of successful HPSs.

**Box 5.2: Components of an Effective School-based Intervention
(Source: Allensworth, 1994)**

- Uses multiple theories and models when planning interventions
- Focuses on priority health behaviours
- Expands the curriculum
- Uses multiple strategies to address "problem" behaviour
- Coordinates school and community health promotion activities
- Coordinates the whole-school programme through all subjects
- Promotes active student participation and use of active learning methods
- Focuses on the development of life skills
- Implements a wider view of all aspects of school life
- Promotes close cooperation with parents

Effectiveness of the Health-promoting School Concept

If the HPS indicators reflect the *process* of health promotion in schools, then the HPS approach can be regarded as another way of schooling rather than an add-on programme (St Leger et al., 2007; Hoyle et al., 2010). A paper by Joyce et al. (2017) asserts the importance of monitoring data to motivate change. The framework adopted by the HKHSA Scheme to measure the efficacy of an HPS evaluates whether the key HPS concepts and principles can be translated into outcomes conducive to student well-being from both the health and education perspectives. This evaluation framework enables the analysis of inputs and activities as part of a system of monitoring and evaluating the healthy initiatives as well as the outcomes to be attained at different levels. Therefore, the comprehensive school profile adopted by the HKHSA Scheme promotes this style of monitoring and evaluation, leading to quality improvements in student health and well-being as well as in the school environment and management conducive to health (Lee et al., 2005a; Lee et al., 2006; Lee et al., 2007b; Lee et al., 2008; Lee et al., 2014a). In fact, schools that have received the gold award of the HKHSA Scheme have shown sustained positive changes in the health of students and staff, and successfully address the intertwined social, educational, psychological, and physical health needs of school children (Lee et al., 2018a). The development of an HPS requires a school to undergo a step-by-step evolution from capacity building and linking

Figure 5.2: Stepwise Evolution of the Health-promoting Schools Movement in Hong Kong

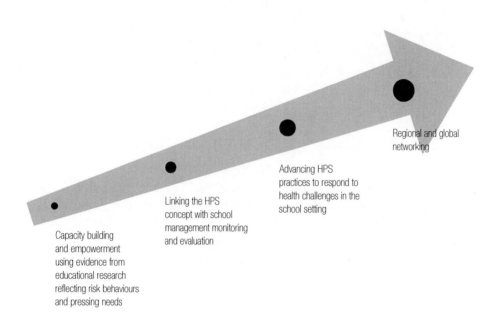

Regional and global networking

Advancing HPS practices to respond to health challenges in the school setting

Linking the HPS concept with school management monitoring and evaluation

Capacity building and empowerment using evidence from educational research reflecting risk behaviours and pressing needs

Source: Lee, 2015.

the HPS concept to management up to advancing HPS practices and eventually networking with other HPSs regionally and globally (Figure 5.2).

The HKHSA Scheme itself has also evolved over time and has developed from an "embryonic" stage to a "consolidation" stage (Box 5.3, Figure 5.3), with each stage of development acting as the foundation for the next stage. This focus on growth and change has lead the HPS movement in Hong Kong to become widely known and admired, both regionally and internationally, and consultancy services have expanded out of Hong Kong to provide insight to neighbouring states as well as the WHO (Lee, 2008; Lee, 2009b, 2009c; Chen and Lee, 2016; Lee, 2011b).

Developing a robust framework to monitor and evaluate a school on its health promotion journey will naturally evolve as an audit cycle of assessment,

---

Box 5.3: Stepwise Development of Health-promoting Schools in Hong Kong

The **embryonic stage** (1998 to 2001) involved capacity building and needs assessment on student health (Lee et al., 2000; Lee et al., 2003b; Lee et al., 2004a), leading to the development of the HKHSA Scheme (Lee, 2002; Lee, 2004b).

In the **growing stage** (2002 to 2005), the HPS framework was applied to deal with health concerns, such as the spread of SARS (Lee et al., 2003a; Lee et al., 2008) and the increased prevalence of obesity (Lee et al., 2014b) and mental health issues (Wong et al., 2009). In this stage, the scheme was expanded to include early childhood education settings, and a mentorship scheme was established (Ho et al., 2007).

During the **consolidation stage** (2006 to the present), research findings were published demonstrating the effectiveness of the HKHSA in promoting health literacy (Lee et al., 2008; Lee, 2009d), enhancing the well-being of students (Lee et al., 2006), and creating a healthy school environment (Lee et al., 2008). In 2010, the Quality Education Fund of the Hong Kong Special Administrative Region Government commissioned the CHEHP at the Chinese University of Hong Kong to develop a thematic network of HPS to expand the initiative. Studies have shown that students at HPSs have improved mental health (Lee et al., 2016).

---

implementation, and performance, as outlined in Figure 5.4. The journey starts with a baseline assessment to identify the needs of the school and areas for improvement. Based on the findings of this initial assessment, strategies can be developed to improve the school health profile through changes in the school environment, revisions in school policies and organisational practices, increases in capacity building for students and staff (to promote action competencies for health), enhanced mobilisation of community resources, and extension of services for health promotion. Implementation of the framework established to enhance the school health profile should correlate with improved student health and performance. The framework and results can then be re-assessed to ensure sustained quality. Repeating this audit cycle will ensure continuous quality improvement in the HPS.

Effectiveness of the HPS concept ultimately depends on the willingness of the school to change, and change in any context requires motivation. A correlation study was conducted by Lee et al. (2019) to identify the HPS performance

Figure 5.3: Major Events in the Health-promoting School Movement in Hong Kong

	2010 Quality Education Fund Thematic Network of Healthy Schools Established (2010–present)
3rd International Training Workshop on Health Promoting Schools	
Consultancy Follow Up to Laos	**2009** Health-promoting Schools Building on Project Conducted (2008–2010)
Dietary Pattern and Nutritional Status in Macao School Children Assessed	**2008** Web-based Version of "Health Promoting School Self-Evaluation System" Established (2008–2010)
	Parents College of Health (2008–2009)
Smart Kids Fitness Project (2007–2008)	**2007** 2nd International Training Workshop on Health Promoting Schools
Health Promoting School Mentorship Scheme Established (2005–2007)	
Promoting and Strengthening Resilience in Schools Initiative (2005–2006)	**2006**
Healthy Schools (Pre-school) Award Scheme Launched	**2005** "Health Promoting School Self-Evaluation System" Established
	Colourful and Bright Fruits and Vegetables Project Initiated (2004–2007)
Schools prepare for outbreaks of influenza	
International Training Workshop on Health Promoting Schools	**2004**
Consultancy Project to Laos	
	2003 Certificate Course in Health Education and Health Promotion for Early Childhood Educators School against SARS Launched
Hong Kong Healthy Schools Award Scheme Launched	**2001**
	1999 Youth Risk Behavioural Surveillance Initiated
Professional Diploma in Health Education and Health Promotion for School Educators Launched	
	1998

Source: Lee et al., 2014a.

Figure 5.4: Cycle of Monitoring and Evaluation of a Health-promoting School

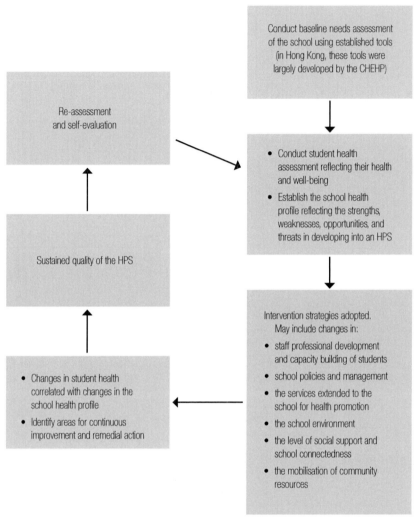

Source: Lee, 2018b.

indicators with the most significant impact on various health-related outcomes. Not surprisingly, these indicators correspond to the primary factors motivating positive change in the school setting (Table 5.2) and can, therefore, also be used as educational outcomes as they reflect school improvement.

Table 5.2: Key Indicators for Motivating Change under Each Key Area

Healthy School Policies

PO 2.1**	Policy on healthy eating
PO 2.2**	Policy on safe school
PO 2.3*	Policy on harmonious school
PO 2.4**	Policy on active school

School's Physical Environment

PE 1.1	School ensures students' safety whenever students are under their care
PE 4.1	School has a system in place to ensure that all food sold or served in school promote healthy eating

School's Social Environment

SE 2.2*	School has a system for the prevention, and management of unacceptable behaviour in school both among students and encourages staff to set personal examples for cultivating students' positive actions
SE 3.2	School has a system in place to look after students and staff with emotional needs or unexpected traumatic life events

Action Competencies on Health Living

AC 1.1	School adopts a systematic approach to conduct health education
AC 1.3	School tries to ensure all students have opportunities to actively engage with each topic, according to their age
AC 2.1	School uses a variety of innovative and student-orientated strategies and formats when implementing health education and promotion activities
AC 3.2*	There are school staff who received professional training in health education or participated in discussions on the development of health promoting school
AC 3.3	School staff participate in different health education workshops or seminars, and have opportunities to collaborate with other teachers and exchange ideas to enhance the teaching of health
AC 3.4	School provides diversified health education resources for staff, and such resources are organised and managed well
AC 4.3	School provides health-related information and resources for family members and the community

Community Links

CL 1.2	School consults parents for recommendations on Healthy School development and encourages their active participation in the joint discussion on the formulation and review of Healthy School policies
CL 2.2	School consults community members or groups that possess substantial understanding of the school for recommendations and professional advice on Healthy School development and involves them in assessing the school's developmental needs and discussing arrangements for corresponding plans and projects
CL 3.2*	School links with community bodies and works with them to promote community health education activities
CL 3.4**	School supports staff to participate in various exchange activities in health education

School Health Care and Promotion Services

HS 2.3	There was a provision of basic health care services and management

*Primary Schools only, ** Secondary Schools only

Source: Lee et al., 2019.

The next chapter will discuss how the HPS model can facilitate links between education and health and how schools can make use of the HPS framework to improve not only health and well-being of students but also enhance school management to create a healthy learning environment.

Chapter 6

The Significance of Student Health and Health-promoting School Effectiveness in Hong Kong

Albert Lee, Amelia Lo, Vera Keung, Amy Kwong, Ceci Chan, Hedy Tse, Calvin Cheung, and Queenie Li

Through his research about Health-promoting Schools (HPSs), City-super gained a deeper understanding of the framework and theory underlying a school's health journey. The next step was to better understand the practical components linking health and education and how individual schools can mediate the holistic development of students and the healthy management of school personnel and infrastructure. City-super thus sought out experts in the field to discuss the complexities involved in the development of an HPS and how success is measured, focusing on adolescent obesity as a case study and effective HPSs in Hong Kong.

The Significance of Student Health and Well-being for Education

Linking Education and Health

In 1986, Aarø et al. showed that students that are more engaged in school are more likely to succeed academically and to display positive behaviours, while alienated students are more likely to engage in risky behaviours. Thus, it is natural to conclude that if a school provides a comprehensive educational and social experience for students, it can maximise educational and health benefits. St Leger and Nutbeam (2000b) further explored this relationship between health and education by mapping the structure of school health promotion from both the health and education perspectives. Their study highlighted the increasing co-incidence of school-related outcomes, school-based interventions, and inputs affecting the education and health outcomes of students (Table 6.1). A review conducted by the Institute of Public Health (IPH) of Ireland has also shown education as an important social determinant of health (Higgins et. al., 2008). Based on their findings, the IPH outlined a relationship between education and health (Figure 6.1). They also specified a need for shared responsibility for health and the identification of appropriate and effective interventions to improve student health.

Emerging Issues in Adolescent Health

In the editorial of a special issue of *Journal of Adolescent Health* on emerging issues in adolescent health, Blum and Dick (2013) highlighted a connection between the policies and programmes implemented in a school to the biology and psychology of adolescent development (Table 6.2). They summarised their findings as follows:

1. Common determinants (e.g., pathways in the brain) exist, and there are inter-relationships between these determinants and risk behaviours, such that the determinant impacts the propensity towards a behaviour and vice versa. For example, growing up in a persistently violent environment impacts brain development, which in turn affects cognition, emotional reactivity, mental health, and drug use, which in turn affects violence and sexual behaviour.

2. If we have a better understanding of biological, social, environmental, and familial risks that a young person is confronted with during adolescence, then it is possible to develop more individualised prevention and interventions.

3. It is important to re-think the concepts of mature minors and informed consent by adolescents in light of the evolving understanding of brain maturation.

These findings indicate that the science of adolescent development should influence policies and programmes, with the goal of preventing non-communicable diseases (NCDs) and negative behavioural modifications as well as enhancing health outcomes for young people.

Table 6.1: Mapping Linkages between Health and Education

Health Perspective	Education Perspective
Health Goals	*Education Goals*
• promote physical and mental well-being	• autonomy
• reduce morbidity and mortality rates in cardiovascular diseases, cancer, injury, and mental illness	• independence
	• citizenhood
School-Related Outcomes	
Lifelong Learning	*Lifelong Learning Skills*
• ability to develop knowledge and skills appropriate to life stages and life events	• ability, capacity, and commitment to engage with formal education and training opportunities
• parenthood	• learning from life stages and life events
• management of chronic diseases	
• coping with stressful life events	
Competencies and Behaviours	*Competencies and Behaviours*
• health-enhancing actions	• literacy
• regular physical activity	• numeracy
• balanced diet	• problem-solving
• non-smoking	
• appropriate use of alcohol	
Specific Cognate Knowledge and Skills	*Specific Cognate Knowledge and Skills*
• accessing and using health information and services	• in sciences, languages, social sciences, creative arts, and technology
• social and political skills	
• health literacy	
• consumer health skills	
Self Attributes	*Self Attributes*
• enhanced self-esteem	• personally and socially responsible attitudes and practices
• management of interpersonal relationships	
School-Based Interventions	
Classroom Teaching and Learning	*Classroom Teaching and Learning*
• the formal health curriculum	• integration
• biological and behavioural focus	• coverage
	• time allocation
	• skills development
Creating a Supportive Physical Environment	*Creating a Supportive Physical Environment*
• areas for play and physical activity	• students, staff, and parents enhancing school facilities
• school buildings that are light and safe	• acknowledging students' art and cultural creations
• upholding occupational health and safety standards	
Creating a Supportive Social Environment	*Creating a Supportive Social Environment*
• setting a climate to support mental health	• care, trust, and friendliness
• encouraging students to discuss related health issues	• encouraging student initiatives and participation
Implementing School Policies	*Implementing School Policies*
• food choice	• discipline
• mandatory reporting of child abuse and infectious diseases	• equity
• safety	• safety (physical and emotional)
• drugs	

Table 6.1: Continued

Providing School-Based Health Services	*Providing School-Based Health Services*
• screening	• basic first aid
• immunisation	• personal relationship counselling
Collaborating with Parents and the Local Community	*Collaborating with Parents and the Local Community*
• parent organisations	• parent and teacher organisations
• local government	• service organisations
• health agencies	

Inputs

Curriculum Products	*Curriculum Products*
• topic specific	• integration of themes and topics
• behaviourally oriented	• influenced by teaching and learning theories and practices
• emphasis on outcome evaluation	• emphasis on process and outcome evaluation
Professional Development	*Professional Development*
• for teachers, school health and welfare personnel	• for teachers, school health and welfare personnel
• building health knowledge and confidence	• developing skills in teaching and learning processes
• creating awareness of health issues and health resources	• understanding health within the community and various social contexts
Public Policy and School Organisational Practices	*Public Policy and School Organisational Practices*
• rules and regulations (e.g., infectious diseases, child abuse priorities)	• rules and regulations
• health and safety requirements	– to enhance school ethos
	– to uphold discipline and relationship standards
	• priorities and time allocation for the health curriculum

Source: St Leger and Nutbeam, 2000b.

Figure 6.1: The Relationship between Education and Health

Source: IPH, 2008.

Table 6.2: New Insights from New Research

New research strengthening our current understanding

- Pathways are identifiable, mapping how one factor or behaviour affects the others, leading to a negative cascade.
- The adolescent brain is still somewhat malleable, and with appropriate interventions, some rewiring is possible.
- Environments play a key role in determining behaviour, and from an evolutionary biology perspective, being accepted by peers is central to group dynamics.
- Environmental factors interact with both genomic and epigenomic controls of gene expression, affecting morbidity and mortality in adolescence and beyond.

New research modifying our current understanding

- Sensation seeking and risk-taking are heightened in adolescence.
- There is a blunt response to punishment and a heightened response to rewards.
- In the heat of emotional arousal (hot cognition), adolescent reasoning is inherently different from adults.
- Hyper-palatable calorie-dense food activates reward pathways similar to other addictions.

New research stimulates new ways of thinking

- Young people are more likely to have their decision-making derailed under emotional, exciting, or stressful circumstances.
- Young people are more likely to be motivated by rewards than punishment.

Source: Blum and Dick, 2013.

A paper by Spear (2013) on adolescent neuro-development reveals that the adolescent brain has elevated activation of reward-relevant brain regions and sensitivity to aversive stimuli may be attenuated. Adolescent brain development is still tilted towards plasticity so the functional transformation in the brain, along with increasing hormone levels and other biological changes, interact with cultural, economic, and psychological forces to shape how adolescents think, feel, and behave. In fact, certain adolescent-typical behaviours, including risk-taking behaviours, may be in part biologically driven by a brain that reacts differently to stimuli because of developmental transformations in relatively ancient brain systems (Spear, 2013).

A similar focus on biology was adopted by Wang et al. (2013). This study highlights new opportunities for developing early prediction and prevention paradigms based on dynamic epigenetic mechanisms in response to both internal and external environmental stimuli (Box 6.1). It raises many important questions, such as to what degree do early life adversities (poor nutrition, prenatal or postnatal second-hand smoke, endocrine disruptors, stress, low social economic, etc.) affect the development and persistence of obesity? To address this particular question, it is essential to investigate what developmental time windows are the most sensitive to environmental exposure, metabolic re-programming, or reversibility of obesity, and what early life risk factors are biologically embedded and how do they cause

**Box 6.1: Epigenetics and Early Life Origins of Chronic Disease
(Source: Wang et al., 2013)**

Human health is interconnected throughout our lifetimes, from conception to foetal life, to early childhood and adolescence, and on into adulthood and our senior years. Each stage presents its own unique health needs and problems, yet each of them is interconnected. There is a growing recognition that early life experiences and adversities may have a profound impact on later growth, development, health, and disease development. This paradigm renders it critical to understand which early life experiences and exposures are biologically embedded and how they cause lifelong consequences.

Obesity is a global public health problem. Growing epidemiological and animal studies suggest that developmental programming of human neuroendocrine systems and metabolism by the perinatal and early postnatal environment is associated with an increased risk of obesity in later life. For example, nutritional and hormonal status during pregnancy and early life may affect the development of the organs involved in the control of food intake and metabolism, particularly the hypothalamic structures responsible for the establishment of digestive behaviour and regulation of energy expenditure. This "developmental programming" appears to be largely independent of genomic DNA sequence and is likely to be mediated by epigenetic mechanisms.

Epigenetics refers to the study of mitotically or meiotically heritable changes in gene expression that occur without changes in the DNA sequence. Epigenetic alterations can influence disease development through dynamic transcriptional activities from gametogenesis to embryogenesis and throughout one's life. Evidence from animal models and humans indicates that the intrauterine period is the most sensitive time for the establishment of epigenetic variability, which in turn influences the risk of developing a range of disorders that develop later in life. The epigenome at birth reflects a net result of underlying genetic variations, in-utero environmental exposures, and stochastic epigenetic changes. Throughout our lifetime, our body's cells and organ systems constantly react and adapt to internal and external environments. While our gene sequence will not change (except in the case of mutations), epigenetic alterations (controlling gene expression) are dynamic over time, and epigenetic changes are reversible. Studies have implicated aberrant epigenomic changes in the aetiology of human diseases, including various forms of cancer as well as cardiovascular and autoimmune diseases. It is likely that epigenetics is the vital link between genotype and the environment, phenotype and disease, and may transform our understanding of disease aetiology and our approach to prevention and treatment of non-communicable chronic diseases.

lifelong or even trans-generational consequences. Indeed, Potenza (2013) reviewed the biological models of addiction and highlighted the interactive influences of genetic and environmental factors to addictive behaviours of adolescents. The study went on to provide supportive evidence of preventive strategies targeting risk factors and enhancing protective factors at the individual, familial, and community levels. Adolescence is a time of considerable brain development and behavioural changes and is also a period of significant vulnerability to addiction. Multi-level interventions going beyond simple behavioural approaches are also supported by Lee and Gibbs (2013). Their study focuses on the neurobiology of food addiction and obesity and provides preventive options to tackle obesity in adolescents (Figure 6.2). They argue that the obesogenic environment can be eliminated by tackling the distal and proximal determinant factors.

Similarly, the Studying Impact of Nutrition and Growth (SING) Project explored the impact of socio-demographic factors on health (Lee et al., 2017), specifically the correlation between sub-optimal growth and nutrition status and factors such as dietary patterns, parenting skills, health literacy of parents, household environment, and sub-optimal breastfeeding. The SING Project stresses the need for a research model which incorporates distal, intermediate, and proximal determinant factors to study health outcomes (Figure 6.3). As the obesogenic shifts on dietary composition are taking place at a much faster rate than the potential benefits in low-income countries as a result of the adverse effects of rapid urbanisation (Dixon et al., 2007), it is essential to utilise models that consider the complexity health from biological and environmental perspectives. This is ultimately the goal of the broader Healthy Settings Approach as an ecological model of health promotion in which health is determined by complex interactions between environmental, organisational, and personal or biological factors.

The continued research on the biology of adolescent obesity has encouraged the WHO to prioritise interventions addressing the common social determinants of health-risk behaviours of adolescents and to place greater importance on balancing actions directed to influence individual behaviours with those targeting the policy and regulatory environment (Bustreo and Chestnov, 2013). These efforts further reinforce the significant impact of the environment on adolescent health and how school policy and organisation influences health behaviours. Thus, the emerging issues in adolescent health only make a school's journey towards becoming an HPS that much more important.

Figure 6.2: Home-School-Community Model to Enhance Positive Adolescent Neuro-development with regard to Diet and Exercise

Home
- Avoid using unhealthy foods (e.g., sweets, soft drinks) as rewards for positive behaviours and withdrawing them as punishment
- Create a joyful and rewarding environment to be physical active, eating healthy food products, and engaging in outdoor activities
- Rewards for buying healthy food products and restriction of "pocket money" to buy unhealthy food
- Bonus systems for healthy eating and being physically active
- Withdraw rewards on excess time on TV and Internet and sedentary lifestyle, and overconsumption of "junk" food
- Be attentive to hunger and satiety cues

School
- Rewards for healthy eating and participation in exercise with log diary to maintain a record
- Create opportunities for students to gain pleasure from healthy eating and outdoor activities (e.g., visit an orchard for fresh fruit tasting, camping)
- Conduct and explain research linking unhealthy eating, physical inactivity, and obesity to impaired learning
- Establish a positive school culture for healthy eating with teachers and prefects as role models
- Promote health literacy as an important learning outcome

Community
- Awards for healthy eating venues
- Price incentives for consuming healthy foods
- Incentive for selling healthy foods
- Proper nutritional labelling with warnings concerning unhealthy ingredients
- Media coverage explaining the benefits of healthy eating
- Bonus points for redemption on buying healthy food products
- Only have healthy foods at community activities
- Make consuming unhealthy food the more difficult choice

Source: Lee and Gibbs, 2013.

Figure 6.3: The Distal, Intermediate, and Proximal Factors Correlated to Obesity-related Health Outcomes

Distal Determinant Factors	Intermediate Determinant Factors	Proximal Determinant Factors	Outcomes
Mechanism to promote healthy eating (e.g., policies, guidelines)	Action competency on diet and nutrition	Dietary behaviours	Diseases related to imbalanced diet
Engagement of different stakeholders	Community resources to support healthy eating	Nutritional counselling services	Obesity
		Screening for under or overweight	Medical conditions caused by obesity
		Healthy eating environment and culture at home, school, and community	

Source: Lee et al., 2018b.

Health Literacy

A positive culture for health will naturally facilitate a higher level of health literacy, helping individuals to build up personal, cognitive, and social skills which determine their ability to access, understand, and use information to promote and maintain good health (Nutbeam, 2000). School is an important setting for students to achieve health literacy (St Leger, 2001). Programme experiences and research findings worldwide suggest that adolescents need accurate information about their health and development, life skills to avoid risky behaviours, counselling services, acceptable and affordable health services, and a safe and supportive environment (WHO, 1999). Schools should emphasise critical thinking to help students understand the why, when, where, what, and how in relation to school health services (Lee, 2009d). Health literacy influences behaviour and the use of health services impacts health outcomes. Thus, decreasing health costs in society and advancing health literacy will progressively allow for greater autonomy and personal empowerment (Sørensen et al., 2012). The process of health literacy can be seen as a part of an individual's development towards improved quality of life. Health literacy is therefore not simply the ability to read, and basic literacy and numeracy skills (as well as the cognitive development associated with these skills) are fundamental requirements for health literacy (Protheroe et al., 2011). Education and the school environment plays an important role in helping students develop a high level of literacy so they can have a healthy life in the future. In Hong Kong, the development of a healthy lifestyle is one of the key learning goals laid down by the Hong Kong Education Bureau.

The Colourful and Bright Fruits and Vegetables Project was launched by the Centre for Health Education and Health Promotion (CHEHP) at the Chinese University of Hong Kong to develop a sustainable policy and mediate environmental change to promote consumption of fruits and vegetables in primary school students (Lee et al., 2010a). This project differed from other fruits and vegetables promotion projects in that it was the first of its kind to embrace health promotion strategies using the Healthy School concept. It emphasised environmental and policy changes in addition to changes in individual knowledge and attitudes. Thus, it was essential to assess the success of the project. This assessment was conducted using student questionnaires. The analysis of the questionnaire survey showed a statistically significant improvement in nutrition knowledge, with 58.7% students received a passing Knowledge Score at baseline compared to 73% in the post-assessment analysis ($p<0.001$) (Lee et al., 2010a). Longitudinal comparison shows that a significantly higher proportion of students reported that they were consuming adequate amount of fruits and vegetables. The weighed lunch survey showed an overall increase of 63.3% ($p<0.001$) in vegetable consumption by students at lunch-time. The consumption of high-fat and high-sugar snacks by the students was also reduced in the longitudinal study. With the consumption of soft drinks and sugary drinks showing the most significant reduction, followed by ice cream and desserts.

More than half of the schools involved in the Colourful and Bright Fruits and Vegetables Project reported that they had strengthened the monitoring measures on the school lunch supply and snack shop management during the project. A 5-day school lunch menu review showed an improvement in nutrition quality of the school lunch supply, namely an increase in vegetables and a reduction in the fat and salt content of the lunch boxes. The weighed school lunch survey results indicate that there was a statistically significant increase of 23.6% ($p=0.007$) in the mean weight of vegetables supplied at lunchtime (Lee et al., 2010a). In addition to these measured changes in the schools and students, the health knowledge of parents also significantly improved according to the survey. Taken together, this project embraced health promotion strategies using the HPS concept, focusing on improving school eating policies and environment, training teachers and parents, involving families and the community, and promoting a comprehensive nutrition education programme and active student participation. The results demonstrate how the HPS framework can be used to create a supportive environment, mediate policy changes, and enhance personal health skills to improve healthy eating and combat childhood obesity (Lee, 2009d). Box 6.2 outlines a case study of one school that participated in the programme.

While the result above focus on obesity, an NCD, implementing the HPS concept has also been shown to improve students' health knowledge and practices to prevent communicable diseases. A study conducted after the SARS epidemic in Hong Kong also showed that students studying in schools that had received a Healthy School Award were found to be better in their personal hygiene practices, have a greater knowledge of health and hygiene, and better access to health information compared to students not studying in award-winning schools (Lee et al., 2008). The award-winning schools were also reported to have better school health policies, higher degrees of community participation, and more hygienic environments.

Healthy Plan-Net: Advancing Health Literacy to Meet Health Education Needs

The HPS model has been proven to be effective in improving school health literacy at both the individual and system levels (Nutbeam, 2008). To further advance health education needs, the Healthy Plan-Net model is conceptualised on the idea of health literacy being an asset (Lee et al., 2018b). It draws on the following theories:

- Functional literacy: basic skills in daily life, such as self-management, assessing information, and services;

- Interactive literacy: cognitive and social skills to extract different forms of information and derive meaning from different forms of information, including problem-solving skills, choice, and decision-making skills) and

- Critical literacy: understanding and personalising health information and appropriate application of relevant health information, including critical thinking, goal setting.

Box 6.2: Promote Healthy Eating and Minimise Risk Behaviours by Adopting the Health-promoting School Framework: A Case Study (Source: CHEHP, CUHK)

At one school that participated in the Colourful and Bright Fruits and Vegetables Project, both the school principal and the coordinating teacher had previously completed professional training in health education and health promotion and have a strong commitment to promoting better health and development of their students and staff. Guided by the HPS framework of the HKHSA Scheme, the school incorporated health concepts in its management, curriculum, and environment. The school set and regularly reviewed various health policies, including comprehensive healthy eating guidelines. A school lunch monitoring committee and tuck shop (snack shop) committee had been set up to monitor the school's meal service and snack food provisions with the support of the CHEHP. This also included receiving feedback from students and parents. Healthy snack marketing and promotion activities were organised regularly. The school also banned soda drinks and crisps in 2003. Health education was accorded a high priority in the school curriculum and activities. The school used a nutrition education teaching kit provided by the CHEHP in the General Studies class. The school utilised an integrated curriculum and project learning on various health topics, including healthy eating, physical activity, and mental health. The school arranged morning exercise, inter-class eye exercises, and a special activity called the Daily Big Strides Award Scheme to increase student activity levels. A Health Education Resource Centre was established at the school in 2004 and was managed by the trained students and parent volunteers. It has become not only a resource centre but also a training centre for students and parents of the school and also their partner schools. The CHEHP conducted the Student Fruit and Vegetable Ambassador Training Programme and Parent Volunteer Training Programme, and the trained ambassadors and parents were actively involved in conveying health messages to their peers and assisted in carrying out the nutrition promotional programme in the school. The school has maintained an excellent working relationship with parents, local community groups, and neighbouring schools in the same school district through sharing their experiences and resources at regular health talks, an annual health carnival, and school visits and discussion forums on healthy schools or healthy pre-schools. With the support of the CHEHP, the school started to support a neighbouring pre-school to develop into a health-promoting kindergarten in 2003.

Impact and Outcomes of the Project

The school was presented with the gold award for having achieved the WHO's standards for an HPS in 2005. There was evidence of improved dietary and exercise habits and mental wellness. Decreased consumptions of high-fat snacks (such as chips and crisps), soda drinks and other sugary drinks, and chocolate and candies were observed. A nearly two-fold increase in supply and a three-fold increase in consumption of vegetables at lunchtime was recorded since the baseline weighted lunch consumption measurement in May 2004. Notably, fighting and disagreements between Primary Four boys decreased from 22.7% to 3.8% within 2 years after joining the HKHSA Scheme. A significant decrease was also observed in the percentage of student reporting suicidal ideas, plans, or actions. The school's health policies, curriculum, and links with parents and the community were strengthened. Parents were provided with more opportunities to participate, support, and cooperate with the school to ensure the balanced development of their children. The social and physical environments were also improved. The school collaborated with another gold award-winning secondary school and built a healthy school network to share good practice of developing and implementing the HPS concept with other schools and kindergartens in the district. The network supported 20 primary schools and pre-schools on their health journey at that time. The school's efforts also inspired schools in other districts to adopt the HPS framework or to act as mentors for pre-schools.

The Healthy Plan-Net (Figure 6.4) integrates these theories with the components of comprehensive school health adopted for HPSs in Hong Kong (Lee, 2009b). This integration will advance health literacy as it will enable individuals to exert greater control over their health and the personal, social, and environmental determinants of health (Nutbeam, 2008).

The effectiveness of such a holistic Healthy Plan-Net in improving health literacy in relation to healthy eating has been shown by Lee (2009d). In a randomised control study among Chinese diabetic patients in Hong Kong, patients who received an intensive health literacy intervention (based on self-management skills and improvement of self-efficacy) had significantly improved eating habits at the time of follow-up (Lee et al., 2010a). Therefore, a Healthy Plan-Net can be used to empower individuals in healthy living planning in making wise and healthy decisions in daily life.

For a Healthy Plan-Net to be implemented, a needs assessment must first be conducted. A needs assessment is defined as "the process by which the programme planner identifies and measures gaps between what is and what ought to

Figure 6.4: The Healthy Plan-Net Model

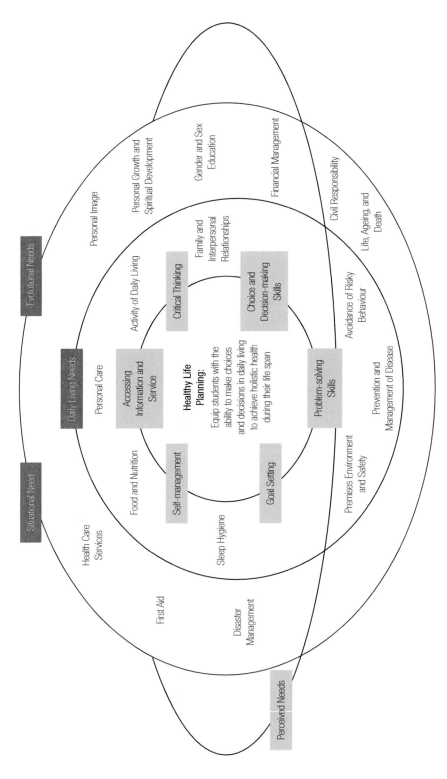

Source: Lee et al., 2018b.

be" (Jordan et al., 1998). In short, the purpose of a needs assessment is to identify what clients require and decide whether these requirements are met. There are two types of health needs:

- Service needs to be perceived by the health professionals (Actual Needs), and

- Service demands determined by the number of clients (Perceived Needs).

In addition to identifying needs, a needs assessment also provides information to help regiment the target population according to demographic variables such as age, sex, socio-economic status, health behaviours, and attitudes. Such regimenting allows planners to design a programme for a specific sub-group, which is an important marketing strategy. For example, sometimes more emphasis must be placed on a Perceived Need to satisfy individual desires, while less focus is put on an Actual Need. However, there may be other occasions that an Actual Need overshadows a Perceived Need. Actual Needs can be further categorised into Daily Living Needs, Evolutional Needs, and Situational Needs, which also allows for further regimenting that focuses more closely on the Actual Needs while still reflecting the individual circumstances and situation.

The Healthy Plan-Net model aims to integrate health literacy with the components of comprehensive school health education to meet the Actual and Perceived Needs for health education. The outer layer of the Healthy Plan-Net (Figure 6.4) illustrates the individual preferences and Perceived Needs, while the inner layers refer to the Actual Needs. It is essential to appreciate the interactions and constrains of the Actual Needs and Perceived Needs during different stages of life. For example, by cultivating the six domains of health literacy in the inner circle, students would improve health literacy in the components in the second inner circle (e.g., the activity of daily living, avoidance of risky behaviours) to meet their Daily Living Needs.

Advancing their understanding of the components of the third layer of the Healthy Plan-Net model (e.g., Life Ageing and Death, Understanding Health Services) would improve their health literacy to meet the Situational Needs and Evolutional Needs. This would achieve holistic coordination and balance between the Actual Needs and Perceived Needs at a macro-level by integrating health learning to cultivate the six domains of health literacy. At this stage, students should be able to understand the complexity of healthy living. This increased knowledge should, in turn, allow students to enhance their capability to make healthy choices and decisions in daily life in order to achieve optimal health and well-being.

Health-promoting School Effectiveness

The core business of schools is enhancing teaching and fostering learning, and there is strong evidence to show that healthy students learn better. In addition, there is evidence that the improvement of student health status and action competencies lead to improved learning outcomes (Feinstein et al., 2008; Taras, 2005a, 2005b; Taras and Potts-Datema, 2005; Warwick et al., 2009). HPSs enhance the key features of effective schools, as they provide students with opportunities to build their education and health assets (St Leger et al., 2010).

The document by the International Union for Health Promotion and Education (IUHPE, 2009) on HPS principles and the various works outlining the system indicators for the Hong Kong Healthy School Award (HKHSA) Scheme (Lee, 2002; Lee et al., 2007c, 2007d) highlight how different elements of HPSs substantiate the key components of effective schools (Table 6.3). Lee and Cheung (2017) also highlighted the positive effects of structured school health programmes, such as the HPS model, on educational outcomes as well as their capacity to change professional cultures and communities in schools and students' physical, emotional, social, and spiritual health. The paper goes on to point out that the Assessment Tool for Affective and Social Outcomes (ATASO) in Hong Kong reflects the social developments of the students in school and resembles the core areas of action competencies and school social environment, two key areas of the HKHSA (Lee and Cheung, 2017). The positive experience and effectiveness of HPSs in Hong Kong has driven the curriculum to focus more on the impact of health on individuals and society. In fact, in 2007, the new senior secondary school curriculum incorporated a model of Public Health and Disease Prevention under the Liberal Studies subject (Curriculum Development Council and the Hong Kong Examination Authority, 2007a). A new elective subject, Health Management and Social Care (HMSC), was also introduced (Curriculum Development Council and the Hong Kong Examination Authority, 2007b). Personal health management and the promotion of community health are among the core components of HMSC.

Table 6.3: Effective School Activity in Coordination with the Principles and System Indicators of the Health-promoting School Model

Effective School Activity	System Indicators of HPSs (Lee et al., 2007c, 2007d)	Principles of HPS (IUHPE, 2009)
Using learning and teaching methods that are evidence-based	The school should implement a health education curriculum and activities appropriate to the ages and needs of the students in order to increase their understanding of the Key Health Content Areas.	• Enhance learning outcomes of students • Set realistic goals built on accurate data and assessment standards
Actively involving students in creating a learning experience	The school should create a suitable learning and teaching environment to stimulate and facilitate the learning process.	• Involve student participation and empowerment • Seek continuous improvement through ongoing monitoring and evaluation
Facilitating cooperation between students	The school should involve students in policy-making.	
Providing prompt feedback to students	The school should use various methods to evaluate the learning outcomes of students and teaching effectiveness.	
Investing in capacity-building experiences for all staff	The school should develop a policy regarding health education training as well as encouraging and facilitating staff to have such training.	• Link health and education issues and systems • Address health and well-being issues of all staff
Establishing and promoting high expectations	The school should promote the development of students' skills in leadership, communication, and interpersonal relationships.	• Set realistic goals built on accurate data and assessment standards
Respecting diverse talents and ways of learning	The school should encourage students and staff to respect and value each other's individuality and differences among cultures, genders, religions, disadvantaged groups, and races.	• Integrate health into the school's ongoing activities, curriculum, and assessment standards • Promote the health and well-being of students
Permitting adequate time for learning tasks	The school should try to ensure all students have opportunities to actively engage with each health topic, according to their age.	
Ensuring there is consultation between parents, students, and teachers in establishing the school's direction	The school should use a system to ensure close communication with parents. Opportunities should be provided for parents to work with the school, especially in health education and health-promotion activities.	• Collaborate with parents and the local community • Set realistic goals built on accurate data and assessment standards
Establishing programmes and facilities for students with special needs	The school should have a system in place and carry out appropriate actions to aid students with special needs.	• Uphold the concepts of social justice and equity • Provide a safe and supportive environment • Seek continuous improvement through ongoing monitoring and evaluation • Collaborate with parents and the local community
Providing clear leadership from the principal and school head in establishing a school climate of trust, respect, collaboration, and openness	The school should consult parents for recommendations on Healthy School development and encourage their active participation in the joint discussion on the formulation and review of Healthy School policies. The school should have a system in place to ensure equal opportunities among students and staff.	

Successful implementation of the HPS concept is reflected by the achievements in the HKHSA Scheme. The implementation of the HPS model has been shown to improve the health and well-being of students and school culture, policies, and organisation and to be more conducive to student health (Langford et al., 2014). The experience of building up the HKHSA Scheme as a quality HPS programme has demonstrated that only complex, multifactorial, and innovative activity in many domains (curriculum, school environment, and community) with substantial building up of the professional capacity of teachers and school culture will result in effective school health promotion and altered health behaviours. The HPS model provides a sound intervention framework for multi-level interventions addressing health, education, and social issues of children and adolescents (Figure 6.5). Through the HPS concept, it is feasible to establish a professional and community culture that in turn creates a healthy teaching and learning environment (Lee, 2019c).

The HPS model can be used to establish a healthy school environment and culture to enhance the health and well-being of students. As the next chapter will show, it is also important to have a similar model implemented in the workplace to enable workers to maintain positive health when they enter the workforce.

Figure 6.5: Health-promoting Schools and Intervention Framework

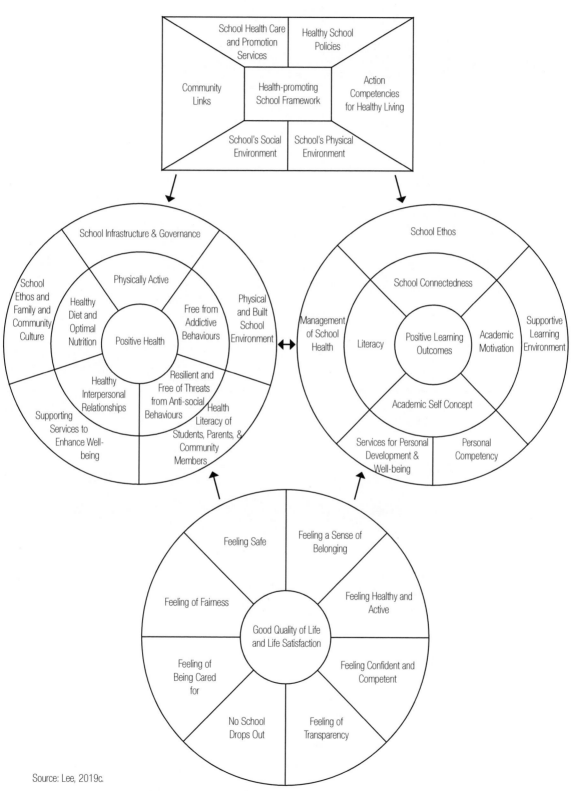

Chapter 7

Health-promoting Workplaces: Concept, Evaluation, and Monitoring

Albert Lee

City-super had by now gained a deep understanding of how effective health promotion could be implemented in a school setting. However, to effectively impact population health, he still needed to explore another important setting: the workplace. He also needed to advise the City Mayor how the health care system should be re-oriented towards health promotion. City-super was introduced to a study by Chu et al. (2000) that used Volkswagen as a model of a Health-promoting Workplace. A Health-promoting Workplace should not be neglected for sustainable growth and development of a city. City-super used this study as the foundation for his research on the concept, evaluation, and monitoring of Health-promoting Workplaces.

Health-related production loss in the workplace can be explained to a larger extent by staff health as opposed to work environment-related factors and is a valid measure capturing the true effects of workplace illness. Indeed, health-related production loss is strongly associated with work ability, meaning that *presenteeism* while sick (i.e., continuing to work at a lower ability while ill) is a costly matter for employers (Karlsson et al., 2015). The number of days absent due to sickness was previously the only factor considered by employers and society when estimating the cost of production loss, but studies have shown that the costs related to the consequences of employees attending work despite being sick could be at least twice as high as the cost of employees taking sick leave (Collins et al., 2005; Stewart et al., 2003). Therefore, the cost of presenteeism while ill has to be considered from a broader societal perspective.

Research has shown that effective worksite health-promotion programmes offering multiple risk-factor interventions combined with group participation and individualised risk reduction counselling to high-risk employees are effective (Pelletier, 2001). This effectiveness is determined based on enhanced clinical outcomes (Pelletier, 2001) and positive cost outcomes (Aldana, 2001) as well as in the increased health awareness, reduced risks, enhanced disease prevention, and reduced demand for health services in the workforce. Health-promotion strategies should aim at providing a more conducive work environment to facilitate individual behaviour changes, and they should be supported and sustained through modification of work policies. Management's support is often needed to implement or modify work policies that promote and sustain healthy lifestyle behaviours (Moy et al., 2006). Occupational health policies should be re-orientated towards creating a healthy workplace environment which can induce many positive changes, such as enhanced physical health of the workforce, increased job satisfaction, and reduced absenteeism, which in turn improve productivity and the quality of working life (WHO, 1995). The Health-promoting Workplace concept is becoming more important and more relevant as private and public organisations increasingly recognise that future success in an increasingly globalised marketplace can only be realised with a healthy, qualified, and motivated workforce, and the development of a health-promoting workplace will be a pre-requisite for sustainable social and economic development (Chu et al., 2000). The WHO's Global Healthy Work Approach (WHO, 1997c) calls for the development of a comprehensive approach for the promotion of health of all working populations. The approach is based on four fundamental complementary principles: health promotion, occupational health and safety, human resource management, and sustainable development. Multi-sectoral partnerships and the involvement and cooperation of key actors not only from within a specific workplace but from all areas that influence working life are the fundamental principles.

The European Network for workplace health promotion was formed in 1996 comprising all 15 member states and the European Economic Area (EEA) countries. The EURO Network for Workplace Health Promotion adopted the Luxembourg Declaration on 28 November 1997 to announce their shared understanding of the aims, strategies, and measures of the European Network for workplace health promotion. The member organisations agreed on the future development and dissemination of workplace health promotion, effective coordination and cooperation at all levels. Germany was entrusted with the task of setting up the requisite infrastructure (Federal Institute for Occupational Safety and Health, 1996). Thus, the German company Volkswagen has made for an interesting case study (Chu et al., 2000) which illuminates issues that can occur during the successful implementation of workplace health promotion.

Model of Good Practice: Volkswagen AG

Volkswagen AG (VW) is a leading German car manufacturer with its head office in Wolfsburg, Germany. VW employed 98,000 people in 2000, when the case study was published. Health protection and health promotion, as integral parts of health management, are two of VW's corporate objectives. Health management is understood to be a continuously developing process based on the principles of active participation, solidarity, and subsidiarity (whereby self-help takes precedence over corporate support).

VW's health management programme consists of a series of obligatory modules that are implemented in all subsidiaries as well as some optional modules that can be used to meet specific needs. The priority of all activities is on work organisation and job design. These include:

- innovative working-time models (working-time accounts);

- introduction of new forms of work organisation;

- corporate regulations to prevent sexual discrimination and mobbing; and

- ergonomic job design, which involves the employees and health specialists within investment decision procedures including the planning of new equipment.

The active participation of employees is realised through

- health circles in many company sectors (problem-solving groups with the task of identifying health-related problems and possible measures for improvement);

- extended job inspection routines involving employees;

- regular employee surveys on health matters; and

- special training modules for health and safety education.

A crucial success factor for workplace health promotion is the support of senior management and its integration into improvement processes. At VW, a company-wide health-related control system was established in 1992 which analysed the causes of ill-health on a regular basis. The results of these programmes were then discussed and acted upon by management. In addition, management at VW deals with the subject of preventive healthcare through regular discussions with staff. An important aspect of this system is that when an employee returns to work after a lengthy absence due to injury or illness, an individual rehabilitation plan will be prepared in collaboration with all appropriate offices. Employees are given medical treatment and sports pedagogical counselling in the company's own rehabilitation centre. All these module-based measures are complemented by services relating to a healthy lifestyle.

The success of the health management system at VW was measurable:

- Absenteeism was halved between 1986 and 1996, which translates into a reduction in the average number of days lost (per employee) of 24 days in 1986 to 12 days in 1996.

- There was a positive increase in work attendance rate (reduction of lost days) from 91.7% in 1988 to 95.8% in 1996.

- Personnel costs of roughly DM 90 million (US$50 million) were saved per year by 1 percentage point increase in the health rate.

As the case study by Chu et al. (2000) shows, VW is a model of good practice illustrating the effectiveness of comprehensive workplace health interventions. A systematic review of 39 organisational-level workplace health interventions has revealed that success rates were higher for the more comprehensive interventions which tackled material, organisational, and work-time-related conditions simultaneously (Montano et al., 2014). Favourable health outcomes were reported for self-rated mental and general health, and for reduction of injury rates. These studies further highlight the paradigm shift in health-promotion activities in the workplace from focusing on a single illness, risk factor, or lifestyle change of individual workers in the 1970s to more comprehensive "wellness" programmes in Western industrialised countries in the 1980s (Chen, 1988). This shift is representative of our growing understanding of the wider determinants of health and the organisational and environmental influence on the health of employees (Chu and Forrester, 1992). In Hong Kong, this knowledge and case studies of global companies have translated into the Healthful Company Initiative.

Healthful Company: A Hong Kong Initiative

In 2013, the Healthful Company Initiative, a platform for advancing workplace wellness, was launched in Hong Kong. The initiative is led by Health Action, a company that also publishes a magazine, *Health Action*, capturing the key health information for the public based on interviews with leading health care professionals in Hong Kong and guided by a panel of public health officers and corporate social responsibility experts (Lee, 2014a). To implement the Healthful Company Initiative, Health Action provided their "My Passport to Health @Work" guide to employees of participating companies to help them reflect and improve their personal health status. The Passport includes content to help better the employee's physical health in three categories:

- Lifestyle — including diet and nutrition, sedentary lifestyle and exercise, sleep, smoking, alcohol and drug abuse, hygiene, and breastfeeding;

- Health Seeking — including recommended health care screening, vaccination, cardiovascular risk factors, and cancer screening; and

- Occupational Health — including musculoskeletal health and eye health.

The Passport also includes content focused on psycho-social health of the employee, such as: emotional resilience, stress management, work-life balance, and emotional intelligence.

Through the Healthy Company Initiative, Health Action has also developed a system of accreditation for companies to become Health-promoting Companies (Box 7.1). Scores can be tabulated based on the survey, and the companies can receive credentials according to their level of achievement. The survey provides data reflecting the development of a health-supportive

---

Box 7.1: Healthful Company Accreditation Survey Questions
(Source: Lee, 2014)

General Workplace and Organisational

1. How many employees in your company have a formal job description that covers workplace wellness activities in the list of responsibilities? (Includes assessing employee health needs; health promotion; occupational health and safety; first aid; absentee management; stress reduction activities; ergonomic assessments; participating in a wellness committee; volunteering; developing workplace policies for wellness issues; developing flexible hour schedules for staff members; maintaining the light, sound, temperature, and air-quality conditions in the office, etc.)

2. How much does your company spend on workplace wellness per annum, as a percentage of your company's annual operating budget? (Includes health insurance premiums, Employee Assistance Programme (EAP) premiums, and the costs associated with any employee health or occupational health and safety activity.)

3. Does your company publish a sustainability report each year?

4. Does your company have a general, company-wide workplace wellness policy in place? (A workplace wellness policy formally outlines the company's approach to providing a working environment that promotes the optimal health of employees.)

   a. Does it include health components? (e.g., involving health promotion, health-risk reduction, health screening, nutritious food, vaccinations)

   b. Does it include safety components? (e.g., involving ergonomics, work-related hazards, basic hygiene, and sanitation)

   c. Does it include environmental components? (e.g., involving the physical workplace, environmental protection, handling of hazardous materials)

5. Does your company have an active workplace wellness or health, safety, and environment committee with members from all levels or departments?

6. Does your company offer permanent employees a private health insurance plan, covering outpatient and inpatient expenditures?

Physical Health Questions

7. Does your company provide physical rehabilitation services, income support, and suitable duties for employees who are injured in the workplace?

8. Does your company provide employees with first aid supplies and have staff members who are trained in first aid present at all times?

9. Does your company provide employees with ergonomic chairs (that provide good back support) and other ergonomic devices, such as footrests, wrist pads, telephone headsets, etc.?

10. Does your company provide employees with free or subsidised vaccinations for pneumonia?

11. Does your company provide employees with free or subsidised vaccinations for seasonal influenza?

12. Does your company have a policy of providing healthy food and beverage choices during meetings and other occasions when food is served?

13. Does your company regularly provide fresh fruit or other healthy snacks or beverages to employees free of charge?

14. Does your company provide employees with a team sports programme, in-house exercise classes, office gym equipment, or free or subsidised gym memberships?

15. Does your company have an HIV/AIDS workplace policy in place, covering non-discrimination, awareness, prevention, and health support?

16. Does your company provide employees with a free or subsidised annual health check-up, covering disease risk assessment and screening, which is performed by a health professional or family doctor? (A health check-up covers items such as hip-to-waist ratio, cholesterol levels, blood pressure, blood glucose level, etc.)

17. Does your company provide employees with written information or training sessions on (tick where appropriate):

    ☐ Healthy eating

    ☐ Exercise and physical activity

    ☐ Smoking cessation

    ☐ Safe levels of alcohol consumption

    ☐ Sleep

    ☐ Breastfeeding

    ☐ Sexual health

    ☐ First aid

    ☐ Recognising and responding to the signs and symptoms of a heart attack

    ☐ Recognising and responding to the signs and symptoms of a stroke

    ☐ None of the above, but the company commits to achieving this goal in the next year

Psycho-Social Questions

18. Does your company provide opportunities for employees to participate in decisions about workplace issues that affect job stress, such as project timelines, headcount, etc.?

19. Does your company provide employees with relaxation services, such as massage, or dedicated on-site space where employees can engage in relaxation activities, such as meditation, tai chi, or yoga?

20. Does your company have an anti-bullying policy in place?

21. Does your company have a Code of Professional Conduct in place, which addresses interpersonal behaviour and dispute resolution?

22. Does your company sponsor or organise company-wide social events throughout the year?

23. Does your company have a corporate community investment strategy in place, covering employee volunteering, charitable donations, and community partnerships?

24. Does your company allow employees to work flexible hours?

25. Does your company provide employees with written information or training on work-life balance?

26. Does your company have a work-life balance policy in place? (A work-life balance policy formally outlines the company's approach to supporting staff to meet their personal commitments to community, home, and loved ones. It covers flexible working schedules, maternity leave, paternity leave, adoption leave, and so on.)

27. Does your company provide employees with stress management education or programmes?

28. Does your company provide employees with free or subsidised clinical screening for depression, performed by a mental health professional or family doctor?

29. Does your company have an EAP or any other kind of free counselling service in place for employees? (An EAP is a confidential counselling service designed to help employees cope with personal problems that adversely affect their lives, behaviour, performance, or job satisfaction.)

and caring workplace culture, which is an important outcome evaluation apart from improvement of health and well-being of workers (Hawe et al., 1990). The evaluation of a comprehensive workplace health-promotion programme is challenging because it involves monitoring and assessing not only overall health outcomes but also changes in the workplace environment and culture, the effectiveness of different strategies, and health programme-specific achievements (Chu et al., 2000). Hawe et al. (1990) have described the three types of evaluation outcomes for health promotion at the workplace (Box 7.2): process, impact, and outcome. The Healthful Company survey can be used to evaluate the process by reflecting whom the programme is reaching and what aspects need to

---

Box 7.2: Evaluation of Outcomes
(Source: Lee, 2014)

Process Evaluation: Evaluate the implementation of strategies (e.g., how were the activities received, how satisfied were the participants, what was the quality or appropriateness of the programme delivered, what aspects of the programmes should be improved, and whom has the programme reached, etc.)

Impact Evaluation: Evaluate the immediate effects of specific programme activities (e.g., the extent of changes in increased awareness, knowledge, beliefs, skills, and behaviour of participants; the increase of morale; the reduction of salt consumption due to healthy canteen provisions, etc.)

Outcome Evaluation: Evaluate the long-term effects of the programme (i.e., the improvement of the health and well-being of workers, the development of a health-supportive and caring workplace culture). In this regard, it would be useful to develop a set of indicators to collect baselines of workplaces and to assess outcomes.

---

be improved, while it can be used to assess the impact by evaluating the policies on a healthy working environment. The survey reflects outcomes by evaluating the development of workplace culture to support health and caring. The survey can also be used to provide a set of indicators for baseline assessment.

Khanal et al. (2016) has reported the effectiveness of a workplace health promotion programme in New South Wales, Australia. This programme is an example of how a large-scale workplace programme can be evaluated using data from multiple source collected for different purpose. The programme used a Brief Health Check conducted online, which was shown to be a valuable mean of assessing workplace and employee health. The Healthful Company Initiative adopts a similar face-to-face health check. The data from these checks can then be used to enhance the uptake of different components of the programme in achieving the ultimate goal of employee and company health.

Conclusion

Implementation of a workplace health promotion needs to be more flexible than a traditional approach (Khanal et al., 2016). Corporations interested in enhancing workplace and employee health can reference specific model companies, such as VW, or other initiatives, such as Healthful Company in Hong Kong, to implement health promotion at the workplace and implement corporate wellness programmes. Figure 7.1 shows the cycle of implementation to meet the needs of both the corporation and its employees. The impact of a corporate staff wellness can include changes in

- Spiritual well-being — enhanced interpersonal relationships and communication;
- Social well-being — enhanced connectedness;
- Psychological well-being — enhanced self-esteem and self-confidence; and
- Physical well-being — enhanced energy and dynamics.

There is also a distinct relationship between corporate governance and staff wellness at multiple levels, whereby increased staff wellness impacts:

- Human Resource Management — meeting the needs of the employee (in reference to Maslow's Hierarchy of Needs);
- Total Quality Management — working environment, job satisfaction, quality of life for employees, and caring for staff;
- Safety and Security of the working environment;
- Entrepreneurial spirit — building social capital and social enterprise.

Enhancing these areas then feeds back to positively impact employee wellness in an ever-growing cycle between the employees and corporate management. The increased levels of each employee's sense of security and devotion to the company as well as their level of collegiality and the overall dynamics of the workforce will impact the efficiency and productivity of the company (Figure 7.2). Ultimately, it is necessary to look beyond absenteeism and presenteeism and focus on the corporate gains that can be mediated through a comprehensive shift towards overall company wellness.

While the Health-promoting Workplace concept can be applied to almost all work-related settings, one workplace that requires a closer look is health care organisations. Chapter 8 uses cases studies in Hong Kong to investigate how health promotion can be enhanced in the health care setting.

Figure 7.1: Cycles of Implementation of a Corporate Wellness Programme

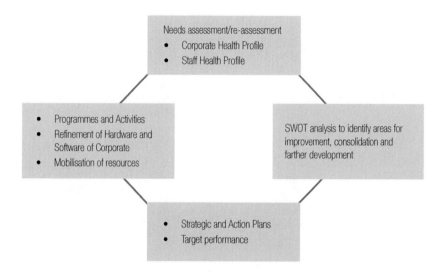

Source: Lee, 2019d.

Figure 7.2: Workforce and Productivity

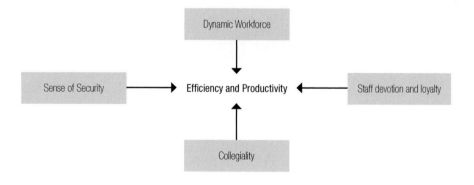

Source: Lee, 2019d.

Chapter 8

Health-promoting Healthcare Organisations: Hong Kong Case Studies

Albert Lee and Yick-hay Chow

Although City-super now has a better understanding of how different sectors, including schools and workplaces, facilitate the improvement of population health, he was puzzled why the health sector in his city had such little input. City-super was advised to explore the concept of a Health-promoting Health Care Organisation, looking beyond the context of health promotion in hospitals. During his research, he found a study by Green et al. (2001) on the "Ecology of Medical Care Revisited", which indicates that only a minority of the population seeks help from hospitals for their health problems. This supports City-super's aim of promoting health more widely to include services beyond the hospital setting. He was then introduced to the Kwai Tsing Healthy City Signature Project in Hong Kong, which links different types of health services to improve the health of the local population. The success of this project has become the cornerstone for the development of a district health initiative, making it an excellent case study for City-super.

A Health-promoting Hospital vs Health-promoting Health Services

In the past, hospital care has mainly focused on acute care for the sick and injured, with health statistics primarily reporting mortality and morbidity rates, which only capture the tip of the clinical iceberg (Green et al., 2001; Lieu et al., 2009; Denaxas et al., 2016). Territory-wide primary care morbidity data for Hong Kong was first available in 1994 (Lee et al., 1995) and a second territory-wide study was conducted in 2007 (Lo et al., 2010). A youth risk behavioural survey was first conducted in 1999 by the Centre for Health Education and Health Promotion (CHEHP) at the Chinese University of Hong Kong (Lee et al., 2004a). Later, in 2004, the Surveillance and Epidemiology Branch at the Centre for Health Protection, Department of Health in Hong Kong, set up the Behavioural Risk Factor Surveillance System (BRFSS), and the first survey was conducted in 2004. Although these studies have played an important role in the collection of health data, health promotion has not been a priority and has always been regarded as part of public health rather than an essential aspect of day-to-day clinical practice. Clinicians, especially in a hospital setting, have largely ignored the ecology of health care and have underestimated the burden of health problems managed outside of the hospital setting, many of which are preventable with proper care (Green et al., 2001). The Health Impact Pyramid described by Frieden (2015) shows that public health care should focus on denominators (i.e., of the people who could benefit from an intervention, what proportion actually do). Improvements at the base of the pyramid (which often focus on tackling socio-economic factors and changing the general circumstances so each individual's default decisions are healthier) generally improve health for more people at a lower unit cost compared to interventions at the top (such as clinical interventions and individual counselling) (Frieden, 2015). The rise of consumerism has resulted in greater advocacy for patients' rights and provision of patient-centred care. Hospital services can no longer be confined to the acute management of illnesses. The Commission on Social Determinants of Health (CSDH) has observed significant improvements in health worldwide over the past 30 years, primarily through three routes: improvements in daily life, actions to address the inequitable distribution of resources, and increased public awareness of determinants of health (Marmot et al., 2008).

The Knowledge Network on Urban Settings (KNUS) published a report for CSDH in 2007 (Kjellstrom et al., 2007) and made five key recommendations to improve health:

- Build social cohesion

- Improve environments for health

- Make primary health care accessible to all

- Use healthy settings as vehicles

- Implement proactive and coordinated urban planning to promote good urban governance

This report and its recommendations raise an important discussion concerning the distinction between Health-promoting Hospitals (HPHs) and Health-promoting Health Services. The HPH movement focuses on building up hospital environments as organisational settings for enhancing health and health promotion (Pelikan et al., 2010). Population health cannot be improved simply by providing health services focusing on particular diseases or organs, and primary health care has been shown to be the independent factor associated with positive health outcomes while other socio-demographic variables are controlled. One thematic KNUS report highlighted the importance of synergy between healthy settings and primary care organisations (Lee et al., 2007a). Apart from the availability of quality primary health care, other health services must also be widely accessible, particularly for disadvantaged groups in the population, and a universal approach might not fully address questions of inequity. The HPH concept should therefore be expanded to include other health services beyond primary care to bring those disadvantaged groups into contact with essential health care services. In fact, hospitals are a key setting for health promotion through other health services as they have a large workforce with close contact with patients at times of heightened awareness about their health and illness. Hospitals also maintain close links to their local community, which allow them to act as an example to other organisations.

This chapter highlights three case studies in Hong Kong. One case concerns a major hospital developing as a HPH in synergy with other healthy settings (Lai, 2010). This case also highlights the strong role of hospital settings in supporting the broader Healthy City movement in Hong Kong (Chow, 2018). The second case study concerns health promotion in primary care through a collaboration between a formal health care organisation and a non-government organisation (NGO) to promote patient self-management of diabetes mellitus (DM), a non-communicable disease (Lee et al., 2010b). A report by the Economist Intelligence Unit (2019) emphasised self-care as having the potential to improve health outcomes for people in addition to easing the strain on stretched healthcare budgets. The third case study focuses on the SARS epidemic and outbreaks of influenza in Hong Kong and how primary care organisations can mediate community resilience against potential threats of communicable and infectious diseases (Lee and Chuh, 2010). This experience contributed to a World Health Organisation (WHO) consultancy study on the "Municipality Response to Influenza Pandemic" (Lee and de Leeuw, 2009).

The Evolution of a Health-promoting Hospital in Hong Kong: Kwai Tsing as a Case Study

Hong Kong is a Special Administrative Region of China and has its own judicial and administrative system. The Food and Health Bureau acts as the Ministry of Health, overseeing government policies related to health. The Hospital Authority (HA) is a statutory organisation funded by the Government to provide hospital care in the public sector, accounting for around 90% of market share. General Outpatient Clinics (GOPCs) in the public sector account for about 20% of all General Practitioner (GP) services, and from 2004, the HA took over from the Department of Health in providing GOPC services. The Department of Health is the primary party responsible for health-promotion initiatives, but it only holds 10% of the health budget. Therefore, many health-promotion movements have been initiated by NGOs and other institutions (Lee et al., 2007e). As hospitals in the public sector hold the majority of the market share and the health budget, they should be considered the main catalyst for the Healthy Settings movement — or the main obstacle, if perceived as a threat.

The Healthy City project in Kwai Tsing District (KTD) was initiated by a senior management team of the Princess Margaret Hospital (PMH). The team included the then hospital chief executive, the head of Nursing Services, and the director of Community Services. The Kwai Tsing Healthy City project also developed in parallel with other health-promotion programs, including that for HPHs, Health-promoting Schools (HPSs), Health-promoting Workplaces, and community health care. The project has received awards from the Alliance for Healthy Cities (AFHC). This case study will focus on the role of PMH and the HPH project and how the initiative acts in synergy with other healthy settings (Chow, 2018; Lai, 2010).

Project Development Based on Needs Assessment

Taking into account the profile indicators developed based on European cities (Nakamura, 2003; WHO, 1997d), a city health profile was created for

KTD by collecting information about the residents' health status, health care service utilisation and satisfaction, lifestyles, personal safety, exercise level, quality of life based on WHOQOL-BREF (Hong Kong Project Team, 1997), and also perceptions about the hygienic environment, security, fire safety, estate and building management, parks and amusement facilities, and culture and leisure facilities with reference to the Community Quality of Life Questionnaire in 2004 (Sirgy et al., 2000; Lee et al., 2004b). KTD created a comprehensive health profile based on the above information and then developed a health plan based on the district's specific needs. The following were some of the key findings:

- The majority (63.7%) of district residents were aware of information concerning safety and health, mainly via television or radio, but only 24.9% had participated or were aware of occupational safety and health.

- About two-thirds expressed satisfaction with the security of the community.

- Around 15% of the sample population reported emotional problems affecting their daily life and working ability. KTD should, therefore, be more aware of residents' mental health issues and create a social support network using community resources to increase awareness.

- Over 60% of the adult population (ages 18–59) did not engage in regular exercise.

- Less than 40% of the residents expressed satisfaction with hospital clinical services and only about 60% expressed satisfaction with local primary health care services in general.

- About 40% were not satisfied with the level of community health education and health promotion.

- Residents expressed the need for more diversified services for the elderly, youth, and families, as well as the need to establish social relationships and self-development programs.

PMH started operating in 1975, serving mainly KTD as well as neighbouring districts with a catchment population over 1 million. It had 1,395 hospital beds with over 1,000 beds for acute care. As demand increased and the cost of health services escalated, a substantial proportion of patients expressed dissatisfaction in various types of services as indicated in the community diagnosis above (Lee et al., 2004b). In response, the hospital felt the need for a paradigm shift in health care delivery towards community-based care with a stronger emphasis on health promotion and disease prevention. In meeting the needs of the community, PMH decided to use the HPH concept to help establish a framework for related projects and health-promotion initiatives with the following aims:

- To make the hospital a healthier working and living environment for its large workforce and for patients

- To expand rehabilitation programmes and integrate health promotion and education, disease prevention, and rehabilitation services with curative care

- To provide information and advice on health issues

- To shift the hospital from being solely a place of treatment to one where prevention and health gains are valued

- To encourage an active and participatory role for patients according to their specific health potentials

- To improve communication and collaboration with existing social and health services in the community, fostering patients' rights

- To promote a healthy environment within the hospital

- To create supportive, humane, and stimulating living environments especially for long-term patients

- To enhance the provision and quality of information, communication, and educational programmes as well as offering skill training to patients and relatives

PMH was the main driver not only for the implementation of the HPH concept but also for the Healthy City movement in KTD. The minimisation of hospital admission and care in the community had been the strategic direction of the hospital to cope with the increasing health burden. The Kwai Tsing Safe Community and Healthy City Association (KTSCHCA) was established in 2000 in a collaborative effort of the District Council, PMH, Kwai Chung Hospital, the Occupational Safety and Health Council, and various Government departments, NGOs, corporations, academic institutions, and other key stakeholders. The KTSCHCA became a member of AFHC in 2004 and was accredited as a WHO Safe Community. Since early 2000, the KTSCHCA has adopted the Healthy Settings Approach to develop a district-based health system linking and coordinating various programs, including Safe and Healthy Homes, Safe and Healthy Estates, Safe and Healthy Elderly Homes, Safe and Healthy Schools, and Safe and Healthy

Workplaces, to become a Safe and Healthy Community. The hospital continued to integrate health education in daily clinical work, supporting community health promotion through the Safe and Healthy City programmes and Community Health Resources Centre. The hospital actively promoted the health and well-being of its staff through specific Health-promoting Workplace initiatives. Figure 8.1 shows how the HPH movement in KTD led to a cascade effect on other settings, allowing them to synergise to create a safe and healthy community. The KTSCHCA won the AFHC Pioneer in Healthy Cities Award in 2010.

In the 2013 Policy Address of Hong Kong's Chief Executive, a one-off allocation of HK$100 million (equivalent to approximately US$13 million) was earmarked to each District to initiate projects under the Signature Project Scheme (SPS). The Kwai Tsing District Council decided to use these funds on an SPS project titled "Enhancement of Community Healthcare". Building on years of experience in promoting safety and health in the community, the KTSCHCA proposed to establish a Medical-Welfare-Community Collaborative Model to capitalise on its intersectoral partnerships and multidisciplinary platform to build a sustainable, safe, and healthy community in KTD. The model adopted patient-centred care to provide a more effective way of improving health care for the residents, especially those with chronic diseases (Figure 8.2). During the 2016 Global Conference of the AFHC in Korea, the Kwai Tsing SPS won the AFHC Award for Creative Development of Healthy Cities under the Good Health System category. Similarly, at the 2018 Global Healthy Cities Conference in Malaysia, the AFHC granted two awards to the Kwai Tsing SPS: the AFHC Award for Creative Development in Healthy Cities (Healthy Settings and Non-communicable Diseases Control) and the AFHC Award for Progress of Healthy Cities with Strong Action (highest level).

Integration of Health Education in Daily Clinical Work

The goal of educating patients and their families is to improve patient health outcomes by promoting recovery, speedy returns to function, healthy behaviours, and patient autonomy in their care decisions. During the last few decades, the growth of consumerism and the self-help movement has encouraged people to take responsibility for their own health, while simultaneously pushing nurses and other health care professionals to actively pursue patient education as an important aspect of patient care. Indeed, there is evidence that health outcomes are worse when health care professionals control patient health decisions without other

Figure 8.1 Linking Up Healthy Settings

Source: Lee and Wei, 2018.

input (Kaplan et al., 1985). PMH has re-oriented their view of patient education from the basic provision of information towards a more enriched discussion with patients and their family members concerning their capacity and responsibility in managing their illnesses. This shift was accomplished through the implementation of various initiatives such as:

- conducting a nursing assessment for all patients upon admission to determine their health knowledge;

- including patient education in all care paths and practice protocols;

- making standard materials for patient education available in both hard copy and electronic forms;

- presenting health information in display panels, exhibits, and racks available in all workplaces;

- increasing community nursing services, including providing an assessment and health advice at every visit and educating patients, families, and caregivers;

- enhancing outpatient clinics to include education sessions and drug counselling in the waiting hall;

- providing procedural information at the Ambulatory Care Centre;

Figure 8.2 Signature Project Scheme: The Medical-Welfare-Community Collaborative Model

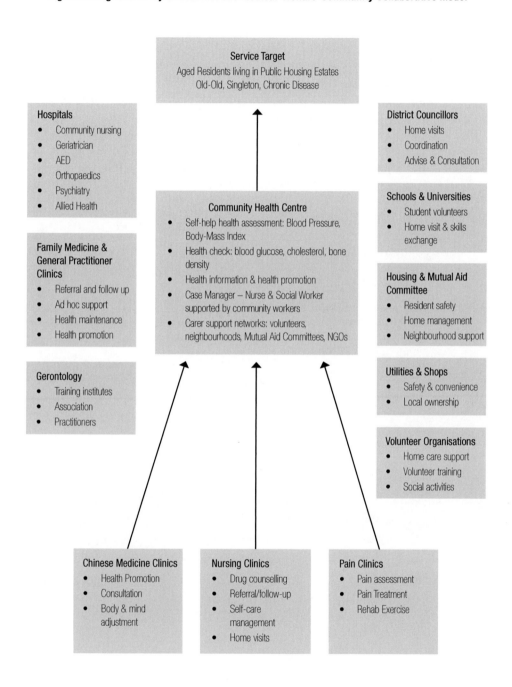

Source: Lee and Wei, 2018.

- conducting education classes and pre-admission clinics for diabetes patients;

- offering educational information sessions concerning procedures, treatments, and aftercare;

- performing pre-discharge assessments; and

- providing information to patients, families, and caregivers on self-care, rehabilitation, medication, and lifestyle modification.

Collaborative Projects for Health in the Community

PMH has developed initiatives in collaboration with other institutions and organisations to enhance health in the community. The services include:

- Photography for diabetes retinopathy

- Pilot for Family Nurse Practitioners

- Fall prevention in the community and elderly homes

- Health galas and prevention sessions for three high-risk dietary factors: high calorie, high salt, and high-fat

- Infection control and CPR training in schools and the community

Family Nurse Practitioners

This initiative further enriched the role of community nurses when they provide outreach services covering comprehensive, holistic, and continuing care. These designated community nurses (titled "the Nurses of Cheung Ching", which is one of the main public housing estates in KTD) were responsible for discharging patients, reviewing cases from primary care clinics, acting as a patient resource for information regarding health issues, and establishing service networks. The ultimate goal of this initiative is to reduce health risks and improve population health as well as empower individuals and groups in health promotion.

Community Fall Prevention Programme

This programme utilised a Community Rehabilitation Practitioner-Physiotherapist Programme to conduct fall assessments and established tai chi classes and activities. The programme involved one NGO with 25 elderly centres. The programme organised 31 tai chi classes for 446 elders. A home-screening programme was also conducted by trained volunteers in 61 homes. A total of 71 elders was screened, and 32 of these were enrolled in the fall prevention exercises classes.

Safe and Healthy Estates

This programme was started in 2002 to promote environmental health and safety in estate management. An inspection team was established to accredit housing estates for the achievements in health and safety. Seven housing estates have been accredited. Through this programme, ten health seminars were held for residents of the estates and eight health check-up events were organised.

Safe and Healthy Elderly Homes

This initiative involved a team of volunteer Safe and Occupation Health Inspectors who visited elderly residents and set up Occupation Safety and Health systems in nursing homes. The team included 34 inspectors, who visited 48 homes and conducted 32 training sessions.

Community Health Resource Centre

A health resource centre was opened to the public. This centre conducted health assessments, maintained a fitness corner and an Occupational Safety and Health corner, and held demonstrations focused on healthy eating.

Staff Health and Wellness Programmes

PMH has been labelled a "caring organisation" and has actively advocated for the physical, psychological, and social health and well-being of its own staff. The hospital has initiated programmes to support physical and mental health as well as emergency services. Physical health programmes include the staff Heart Health Programme and health assessments as well as the Walk for Health plan, tai chi classes, and fitness instruction days (including roping and stair-climbing exercises). Healthy behaviours are also promoted through sessions on healthy eating and health education. Mental health programmes include Workplace OASIS services, staff counselling services, and Quiet Room facilities. Specific sessions have also been conducted focusing on positive thinking, life values, food for thought, "smile prescription", increasing happiness, and using aromatherapy. A Critical Incident Support Team (CIST) and Employee Assistance Programme (EAP) have also been established to provide emergency support to staff facing life crises.

The above programmes serve as examples not only for other hospitals but also for other workplace settings to promote health throughout the community. The Medical-Welfare-Community Collaborative Model has enabled the KTD to work towards a more effective way to improve care for residents by advocating patient-centred services. Since it's initiation, this transdisciplinary SPS has implemented a wide range of community health services focusing on four main dimensions: chronic disease prevention and management, improving functional ability, rehabilitation, and psycho-social adjustment. The Medical-Welfare-Community Collaborative Model is also in line with the Medical-Social-Welfare Model proposed in the 2017 Policy Speech of Hong Kong's Chief Executive. In February 2019, the KTSCHCA was commissioned by the Government to develop the first District Health Centre in KTD to strategically strengthen primary healthcare in Hong Kong (Lee and Poon, 2020).

Control of Non-communicable Diseases: An NGO Case Study

Non-communicable diseases (NCDs) are emerging as significant global health care challenges. In fact, at the General Assembly in 2011, the United Nations called for action to address various NCDs. Diabetes mellitus (DM), for example, is a major cardiovascular risk factor, and maintaining a high degree of glycaemic control is the key to disease management. Although advice is frequently given in general practice, more extensive patient education programmes emphasising self-management skills are generally needed to more effectively improve DM control (Norris et al., 2001), particularly programmes emphasising lifestyle modification to safe and effectively control type 2 DM (Havas, 2009). Self-management programmes should be built on patient-perceived disease-related problems and help equip them with problem-solving skills to boost their self-efficacy and self-confidence in dealing with problems (Lorig, 2003).

In this case study, a programme was initiated to evaluate the effectiveness of a DM self-management programme established by a partnership between a general practice (operated by the HA) and the Hong Kong Society for Rehabilitation (an NGO). The evaluation focused on clinical outcomes, patient self-efficacy, and changes in lifestyle behaviours (Lee et al., 2010b). The objectives of this collaborative programme were to increase a patient's knowledge and skills, motivation to change, self-efficacy, and acceptance and ability to adapt.

The health benefits of the programme were significant. The proportion of subjects with normal glycated haemoglobin (HbA1c) levels increased from 4.5% (3 out of 66 patients) at baseline to 28.6% (19 out of 66 patients) ($p<0.001$) after 28 weeks in the programme. In contrast, HbA1c levels in the control group (DM patients not enrolled in the programme) did not change significantly over the same period (3.9% to 11.8%, $p=0.13$). The results of this evaluation also showed marked improvement in DM self-efficacy and body-mass index (BMI) among those enrolled in the programme. Dietary behaviours also improved significantly. Taken together, this DM self-management programme successfully help patients to better control their disease, improved self-efficacy, and minimised risky behaviour.

This type of chronic care partnership between a formal health care organisation and an NGO demonstrates the potential of different health care sectors to improve population health and develop synergistic actions with partners in the community. Empowering people to look after their own health is essential and, as highlighted by the Economist Intelligence Unit (2019), should be a primary concern in community health-promotion programmes.

Control of Infectious Diseases: Hong Kong's Response to SARS as a Case Study

A study by Wong et al. (2005) analysed the responses to the SARS epidemic in Hong Kong and Toronto, focusing on how primary care organisations can be more effective in preventing and fighting communicable and infectious diseases. SARS, or severe acute respiratory syndrome, has been one of the most significant infectious disease outbreaks in the world. During SARS, one of the strategies to manage the outbreak in Hong Kong was to centralise cases in selected institutions. For example, PMH was initially designed to receive all SARS cases during the Amoy Gardens community outbreak. In contrast, SARS cases in Toronto were allowed to enter a large number of hospitals across the city during the first wave of the outbreak, while all non-urgent hospital activities were suspended. This resulted in a massive backlog of deferred elective surgeries and ambulatory services with immeasurable long-term damage and dissatisfaction among family physicians. This was not the case in Hong Kong. This comparison highlights strengths and weaknesses in the methods used to organise and support the primary care system during an epidemic. This has become increasingly important recently as the world deals with the COVID-19 pandemic.

Similarly, Hong Kong's responses to outbreaks of influenza are also informative. For example, Lee and Chuh (2010) reviewed the role of primary care in facing the threats of an influenza pandemic and how quality and sustainable health care can be maintained during a health crisis. The WHO has outlined six phases in a pandemic or health crisis (WHO, 2009f). Phases 1 to 3 are warning stages and reflect levels of alertness to be prepared for community-level outbreaks. Phase 4 signals the verification of community-level outbreaks and suggests urgent steps should be taken for the rapid containment of the outbreak(s). Phases 5 and 6 correspond to there being sustained community-level outbreaks in different countries and stress the need for a pandemic response to mitigate the impacts on society. For each phase, there are five components of preparedness and response:

- Planning and coordination

- Situation monitoring and assessment

- Reducing the spread of disease

- Continuity of health care provision

- Communication

For each component, there are actions the WHO will take as well as actions that will be launched by individual countries. Furthermore, there are also actions recommended for primary care organisations to take to aid the local community during a health crisis during each phase (Table 8.1). While these actions were established based on the necessary response to an influenza outbreak (Lee and de Leeuw, 2009), they can be extrapolated to help assist primary health care organisations to prevent and fight the spread of any communicable disease.

Conclusion

The three case studies outlined in this chapter illustrate how HPHs and Health-promoting Health Services support the development of other healthy settings

Table 8.1: Roles of General Practitioners in Preparing for and Responding to Outbreaks and Pandemics of Influenza

	Phases 1–3	Phase 4	Phases 5 and 6
Planning and Coordination	Establish local network of GPs Establish rapid diagnostic system for confirmation of influenza type Coordination of related sectors to provide care for a large number of ill patients if needed Preventive measures for high-risk groups (i.e., vaccination and prophylaxis.) Protect health care workers and high-risk carers	Establish a triage system for suspected cases Standardise procedures for handling suspected cases Implement action plan to avoid cross-infection Coordinate with other sectors to care for large numbers of ill patients Identify the vulnerable and at-risk groups for necessary health protection Coordinate care for close contacts	Liaise with national and local health authorities to prioritise primary health care during the pandemic Coordinate care at the primary care level for a large influx of influenza patients and patients with other illness Implement a protocol for home management for those with minor illnesses
Situation Monitoring and Assessment	Participation in influenza sentinel surveillance Establish system of reporting of suspected cases Document travel history and possible close contacts of potential cases	Collect more clinical and epidemiological data from suspected cases Monitor symptoms and signs of flu-like illness in close contacts of confirmed and suspected cases Close monitoring of suspected cases	Assess capacity to manage larger numbers of ill patients Monitor suspected cases Assess the uptake and impact of mitigation measures at the community level Develop alternative health care measures to manage non-infectious diseases
Reducing the Spread of Disease	Reinforce the importance of adhering to infection guidelines in individual households by explaining the rationale for the measures Establish a primary care management protocol for those with flu-like illness Surveillance and monitoring of those with flu-like symptoms including their close contacts Support ill persons isolated at home, their household, and any close contacts	Clinical management of suspected and confirmed cases Manage suspected cases isolated at home, their households, and close contacts Provide health protection for at-risk groups Re-organise clinic schedules to minimise cross-infection with minimal disruption Reinforce individual, household, and societal disease control measures Give advice and provide care to patients returning from high-risk areas and close contacts	Re-designate clinics to manage patients with flu-like illnesses, and other clinics to manage non-infectious illnesses Organise home visits for patients with chronic illnesses and those requiring follow-up appointments to avoid clinic visits Implement prophylactic treatment for high-risk groups
Continuity of Health Care and Provision	Coordinate primary health services to handle increasing demand for flu-like illnesses, cases of NCDs from hospital settings, and home visits for those with minor illness	Activate the primary health care system to manage flu-like illnesses as well as non-infectious illnesses with minimal cross-infection Develop a self-management protocol for minor illnesses	Establish an alternate source of care for stabilised hospital patients with NCDs as well as patients, communities, and health care workers requiring psycho-social support
Communication	Translate national guidelines to meaningful public health initiatives	Explain to the local community what is known and not known, and act as a reliable resource for information	Resource persons for community and feedback of community concerns

Source: Lee and Chuh, 2010.

and the Healthy City at large. They help to control the increasing burden of NCDs, such as DM, heart disease, diseases related to unhealthy diet and physical inactivity, fall injuries, and mental illnesses. This role, as well as that of other healthy settings, is further examined for childhood obesity in the following chapter. Health-promotion in primary health care organisations can also help control outbreaks of communicable diseases. Health-promoting Health Care Organisations are the backbone of a Healthy City, and the synergy with other healthy settings is essential to help build up community capacity and empower the community in health promotion. Furthermore, Health-promoting Health Care Organisations can also play a significant role in helping primary care providers deliver patient-centred care during crises, as shown during the COVID-19 pandemic (Stone, 2020).

Chapter 9

How Can the Healthy Settings Approach Prevent Childhood Obesity? Views of Parents in Hong Kong and Scotland

Albert Lee, Christine Campbell, Tony Yung, and David Weller

During City-Super's research on Health-promoting Health Care Organisations, he came across a focus group study investigating the role of schools, parents, and primary care organisations in preventing childhood obesity. As the prevalence of childhood obesity is on the rise globally in both developed and developing countries, City-super decided to dive deeper into the details of this study, which was conducted in Hong Kong and Scotland. Management of childhood obesity requires significant input from parents, and parents also need support from the community as well as health care professionals. Thus, it is essential to explore the perceived barriers in preventing childhood obesity from the perspective of parents and to examine how to facilitate healthy eating and regular exercise among school children.

Childhood Obesity in Hong Kong and Scotland

Globally, high body-mass index (BMI) accounts for 4.4 million deaths and 134 million disability adjusted life years (DALYs), while dietary risks account for 11.3 million deaths and 241.4 million DALYs (GBD 2013 Risk Factors Collaborators, 2015). Successful obesity prevention requires a combination of approaches, including educational, behavioural, and environmental (i.e., policy) changes along with shifts in the culture of how we approach food, physical activity, and health. The most successful interventions have been implemented in school settings (Huang and Story, 2010; Lee and Keung, 2012). In the United States, Canada, and Europe, coordinated, multi-component school health programmes have been successfully established for obesity prevention (Veugelers and Fitzgerald, 2005; Day et al., 2008; Inchley and Currie, 2003). Both "top-down" and "bottom-up" approaches, involving committed policy makers and energetic community action teams, are needed, but these efforts rarely occur synchronously (Swinburn and Silva-Sanigorski, 2010).

With respective populations of 7 million and 5 million, both Hong Kong and Scotland have developed strong public health initiatives using the Health-promoting School (HPS) concept, putting health into practice for school children to promote healthy eating and regular physical activity (Inchley and Currie, 2003; Lee et al., 2005b; Young, 2005). These programmes involve multiple components (Figure 9.1); however, the school setting is only one piece of the puzzle for obesity prevention, and success also requires significant input from other settings. Evidence has shown that the home and family environment (availability) as well as socio-cultural (acceptability and accessibility) and socio-economic factors (affordability) are associated with behaviours related to diet and exercise (Brug et al., 2010; Ventura and Birch, 2008; Van der Horst et al., 2007, Cullen et al., 2003). Children's knowledge, attitudes, and behaviours towards food and eating are often associated with that of their parents (Ventura and Birch, 2008), particularly their mothers (Yung et al., 2010). Understanding childhood obesity and barriers to prevention from the perspective of parents will provide insight into how different healthy settings could facilitate healthy eating and regular exercise among children.

Using Focus Groups to Understand Childhood Obesity

Focus Group Recruitment

A qualitative approach based on focus group interviews was utilised for data collection to provide the best opportunity to understand the processes involved

Figure 9.1: Using the Health-promoting School Framework to Address Childhood Obesity

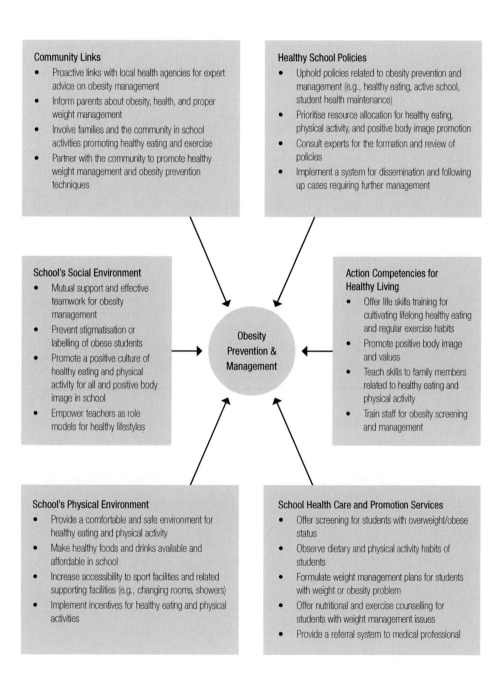

Source: Lee, 2017.

in a given situation and to gain a better understanding of human behaviour and experience. Four focus group interviews were conducted in total for this study. This study received ethical approval in both Scotland and Hong Kong, and written informed consent was obtained from each participant before the interviews. Subjects were recruited in Edinburgh, Scotland, and in Hong Kong. In Edinburgh, parents were recruited via posters in the waiting rooms of two general practices (one within the City of Edinburgh and one outside the city area). A name and telephone number were provided on the poster for any interested parents to call for more information and for the date and time of the focus group interview. They were invited to discuss their views about healthy eating, the role of their general practitioners (GPs) and health visitors (trained nurses who provide information to parents and children during early childhood) in giving advice on this topic, and any challenges they face in their families with regard to food and healthy eating. Eight parents participated in the Edinburgh study, two from the practice within Edinburgh (designated S-1) and six from the practice outside Edinburgh (S-2). The interviews were conducted in August 2006. In Hong Kong, parents were recruited from two schools not involved in HPS programmes (one within the main area of the city and one from a more rural area) via a principal's recommendation. Eight parents participated from the school located within the city area of Hong Kong (HK-1), while six parents participated from the school outside the city (HK-2). The interviews were conducted in March 2007.

Each focus group was audio-taped. Detailed field notes were also taken during the interviews. Interviews were conducted in English in S-1 and S-2 and in Chinese (Cantonese) in HK-1 and HK-2. Those in Chinese were then translated into English. Data were then categorised into different headings and themes and analysed for regularities and patterns. These data were collated and refined during discussions between the study coordinators, to provide meaningful results. Quotations from the interviews are included as directly transcribed and translated, and include the variations in speech pattern, grammar, syntax, tone, and stream of thought inherent in oral interviews.

Reasons Underlying Unhealthy Eating and Inadequate Exercise

Parents in Scotland and Hong Kong indicated that one of the main causes of childhood obesity is the overconsumption of unhealthy food outside the home and that this is largely related to the convenience and low cost of these unhealthy food options.

> Nowadays there are many take away foods and also so many places one would buy ready-made food. Sometimes families would afford to buy so they might not bother to prepare their own food for children. (S-2)

> When eating outside the home, it is difficult to ensure that the food is healthy. (HK-1)

> The vending machine at school is full of junk foods. (HK-1)

Parents also felt that the school setting is the best environment for protecting children from unhealthy eating by limiting the sale of unhealthy foods on school premises and ensuring the availability of healthy food options.

> One primary school has breakfast club. A lot of parents need to work so school breakfast would ensure children at least having a good breakfast … You can pay 2 pounds and your child can have a decent breakfast with the school providing the right kinds of food. (S-1)

> My son's school has a healthy tuck shop and children are encouraged to buy healthy food from the shop such as a fruit bar. Fizzy drinks and sweets are not allowed and abandoned … The school encourages drinking water throughout the day. (S-1)

> Some schools provide free fruits once or twice a week. The tuck shops sell nutrition bars, water, cereal bars. (S-2)

> Parents have suggested relocating the vending machine near the teachers' office for monitoring. Some parents have also suggested replacing them with healthier snacks. (HK-1)

Concerns about unhealthy fizzy drinks were also raised by Hong Kong parents and such beverages were identified as causing childhood obesity.

> My daughter will buy drinks at school when she has finished her water brought from home. It is not easy to control the types of drinks consumed by children at school. Schools should consider replacing the current drinks with healthier drinks. (HK-2)

Parents also viewed advertising as having a major impact on the consumption of foods with high sugar content.

> My child wanted me to buy some food with high sugar content, but he did not like it at the end but wanted to try because of an advertisement. (S-1)

> Promotion of weight and food on TV would also have an adverse effect. (S-1)

Each focus group identified a lack of exercise as another major cause of childhood obesity. In Scotland, this was suggested to be caused by a lack of safety and supporting facilities, while in Hong Kong, the main reason parents identified for this was that more time was being used for academic activities.

> Although I would walk [my child] to school and back, I would not see many parents doing so. Traffic would be a problem for walking down the school and also you will see a lot of drunken people along the road. I have also seen people dealing with drugs and I do not want my children to see them. I will feel safe to send children walking to school if more police are there in the morning. (S-1)

> I do not feel safe to send my child cycling to school. The school head discourages this because of safety reasons. (S-1)

> There are not a lot of events in the community for physical activities for children. There are not many clubs … There is a swimming pool in the area, but it is not open to public access because of no lifeguards. (S-2)

> We can arrange children to local sports activities, but transport is needed. (S-2)

> Some parents still put their children in carriers even for short distances because of convenience and safety. (S-2)

> Some parents mentioned the inadequacy of physical education lessons and that they are sometimes even replaced by academic activities. Some exercise programmes held during the last academic year have disappeared from this year's school calendar. (HK-1)

> The main obstacle for adequate exercise for children is whether parents put the children's physical health at a higher priority than academic performance. (HK-1)

> The heavy demand of school work diminishes the time that children can spend on exercise. There are only two physical education sessions per week during

school … there are some occasions that these lessons would be taken up by academic subjects. (HK-2)

The Concept of Healthy Eating

Parents in both Hong Kong and Scotland felt the importance of cultivating healthy eating habits early on in life. They all realise that their children have been exposed to an unhealthy eating environment. To remedy this, parents in Scotland tended to use internal controls at home, while Hong Kong parents tended to rely on external controls to reverse unhealthy eating patterns.

> My daughter tends to eat sweet chocolate and is fussy about food … [she] tends to eat "rubbish". This has made me more determined to ensure my children eat healthier. As they get older, they will choose their own food, which is usually unhealthy. Therefore I want to establish and encourage healthy eating habits early on in life. (S-1)

> I do not allow fizzy drinks or too many sweets. Our children are less fussy about food and enjoy food more. (S-1)

> When I was a child, I did not have many sweeties. This was not because I was not allowed, but I had to have a proper meal first. I did not eat sweeties on many occasions. (S-1)

> It is best to start low sugar content so they would grow up without too many sweeties. One should always try to make sure that they finish dinner before having sweeties. (S-2)

> Parents generally feel that lunch provided by the school is less healthy than homemade … Children tend to eat mostly meat with only a few vegetables. (HK-1)

Most of the children in Hong Kong opt to have school lunch rather than bring a packed lunch from home. Parents rely on the provision of healthy school lunches to support healthy eating. The traditional views of older Chinese people also impacts the eating habits of school children.

> Some grandparents regard being fat as healthy, so this has exerted additional pressure on parents to give more food to children. It is difficult to balance the grandparents' desires and achieving a healthy weight for the children. (HK-2)

Healthy eating is not an easy choice as a lot of fresh foods including fruits and vegetables are contaminated in Hong Kong. (HK-2)

Health Promotion in Schools and the Community

School and the local community are considered to be important settings for promoting healthy eating and physical activity. Parents in Scotland emphasised the importance of schools being proactive in their integration of health promotion into school activities. They regarded the community as a source of support, skills development, and empowerment for healthy living. However, their local community centre lacked a regular source of funding. Similarly, parents in Hong Kong emphasised schools and the community as sources of health information but indicated differences in the availability of services.

> Schools are really good on promoting physical activities and children are sent to the local sports centre for different sports activities, like gymnasium, football, and dancing, on different nights. Schools should set up an advertisement on healthy eating. Although it might be common sense to me, it is still useful for many people. (S-1)

> It is best if the whole school is involved in promoting healthy eating and exercise. Children tend to eat more at school and are less fussy. It is quite amazing when parents are informed that the food eaten by children at school is usually fruits and vegetables, as they do not eat a lot of those at home. This is due to peer influence and food availability at school. (S-1)

> Schools have a lot of playgrounds supervised by adults and some teachers also play with children. (S-1)

> Some schools provide free fresh fruits once or twice a week … The school menu is healthy. (S-2)

> Health talks are organised by the schools. Radio and television also contain a lot of information on healthy eating and are readily available and accessible. (HK-2)

> Educational television can also be an effective way for children to obtain information about healthy eating. (HK-1)

> The community is trying to push projects to meet the needs of the community. One swimming pool is not open to the public because it lacks a lifeguard. The

community is working on a project to bring in lifeguards. The community is trying hard in the Family Centre to help young mothers and particularly young children to develop healthy lifestyles. They have healthy eating activities in the centre and teach young mothers how to cook healthier. (S-2)

Parents get more information in the Family Centre by sharing with the other parents … They have health visitors coming in to discuss a wide range of health issues … There are also courses organised, such as a demonstration in cooking healthy food. Space is available for activities. (S-2)

It would be good if more playground for games is near the house. It would be good if one would encourage indoor activities for bad weather and outdoor activities for good weather. (S-2)

A lot of activities are initiated by the community, but they have limited funding and need to chase for funding … There is no regular source of funding for health promotion projects in the community. (S-2)

Parents will seek advice regarding healthy eating and exercise from community centres … Student Health Services of the Department of Health also provides information to parents. (HK-1)

Parents believe videos and posters are an effective way of obtaining health information for children with time limitations. (HK-1)

A Medical Information Centre should be established for parents as a resource centre in case of any medical enquires … Alternatively, a medical hotline would also serve the same purpose. (HK-2)

A well-promoted health talk with interesting topics will ensure participation from parents. (HK-2)

The Roles of General Practitioners, Nurses, and Health Visitors

There is a general feeling that GPs are too busy to give advice on health promotion. Parents in Scotland tended to seek advice and support from health visitors.

Only if asked about it, GPs usually do not offer advice. (S-1)

Regarding weight problems and physical activity, I will consult a doctor if I feel that it is a serious problem rather than during a developmental check. (S-1)

GPs would give advice on eating if our children present with related medical conditions. Usually GPs do not give much advice on eating unless we ask. (S-1)

It is not part of GP's job to offer advice on health. They should deal with medical condition ... GPs are medical persons so one cannot just bother them for health advice. (S-2)

Health Visitors are [the] usual source of advice and information ... Health Visitors always offer advice on healthy eating and exercise. They can be approached easily for discussion ... GPs might not know their children as well as the Health Visitors. (S-1)

When my son had problems and worries of overweight, I had the support from [a] Health Visitor to discuss the problems with school. (S-1)

We can discuss food preparation with Health Visitors ... The clinic should employ more people doing the job. (S-2)

Health Visitors usually advise young parents [about] the ongoing health activities at the medical centre. (S-2)

It has taken me 10 months to see a dietician. It would be better if a dietician would come once a week in a community setting to help those families struggling with diet problems. If health professionals coming to the community once or twice a week to discuss various issues with families, this would be very helpful. (S-2)

In Hong Kong, parents tended to seek health advice from doctors or nurses through the Student Health Services where their children have their annual periodic check-ups. However, these services do not include personalised care. The parents expressed a strong desire for their GPs to be more proactive in promoting healthy eating and physical activity for their children as well as to give them advice on various health issues.

It is less common to ask GPs directly about a child's weight problems unless it becomes serious. Doctors from Student Health Services provide a channel for parents to ask about the weight problems of their children. They proactively provide dietary advice to children who are overweight or underweight. (HK-1)

Health advice from GPs is more powerful for the children compared to words from parents. A nurse can help to perform an assessment of weight so doctors have more time to explain or advise parents and children during the consultation. (HK-1)

If GPs can give health talks to students and parents periodically, this would be effective to promote health because some parents might have an incorrect understanding of some health issues. (HK-1)

The younger children are when they receive relevant health messages from their doctors, the easier it will be for them to know more about relevant diseases. (HK-2)

Most parents in the HK-2 group did not think that they would consult their GPs if they or their children encountered weight problems, especially during consultations for other matters such as flu-like illnesses or regular check-ups. However, two parents reported having positive experiences with GPs in discussing weight-related issues.

We would consult a GP if we encounter weight problems … Sometimes when parents have not established a good relationship with their GP, it is rather difficult to start talking about the topic. (HK-2)

My GP takes a proactive role on talking with me regarding healthy eating and exercise. (HK-2)

Some parents indicated that they saw different doctors during their multiple visits to Student Health Services and that they received different pieces of advice.

Doctors from Student Health Services do not necessarily perform better than GPs and some might not talk about the topic of healthy eating or exercise proactively … The attending doctor is different from visit to visit … and patients may not feel cared for, which hinders further communication with them. (HK-2)

While parents from both Hong Kong and Scotland felt that the offices of GPs would be ideal venues for health promotion, they did not feel that GPs were doing enough to work with other health professionals on public health initiatives to promote healthy eating and physical activity.

The GPs and other health professionals are trying to work well with public health initiatives as much as they would but not much resource going to them and not enough staffing … They are overworked operating with limited resources and other issues with higher priorities. (S-2)

It would be better to have more frequent visits to Student Health Services rather than just once a year. There should be another venue for follow-ups and not just annual check-ups. GP offices could be a venue for this. (HK-1)

GPs do not work well with public health initiatives because of their limited time during consultation. (HK-2)

GPs are quite independent of other health providers ... There is news about childhood obesity from time to time. But the involvement from GPs is minimal. The concept of family doctors in Hong Kong is also not very well-established. Families usually collect health information by themselves rather than their GPs. (HK-2)

GPs should put educational pamphlets in their clinics to disseminate health messages. They should also hold some health talks in the community to promote health. (HK-2)

Encouragement from GPs would be very helpful. Some GP offices should put up posters to draw the attention of patients to certain issues such as healthy eating and quitting smoking. (S-2)

If other health services, such as dental services, family planning services, optometry, chiropractors, and other allied health services of the NHS [National Health Services] are under one roof of a GP premise, it would lead to a healthy community in long run. (S-2)

What Do These Focus Groups Tell Us?

Minimising children's exposure to adverse food environments and maximising their exposure to independent mobility will promote healthy eating and physical activity as an effective means of preventing childhood obesity. With respective populations of 7 million and 5 million, both Hong Kong and Scotland can be regarded as developed parts of the world, so parents, in general, will have a reasonably good understanding of what it means to "eat healthy" and will recognise the importance of physical activity for children. The key findings from this focus group study have revealed that parents in both localities have a good understanding of the importance of healthy eating starting in childhood. However, they encountered obstacles to expose children to a healthy eating environment. Convenience and easy access to food outside the home environment was found to be one of the main factors exposing children to an unhealthy eating environment. Like many other cities and countries, Hong Kong and Scotland have also experienced changes in food patterns, moving away from traditional foods to food products with high energy and fat density because of shifts in production and processing practices (Inchley et al., 2001; Dixon et al., 2007; Scottish Government, 2011; Lee and Keung, 2012). This has been accompanied by a rise in the number of supermarkets instead of fresh-food markets, which has been attributed to the lower price offered in the former. There has also been a large increase in animal source foods, added sugar, caloric sweeteners, and edible oil over a short period of time, while the supply and consumption of fruit and vegetables has changed very little (Mendez and Popkin, 2004). Convenience, easy accessibility, and marketing have accelerated this transition as individual choices are strongly influenced by the choices they are presented with (Kahneman, 2003). In fact, an Australian study found that childhood obesity has tripled since 1985, mirrored by increases in the consumption of energy-dense foods and advertisements on television programmes (Carter, 2006).

The school setting is one context that can be used to help protect children from unhealthy eating. In this study, parents in Scotland tended to adopt internal controls to modify eating habits, while Hong Kong parents tended to rely more on external controls. Regarding health promotion in schools and the community, parents in Scotland expressed the importance of a supportive environment for healthy eating and physical activities as well as the need for setting-based health promotion initiatives. In Hong Kong, parents mainly focused on the importance of health information given in schools and the community rather than any particular health promotion initiatives.

Food accessibility can be controlled in settings where managers and administrators have a vested interest in controlling the health of those who use the facilities (Cohen, 2010), so schools are increasingly becoming sensitive to the childhood obesity problem and are taking action to promote healthy food choices, as reflected by comments from parents in Scotland in this study. Schools can become an effective setting for health promotion if the main goal is improving the social and physical environment rather than simply changing the traditional ways of health education in the classrooms (St Leger and Young, 2009; Lee and Keung, 2012; Lee et al., 2014b). Social models of consumption also affect eating, drinking, and sedentary behaviours (Monasta et al., 2010). In the focus group interviews, Scottish parents mentioned a number of school-based initiatives that could be implemented to promote healthy eating and physical activity in line with the HPS concept, which is shown to be effective in the prevention of childhood obesity (Timperio et al., 2004; Bell and Swinburn, 2004; Lee, 2010c; Lee et al., 2014b).

Parents from both Hong Kong and Scotland indicated that they would not seek advice from GPs regarding healthy eating and physical activity for their children during routine medical consultations. Parents in Scotland would instead rely on Health Visitors for support and advice as they felt that GPs should focus on acute medical conditions. Parents in Hong Kong stated that they would prefer GPs to be more involved in community health promotion and that they believed their advice and guidance would have a greater impact. Parents from both locations observed that GPs might not be fully aware of the public health initiatives for obesity prevention within the community. They felt that GP offices should be used for additional health promotion, providing more resources and support. Primary care establishments are another important setting in which preventive measures can be explained and promoted to decrease the prevalence of childhood obesity. Globally, the delivery of preventive services in GP offices is below the recommended levels (Brotons et al., 2005) and these services are even more limited with regard to the prevention of childhood obesity (Lock and Hillier, 2010; Wake and McCallum, 2004).

In several previous studies (Epstein and Ogden, 2005; Mercer and Tessier, 2001; Walker et al., 2007), GPs and nurses indicated that they feel less equipped to tackle childhood obesity and that they were sceptical about the impact of their advice concerning diet and exercise. Some of them felt that obesity prevention was an inappropriate use of their time and should be problem addressed by the family. This separation of roles creates conflict and inconsistent advice. Weight management strategies should include behavioural changes to increase children's physical activity and food choices. While such lifestyles modifications need to be addressed within the family and social settings (NICE, 2006), primary care interventions and GPs must support these efforts. Primary care intervention should move beyond standard GP consultations (McCallum et al., 2007) towards patient-centred assessments, follow-ups, and counselling for diet and exercise. This could also include monthly mail or telephone counselling sessions. For example, in a study by Patrick et al. (2006), such follow-up mail and telephone counselling was conducted for 12 months after assessment and these individuals had a significant reduction of sedentary behaviours and some improvement in daily physical activity in boys and dietary saturated fat intake in girls.

In general, Health Visitors and nurses understand that they have a role to play in preventing childhood obesity and they are comfortable with giving routine advice about diet and physical activity (Douglas et al., 2006). However, many have indicated that they are not aware of the correct recommendations they should be offering to patients. These efforts need to be in sync with recommendations from GPs and other health care providers. Indeed, the role of primary care in obesity prevention should be maximised by tackling the barriers of time, resources, skills, and training. These measures should include multidisciplinary professional input to put public health policies and interventions into daily practice, and aid skills development to help people modify unhealthy behaviours. Public policies in turn need to monitor adverse advertisements and marketing for unhealthy food products. Town planning and development should also be more child-friendly.

Conclusion

To be successful, obesity prevention needs to take place in multiple different settings. It is more cost-effective to develop synergy across settings to complement the deficiencies in one particular setting. The qualitative focus group study presented views on four important themes: (1) the reasons underlying unhealthy eating and inadequate exercise; (2) the concept of healthy eating; (3) health promotion in schools and the community; and (4) the role of GPs, nurses, and health visitors. Convenience and low-cost unhealthy food outside the home were considered to be the main causes of childhood obesity by our study participants. The reason for the lack of physical exercise in Scotland included limited facilities and safety concerns, while in Hong Kong, school children spent most of their time in academic activities, leaving little time for physical exercise. Schools and local community settings were considered important arenas for promoting healthy behaviours. GPs were not considered the first point of help regarding weight problem as they were too busy, despite the parents' feelings that GP offices would be a good venue for health promotion. This study provides insights into how primary care and community settings can work more closely to tackle childhood obesity. The following chapter takes a broader look at the prevention of other non-communicable diseases (NCDs) as well as how using the Healthy Settings Approach supports these preventive measures as a basic right to health.

Chapter 10

The Right to Health Promotion: Revisiting the Healthy Settings Approach

Albert Lee

City-super has realised that the rights of citizens to health promotion should involve more than just providing health services, and that steps should be taken to enhance exposure to determinant factors conducive for health and minimise exposure to determinant factors detrimental to health. As the previous chapters have shown, while some determinant factors of health can be addressed within the health care sector, many others are found in other contexts, including workplaces, schools, and cities. They are embedded in the social, political, and economic systems in these environments. During his research, City-super has learned that a delicate balance must be struck between individual rights and the interests of the entire population. Thus, it is essential to analyse the policies concerning human rights and health in relation to disease prevention and health promotion.

Health as a Human Right

The right to health is a public policy outlined in article 12 of the 1966 International Covenant on Economic, Social and Cultural Rights (ICESCR) and is further spelled out by both the United Nations (UN) Committee on Economic, Social and Cultural Rights (CESCR) and the UN Special Rapporteur on the

Right to Health (SRRH). This policy is echoed in the UN Sustainable Development Goals 2030 (SDGs 2030) (UN, 2015), which establish a vision to make our planet not only more peaceful and pleasant but also to bring equality and equity to mankind irrespective of age, gender, ethnicity, or socio-economic background. SDG 3, which states: "Ensure healthy lives and promote well-being for all at all ages", involves more than just the prevention of premature death but also requires the empowerment of individuals as well as communities to protect themselves from harm and equip them with the capacity to achieve optimal health and well-being.

The right to health requires governments not only to *respect* individual human rights and personal freedoms but to *protect* people from harm from external sources and third parties and to *fulfil* the health needs of the population (Annas and Mariner, 2016). Schrecker et al. (2010) has suggested that "market fundamentalism" has become dominant worldwide, leading to rising poverty and economic insecurity, and that policy makers should rely on the norms, institutions, and procedures established in ICESCR article 12 to counteract this. However, Reubi (2011) expressed doubt about the ability of this international human rights framework to hold transnational corporations accountable. Is this framework the best option to thwart the detrimental impact of the global marketplace? As Reubi (2011) speculates, it may be necessary to critically assess the promises of human rights before promoting them as a solution. A key point that must be considered is the basic, but often complex, concept of balance. Unfortunately, it is not always easy to balance human rights with individual rights, such as balancing the public's right to safety with an individual's rights of autonomy and privacy, and imbalances unfairly limit the permissible means to promote better health. There needs to be a paradigm shift to ground human rights in a plurality of interests, thus generating an obligation to respect, protect, and promote the interests of others, and to focus on common social ethos and on cultivating a culture of compassion (Tasioulas and Vayena, 2015). For contemporary approaches of health promotion to be effective, they should focus on the everyday lives of citizens and combine diverse techniques to strengthen human and social capital (Lee et al., 2007a).

Individual Rights vs Societal Rights

There are concerns whether judicialisation of the right to health is increasing rather than decreasing health inequalities. For instance, this was the primary focus of a study by Biehl et al. (2009), which explains the rise in legal suits filed by Brazilian patients against the state to obtain prescribed antiretroviral drugs. While such lawsuits do secure access to treatment, they often lead to the prioritisation of individual patients, often from higher income groups, leaving the collective needs of patients, which includes lower income groups, unaddressed. Furthermore, the international framework on human rights is ratified by states but not by non-state actors, such as civil society groups, transnational corporations, religious organisations, professional bodies, municipalities, educational institutions, or social services organisations (O'Neill, 2005; Reubi, 2011). Thus, the places and settings where people live, work, study, and socialise are not bound by the same human rights standards. To address this, a means of global governance is necessary to determine health norms and mediate collective action internationally (Gostin, 2014a). Implementing global governance for health would dramatically improve health for all and reduce health inequalities in all sectors, while working towards the highest attainable standards of health for citizens worldwide (Gostin et al., 2015). In this way, formal legal obligations (i.e., the "hard law") can be complimented by normative guidance (i.e., the "soft law") (Gostin and Sridhar, 2014).

The Healthy Settings Approach provides an ideal framework to facilitate the "right to health". Evolving from the Ottawa Charter for Health Promotion (WHO, 1986), the Healthy Settings Approach focuses on building healthy public policy, re-orienting health services, strengthening community action, and enhancing personal health skills and health advocacy. The beauty of the approach is that it can be applied across settings, providing standard guidance to promote health and a means to balance individual rights and societal rights across sectors.

Niessen et al. (2018) identified poverty reduction, equitable education, gender equality, and reduction of inequalities within and between countries as key aspects necessary to attain health and well-being. The same study has positioned health as the primary driver towards achieving the SDGs. The Healthy Settings Approach can be implemented to protect citizens from harmful factors and maintain equitable access while facing the challenges of the "triple health burden" — namely, the emergence of old and new communicable diseases, the spread of non-communicable diseases (NCDs), and the prevalence of mental health issues. The challenge inherent in these three health burdens is how the right to health is balanced. The following sections focus on NCDs and mental health issues, outlining specific legislative and policy decisions as well as the role of the Health Settings Approach.

Prevention of Non-Communicable Diseases

In a *Lancet* commentary, the WHO Director-General provided several shocking statistics: NCDs kill 40 million people each year, accounting for 70% of global mortality, with around 15 million of these falling within 30–69 years of age (Ghebreyesus, 2018). Moreover, 80% of premature deaths occur in low-income and middle-income countries. There is therefore an urgent need to address the growing inequalities in access to resources for prevention and treatment of NCDs through improved regulations across jurisdictions (Niessen et al., 2018). In fact, there is overwhelming evidence that prevention of NCDs is possible when sustained actions are directed at individuals and families simultaneously, while also addressing the broader social, economic, and cultural determinants of health (Marmot et al., 2008). This includes cross-sector engagement involving all parts of the government (Gostin and Wiley, 2016; McKee et al., 2014) to implement legislation and policy efforts aimed at reducing health risks. Three widespread NCDs of concern include: cardiovascular and metabolic diseases; childhood obesity; and exposure to carcinogens, tobacco, and alcohol. The following sections detail how some countries have addressed these NCDs through health legislation.

Reducing Cardiovascular and Metabolic Risks

One example of legal interventions effectively reducing NCD factors can be observed in the Eastern Mediterranean Region (EMR). Citizens in the EMR consume high levels of mean fat (Micha et al., 2014) and the proliferation of screen-based technologies and jobs have led to a more sedentary lifestyle across the region (Al Subhi et al., 2015). Unhealthy diets and physical inactivity are widely known to be major contributors to NCD development. However, the EMR has tried to address the underlying drivers of some cardiovascular and metabolic diseases through regulatory and governance mechanisms promoting multi-sectoral collaboration and accountability as well as tailored interventions in local legal, economic, and social contexts (Gostin et al., 2017). Unfortunately, laws related to diet and physical activity often face greater political and social resistance as this type of legislation is viewed as a restriction of individual choice and indicative of a "Nanny State" (Mackay, 2011; Gostin and Gostin, 2009). Furthermore, research has shown that policies increasing the prices or taxation of potentially unhealthy products, such as tobacco and alcohol, would ultimately impose an unfair financial burden on lower-income households (Sassi et al., 2018). It is therefore essential that the laws and norms established to prevent cardiovascular and metabolic diseases go beyond simple restrictions or coercion and help to create environments that make healthy choices the easy choices. While many citizens consider lifestyle decisions, such as food choice, as being "free" and up to each individual, the environment is a constraining factor, and approaches based on personal responsibility and individual liberty do not always recognise the environmental influences on individual behaviour (Mackay, 2011; Brownell et al., 2010; Hoek, 2008). Thus, for legislation to be successful, it should focus on modifying the social, economic, and physical environment in which people make their decisions (Magnusson, 2008a, 2008b; Swinburn, 2008). For example, government interventions to decrease unhealthy eating habits should first and foremost address environmental factors such as the promotion, pricing, availability, and accessibility of unhealthy foods compared to that of healthy foods (Mackay, 2011).

Furthermore, governments should be transparent about how the legislation will be enforced as well as how any revenue, such as that generated by taxing unhealthy products (i.e., tobacco and alcohol), will be used. Ideally, the revenue should be used to create healthy living conditions, especially for low-income groups, as this will also help garner support from the community. Legislation should also designate appropriate authority and regulatory powers to relevant government entities as well as empower public officials to create supportive environments for NCD control. For instance, civil society can be engaged in monitoring and reporting habits and NCD prevalence in their communities, which can improve the implementation of NCD-related legislation (Gostin et al., 2011). A comprehensive approach to incorporate research, develop guidance tools, and build community support will synchronise with the power of law to improve population health (Gostin et al., 2011).

Preventing Childhood Obesity

Protecting children and adolescents exposed to obesogenic environments has been shown to be an effective intervention to prevent obesity-related premature morbidity and mortality in adults (Reilly and Kelly, 2011). A systematic review by Ho et al. (2012) shows that lifestyle interventions incorporating dietary and exercise components with or without behavioural therapy are a successful means to improve weight and cardio-metabolic outcomes among children. Legislation would facilitate the promulgation of the Health-promoting Schools (HPS) concept, described in Chapters 5 and 6. This school-specific application of the Healthy Settings Approach would help develop health policies, create supportive environments, strengthen community action, and enhance personal skills to combat the risk factors for obesity and other NCDs (Lee et al., 2010a; Lee et al., 2014c). While the school setting plays a prominent role in obesity prevention in adolescents, childhood obesity should also be addressed through other settings (Figure 10.1) as well as through legislation and parental involvement (see also Chapter 9).

The question of whether governments should impose measures to ensure healthy eating and physical activity in schools and other settings to combat childhood obesity sparks significant debate. Similar to such regulations for adults, choices concerning eating and physical activity are regarded as personal decisions, and any limitations on individual freedoms will have pushback. Nonetheless, educational authorities in many developed countries have established principles for school governance to empower school heads and management to adopt appropriate measures to meet health standards. Instead of detailed legislative measures to tackle obesity, schools are requested to reference concepts for health promotion, such as HPSs; to develop school policies related to healthy living; to create a healthy school environment (physical and social); to improve the health literacy of student; and to facilitate the use of appropriate services for health promotion and health protection in the community. Schools should be encouraged to develop holistic and comprehensive strategies to ensure healthy living of their students according to their needs and circumstances. While the quality of these measures cannot be guaranteed without a national framework, allowing schools to maintain their professional autonomy to develop their own appropriate teaching programmes and strategies is essential for preventing childhood obesity and other NCDs. Governments must also work with schools to assess the impact of health promotion measures, which can in turn help the government make further recommendations and to legitimise their implementation. A successful example of this is Hong Kong's use of the Hong Kong Healthy School Award (HKHSA) Scheme in conjunction with the recommendations made in audit reports (HKSAR, 2005). Schools should be encouraged to achieve the status of a HPS and undergo comprehensive assessments of the overall impact of their health promotion measures.

Reducing Exposure to Potential Carcinogens, Tobacco, and Alcohol

Looking beyond cardiovascular and metabolic diseases, cancer is also a leading cause of death globally, and around one-third of cancers are attributed to identifiable

Figure 10.1: Using the Healthy Settings Approach to Prevent Obesity

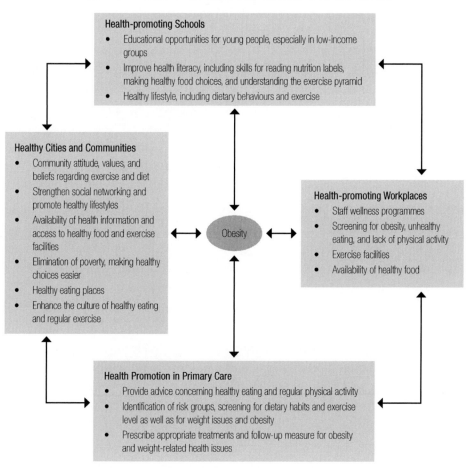

Source: Lee, 2019e.

risk factors like smoking and overconsumption of alcohol (Beaglehole et al., 2011). Moreover, smoking is also a risk factor for chronic obstructive pulmonary disease (COPD) (Lopez et al., 2006), which is expected to be the third leading cause of mortality in 2030 (WHO, 2008). According to a cohort study (Bui et al., 2018), three-quarters of cases are associated with exposure-related childhood illnesses (such as asthma, bronchitis, pneumonia, allergic rhinitis, and eczema). Thus, while smoking as an adult is the primary risk factor for COPD, exposure to parental smoking predisposes children to this and other lung diseases.

These findings support shifting the legal balance towards protecting the health of the population by implementing tighter tobacco control.

Naturally, the tobacco industry argues against stricter tobacco control, stating that tobacco is a legal product and adult smoking is an individual's choice. The Framework Convention on Tobacco Control (FCTC), which was signed by 177 States in 2013, creates binding norms for reducing supply and demand as well as increasing information sharing (Gostin, 2014b). However, the framework also establishes broad principles without specificity and does not detail enforcement procedures. It is the responsibility of the individual State to define and implement the national health policies under the FCTC (WHO FCTC, 2003). This has resulted in differences between entities, which can be exploited. The tobacco industry also relies on the doctrine of expropriation of property found in bilateral investment treaties. Although the regulation of tobacco cannot be justified on the ground of direct expropriation, it still amounts to indirect expropriation as the relationship between health and trade is more equivocal under the FCTC, notwithstanding some wanted "health over trade" in the text (Mamudu et al., 2011). The counter-argument against such legislation is that it creates a precedent that States can forgo their prior treaty obligations and also invites "protectionism". This kind of protection of domestic industry was observed in *Corn Products International, Inc. v The United Mexican States* (ICSID Case No. ARB (AF)/04/01), which questioned the protection of domestic sugar producers through Mexico's adoption of a tax on high fructose corn syrup and legislation to exclude high fructose corn syrup from the soft drink sweetener market. However, if such laws are enacted with the legitimate power of the State for a sound public purpose on a non-discriminatory and proportionate basis, then they should not trigger industrial compensation.

For tobacco control, the FCTC has initiated domestic regulations on advertising and sponsorship of sporting events as well as prohibiting smoking in public places and requiring plain packaging. Domestic courts have relied on the rights to health, life, and a safe environment to upholding tobacco control laws. This includes article 12 of the ICESCR, which guarantees the right of everyone to enjoy the highest attainable standard of physical and mental health and indicates that access to appropriate public health measures to tackle the underlying determinants of health is an important right for the population. Furthermore, in 1998, the FCTC began drafting and negotiating with civil society to create the Framework Convention Alliance (Gostin, 2014b). The goal of a tobacco-free world requires intense social mobilisation with a bottom-up approach towards disseminating information, supporting at-risk communities, and putting pressure on governments and other key stakeholders to act. The Health Settings Approach can be implemented as a vehicle to foster change (Figure 10.2).

Alcohol overconsumption is another risk factor for cancer and other NCDs, and prevention must also be a legislative priority (Beaglehole et al., 2011). It is often a neglected NCD risk factor, even though it is responsible for approximately 2–3 million deaths annually (GBD 2016 Alcohol Collaborators, 2018). The Chief Medical Officers in England recently changed their recommendation for low-risk drinking in men, reducing the maximum intake from 21 to 14 units a week (Welch, 2017). This change was largely based on the accumulating evidence that even light drinking increases the risk of developing various cancers, including colorectal, breast, larynx, liver, oesophagus, oral cavity, and pharynx (Bagnardi et al., 2013).

However, progress in alcohol control has been slow because alcohol advertising is ubiquitous and embedded into the commercial structure of cultural and sports events, and cultural norms permeate social networks (Beaglehole et al., 2011). Like the tobacco industry, the alcohol industry prefers voluntary codes and standards rather than legislation (Bond et al., 2010). A Framework Convention on Alcohol Control (FCAC) has been proposed to encourage countries to use legislation and regulations to reduce alcohol-related harm (Room et al., 2008). An international convention would separate alcohol from other commodities for governments with a more secure basis to implement evidence-based public health measures. The health and social consequences of alcohol extend beyond cancer, and include cardiovascular diseases, death, and injury from road accidents and the health impacts of alcohol-related violence (Room et al., 2008). Alcohol use is associated with reduced right hippocampal volume in a dose-dependent manner, after adjustment for numerous potential confounders (NIH, 2021). This study shows that even moderate drinkers (classified as up to 21 units a week for men at the time of the study) were three times more likely to have hippocampal atrophy than abstainers, while very light drinking (1–6 units a week) conferred no protection relative to abstinence, and higher alcohol consumption was also associated with reduced white matter integrity and a more rapid decline in lexical fluency (a test of "executive function"). Other research findings have strengthened the argument that drinking habits many regard as normal have adverse consequences for health (Welch, 2017; Topiwala et al., 2017).

Figure 10.2: Using the Healthy Settings Approach for Tobacco Control

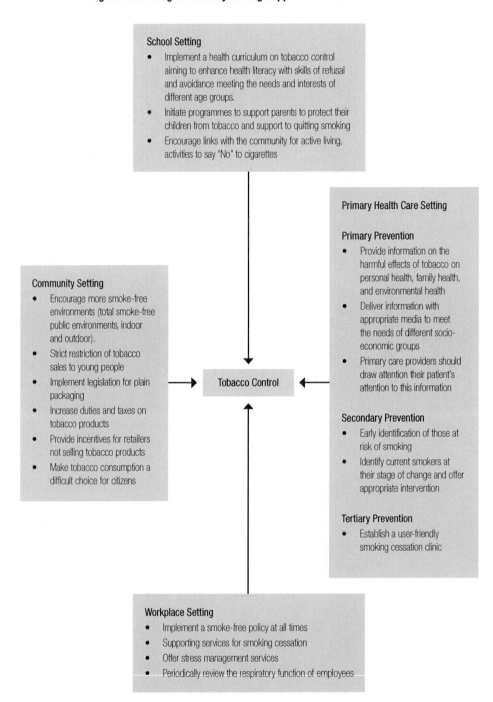

School Setting
- Implement a health curriculum on tobacco control aiming to enhance health literacy with skills of refusal and avoidance meeting the needs and interests of different age groups.
- Initiate programmes to support parents to protect their children from tobacco and support to quitting smoking
- Encourage links with the community for active living, activities to say "No" to cigarettes

Primary Health Care Setting

Primary Prevention
- Provide information on the harmful effects of tobacco on personal health, family health, and environmental health
- Deliver information with appropriate media to meet the needs of different socio-economic groups
- Primary care providers should draw attention their patient's attention to this information

Secondary Prevention
- Early identification of those at risk of smoking
- Identify current smokers at their stage of change and offer appropriate intervention

Tertiary Prevention
- Establish a user-friendly smoking cessation clinic

Community Setting
- Encourage more smoke-free environments (total smoke-free public environments, indoor and outdoor).
- Strict restriction of tobacco sales to young people
- Implement legislation for plain packaging
- Increase duties and taxes on tobacco products
- Provide incentives for retailers not selling tobacco products
- Make tobacco consumption a difficult choice for citizens

Tobacco Control

Workplace Setting
- Implement a smoke-free policy at all times
- Supporting services for smoking cessation
- Offer stress management services
- Periodically review the respiratory function of employees

Source: Lee, 2019e.

We cannot allow manufacturers to abuse the rule of law to safeguard products that damage population health. There are several legal cases in which manufacturers have challenged the infringement of their rights. For example, in 2002, three major Canadian tobacco manufacturers took the Federal Government to court over the Federal Tobacco Act, which included new regulations for comprehensive health warnings (*Rothmans, Benson and Hedges, Inc., JTI-MacDonald Inc., and Imperial Tobacco Limited v Attorney General of Canada*, Canada Montreal Sup. Ct). The Court dismissed the application. The manufacturers appealed to the Quebec Court of Appeal in 2005 and complained that the health warning regulation was *ultra vires* beyond the power of the Canadian Parliament and was an unjustified infringement on their freedom of expression as guaranteed in the Canadian Charter of Rights and Freedoms. The Quebec Court of Appeal found the infringement of freedom of expression groundless and held that the text and photographs of the warnings required by the regulations were not disproportionately harsh with respect to the legislative objective. The manufacturers appealed to the Supreme Court of Canada (2007 SCC 30). The Court ruled that the Federal Tobacco Act was a *justified* infringement of the Canadian Charter of Rights and Freedoms as the risks and suffering associated with tobacco addiction were pressing and substantial.

In defining the rule of law, Lord Bingham explained that "[t]he Law must afford adequate protection of fundamental rights" and discussed eight sub-rules associated with this concept (Bingham, 2000). The rule of law must balance competing ideas, and governments are forced to consider the rights of all the stakeholders. In such situations, many governments have avoided legislative measures in favour of improving health literacy regarding the potential risks of tobacco and alcohol use. Application of the Health Settings Approach to accomplish this will help to build up community action to advocate for their protection from harmful substances and will also help and support individuals in making their own lifestyle changes.

Preventive Strategies for Mental Illnesses

Prevention is the most cost-effective way of managing mental illnesses, but this process is complex as many preventive strategies are beyond the boundary of the health sector. Figure 10.3 illustrates the three tiers of prevention for mental health issues (Baird et al., 2013). Equitable societies should invest in protective factors

Figure 10.3: The Three Tiers of Mental Health Illness Prevention

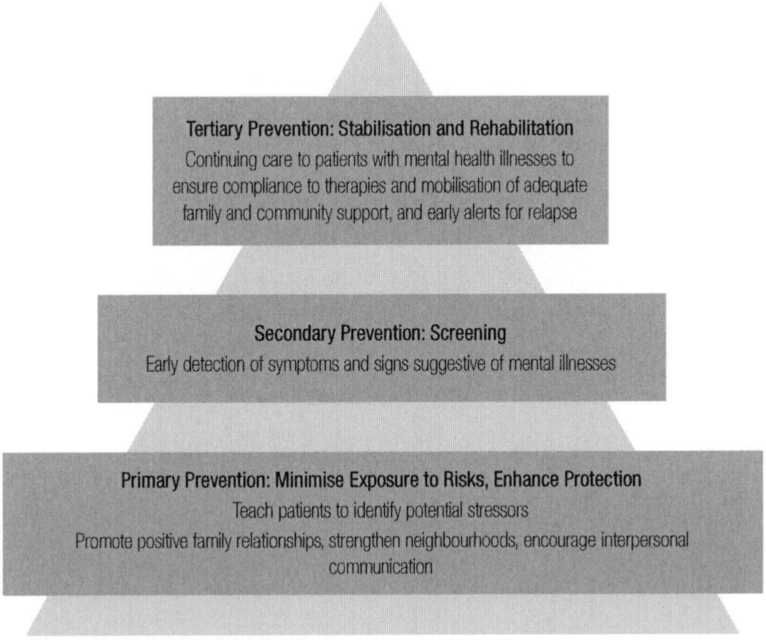

Tertiary Prevention: Stabilisation and Rehabilitation
Continuing care to patients with mental health illnesses to
ensure compliance to therapies and mobilisation of adequate
family and community support, and early alerts for relapse

Secondary Prevention: Screening
Early detection of symptoms and signs suggestive of mental illnesses

Primary Prevention: Minimise Exposure to Risks, Enhance Protection
Teach patients to identify potential stressors
Promote positive family relationships, strengthen neighbourhoods, encourage interpersonal
communication

Source: author.

such as promoting positive family relationships, strengthening neighbourhoods, and enhancing interpersonal communication, while also minimising stressors by meeting the basic needs of the population (e.g., by optimising their living and working environments). Early identification of mental health problems and encouraging health-seeking behaviours is only possible in societies that eliminate the stigmas around mental health issues. Support services must also be available, accessible, acceptable, and affordable for users. Effective implementation of the three tiers of prevention needs to take place in people's living, working, or learning environments. Thus, the Healthy Settings Approach is an ideal framework for addressing mental health issues across the population. Figure 10.4 illustrates how different settings can facilitate well-being with regards to mental health promotion (Lee, 2018c).

Figure 10.4: Using the Healthy Settings Approach to Promote Mental Well-being

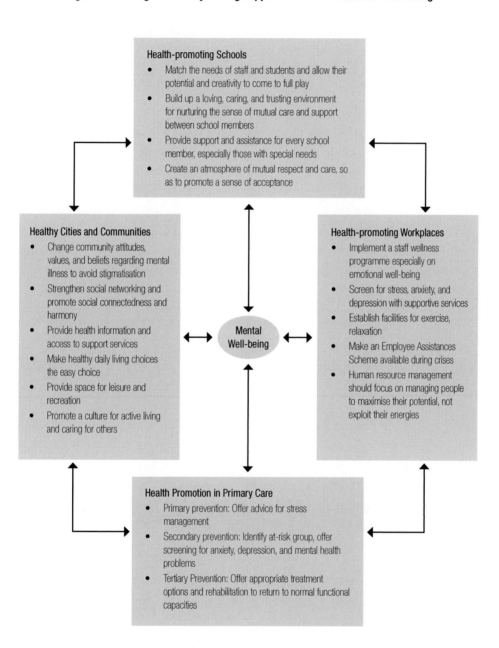

Source: Lee, 2018c.

175

The Right to Health

Social injustice has been identified as a widespread global "killer". Injustice-related deaths are a by-product of the toxic combination of poor social policies and programmes, unfair economic arrangements, and "bad politics" responsible for health inequalities (Marmot et al., 2008). Applying a Human Rights-based Approach (HRBA) would be an effective means to help the poor, vulnerable, and marginalised groups gain access to health-related services and improve their quality of health care (Hunt et al., 2015). It is essential to integrate HRBA systematically in order to develop the capacity of government and civil society actors to focus on human rights during the planning, implementation, and evaluation of health programmes and strategies. A study by Marmot and Bell (2012) of the health inequalities in England identified the importance of linking knowledge to action to ensure all children, young people, and adults are able to maximise their capabilities and have control over their lives, while creating and developing healthy and sustainable settings as well as strengthen the impact of ill-health prevention.

Experience in high-income countries has shown that many households with family members with chronic conditions still carry severe economic burden, even when a well-developed health care system with universal health coverage (UHC) is in place (Jan et al., 2018). UHC is, therefore, not a panacea for protecting households from the economic burdens of health. This is particularly the case if the resources for broader public health and preventive services are inadvertently channelled towards clinical service coverage at the individual level (Jan et al., 2018; Schmidt et al., 2015). Wider government programmes increasing social mobility and alleviating poverty through a safety net such as free education and basic employment rights are required to mediate action. Such programmes must move beyond the health care field and synergise across multiple sectors to enhance coordination with other SDGs (Waage et al., 2015).

In assessing the impact of an HRBA, it is best to move away from relying on a "strict hierarchy of acceptable evidence linking to clinical effectiveness" and use plausible evidence capturing the effects of multiple co-occurring factors (Biehl et al., 2009). This requires both conventional health indicators and new measures for assessing the effects of changes in the legal and policy framework as well as other qualitative changes (Kjellstrom et al., 2007). The right to health should cover more than just conventional health services (Lee, 2020). It should ensure people can live in a healthy environment (physical and psycho-social) with minimal exposure to risk factors, while enhancing opportunities for protection. There has also been a call for greater legal accountability in how the right to health is upheld (Yamin and Lander, 2015). This multi-sector application and assessment as well as the coordination required from policy makers is precisely where the Healthy Settings Approach is focused (WHO, 1986). Thus, the Healthy Settings Approach across multiple settings, as described throughout this book, is essential to assure the right to health for all.

Chapter 11

Concluding Remarks
and the Close of City-super's Story

To conclude City-super's journey, he provided one final recommendation to the City Mayor: to better the health and well-being of citizens, it is essential to emphasise the Healthy Settings Approach in all contexts, including cities, schools, workplaces, and health care establishments. Assessment must move away from using strictly conventional indicators of clinical effectiveness and move towards the use of new measures showing increases in health knowledge, positive behavioural changes, disease prevention, and enhanced access to health information across the community. Community and city leaders must spearhead changes in public policies to enhance environments to support health and preventive health services. Research using focus groups to gather information from the community will encourage support for these policy changes and for broader application of the approach. Applying these measures across multiple settings will create synergy throughout the community, and only then can the "right to health" be recognised for all citizens.

Concluding Remarks

Behavioural, environmental, occupational, and metabolic risks explain half of global mortality and more than one-third of global disability adjusted life years (DALYs), providing many opportunities for prevention (GBD 2013 Risk Factors Collaborators, 2015). Non-communicable diseases such as cardiovascular disease, chronic lung diseases, cancer, and diabetes are major health burdens, and the main drivers underlying these conditions are an unhealthy diet and lack of physical activity or a sedentary lifestyle. These risk factors are often the result of a lack of places and opportunities to be physically active and to purchase healthy foods, or may be due to industry-specific or political opposition to public health interventions (GBD 2013 Risk Factors Collaborators, 2015; Gostin et al., 2017; Patterson et al., 2018). The chapters of this book have illuminated how the Healthy Settings Approach can be used to improve population health by creating a supportive environment in cities, schools, workplaces, and healthcare services. Built environments, internal environments, and social environments are essential aspects of the Healthy Settings framework.

Built environments can be defined broadly as "the human-made space in which people live, work and recreate on a day-to-day basis" (Roof and Oleru, 2008). This includes not only green spaces and parks but also the presence and conditions of sidewalks, traffic flow, cleanliness and maintenance of public spaces, perceptions of safety and community security, zoning and land use mix, and population density. The internal environment refers to the social capital or social networks and interactions that inspire trust and reciprocity among citizens (Leyden, 2003). Social environments refer to factors such as social support, social deprivation, income inequality, racial discrimination, social cohesion and systems, food infrastructure, and green spaces (Gose et al., 2013). It is not difficult to understand the importance of the Healthy Settings Approach in shaping the holistic health of the people in each of these respective environments and how they can apply across settings. Furthermore, using an approach that encompasses all of the environments an individual encounters will allow health promotion to be viewed as more than just disease treatment. It will instead promote the strengthening of community actions for better health, building up of personal health skills to enhance health literacy, and the development of greater health advocacy.

Each chapter of this book has highlighted various initiatives in different settings in different parts of the world that can be implemented to create a better environment. These initiatives are based on the philosophy of "new public health", which requires continually creating and improving physical and social environments and expanding community resources to enable people to support each other and develop to their maximum potential (Ashton and Thurston, 2017). In this way the Health Cities model can be used as a key example. It encompasses all of the other settings and explains how health promotion can be effectively implemented to create synergy between schools, workplaces, heath care services, etc. Failure to make good use of community resources and empowerment of people will impede health promotion. For maximum effectiveness, the Healthy Settings Approach should be referenced during the formulation of public policies. The evidence gathered after an initiative is implemented, whether in relation to the Healthy Cities movement, Health-promoting Schools movement, or other setting-specific programme, should be assessed and used to inform decisions and policies regarding development and design (Carmichael et al., 2020). Taken together, the Healthy Settings Approach facilitates the "right to health" and promoting health in multiple and varied settings concurrently will ensure healthy living throughout the community and, ultimately, the world.

References

Aarø, L. E., Wold, B., Kannas, L., and Rimpelä, M. (1986). "Health behaviour in schoolchildren. A WHO cross-national survey: A presentation of philosophy, methods and selected results of the first survey". *Health Promotion International*, Vol. 1, Issue 1, pp. 17–33.

Aldana, S. G. (2001). "Financial impact of health promotion programs: a comprehensive review of the literature". *American Journal of Health Promotion*, Vol. 15, Issue 5, pp. 296–320.

Allensworth, D. (1994). "The research base for innovative practices in school health education at the secondary level". *Journal of School Health*, Vol. 64, No. 5, pp. 180–187.

Allensworth, D. (1997). "Evolution of school health". In: Allensworth, D., Lawson, E., Nicholson, L., and Wyche, J. (Eds.), *School and Health: Our Nation's Investment. Institute of Medicine (US) Committee on Comprehensive School Health Programs in Grades K-12* (pp. 33–59). Washington, DC: National Academies Press.

Alliance for Healthy Cities [AFHC]. (2010). *Gangnam Declaration for Ubiquitous Healthy Cities.* Fourth Global Conference of the Alliance for Healthy Cities, Gangnam, Gangnam, Seoul, Korea, 26–30 October 2010. Available at: http://alliance-healthycities.com/PDF/GangnamDeclarationUbiquitousHealthyCities_October2010.pdf, last accessed 13 April 2021.

Al Subhi, L. K., Bose, S., and Al Ani, M. F. (2015). "Prevalence of physically active and sedentary adolescents in ten Eastern Mediterranean countries and its relation with age, sex, and body mass index". *Journal of Physical Activity and Health*, Vol. 12, Issue 2, pp. 257–265.

American Academy of Pediatrics. (2004). *School Health: Policy and Practice*. Elk Grove Village, IL: American Academy of Pediatrics.

Amorim, T. C., Azevedo, M. R., and Hallal, P. C. (2010). "Physical activity levels according to physical and social environmental factors in a sample of adults living in South Brazil". *Journal of Physical Activity and Health*, 7 Supp. 2, pp. S204–S212.

Annas, G. J., and Mariner, W. K. (2016). "(Public) health and human rights in practice". *Journal of Health Politics, Policy and Law*, Vol. 41, Issue 1, pp. 129–139.

Ashton, J. (1992). *Healthy Cities*. Philadelphia: Open University Press.

Ashton, J., and Kickbusch, I. (1986). *Healthy Cities: Action Strategies for Health Promotion*. Copenhagen: World Health Organisation, 1986.

Ashton, J., and Thurston, M. N. (2017). "New public health". *International Encyclopedia of Public Health* (2nd edition), Vol. 5, pp. 231–239.

Badland, H., Whitzman, C., Lowe, M., Davern, M., Aye, L., Butterworth, I., Hes, D., and Giles-Corti, B. (2014). "Urban liveability: Emerging lessons from Australia for exploring the potential for indicators to measure the social determinants of health". *Social Science and Medicine*, Vol. 111(C), pp. 64–73.

Bagnardi, V., Rota, M., Botteri, E., Tramacere, I., Islami, F., Fedirko, V., Scotti, L., Jenab, M., Turati, F., Pasquali, E., Pelucchi, C., Bellocco, R., Negri, E., Corrao, G., Rehm, J., Boffetta, P., and La Vecchia, C. (2013). "Light alcohol drinking and cancer: A meta-analysis". *Annals of Oncology*, Vol. 24, Issue 2, pp. 301–308.

Baird, M. A., Riba, M., Lee, A., Galvez, E., and Deneke, D. (2013). "Managing the interface in primary care mental health clinics". In: Ivbijaro, G. (Ed.), *Companion to Primary Care Mental Health* (pp. 1116–1137). London/New York: WONCA and Radcliff Publishing.

Baum, F. (1993). "Noarlunga Healthy Cities Pilot Project: The contribution of research and evaluation". In: Davies, J. K., and Kelly, M. P. (Eds.), *Healthy Cities: Research and Practice* (pp. 90–111). London: New York: Routledge.

Baum, F. (1995). "Researching public health: Behind the qualitative-quantitative methodological debate". *Social Science and Medicine*, Vol. 40, Issue 4, pp. 459–468.

Baum, F. (2003). *The New Public Health* (2nd edition). South Melbourne: Oxford University Press.

Baum, F. (2014). *Addressing Health Inequities in the New Era of Public Health.* Pre-conference Seminar of Global Conference of Alliance for Healthy Cities, 27 November 2014, Hong Kong.

Baum, F., and Cooke, R. (1992). "Healthy Cities Australia: The evaluation of the pilot project in Noarlunga, South Australia". *Health Promotion International*, Vol. 7, Issue 3, pp. 181–193.

Baum, F., Jolley, G., Hicks, R., Saint, K., and Parker, S. (2006). "What makes for sustainable Healthy Cities initiatives? A review of the evidence from Noarlunga, Australia after 18 years". *Health Promotion International*, Vol. 21, Issue 4, pp. 259–265.

Beaglehole, R., Bonita, R., and Magnusson, R. (2011). "Global cancer prevention: An important pathway to global health and development". *Public Health*, Vol. 12, pp. 821–831.

Bell, A. C., and Swinburn, B. A. (2004). "What are the key food groups to target for preventing obesity and improving nutrition in schools?" *European Journal of Clinical Nutrition*, Vol. 58, Issue 2, pp. 258–263.

Biehl, J., Petryna, A., Gertner, A., and Picon, P. D. (2009). "Judicialisation of the right to health in Brazil". *Lancet*, Vol. 373, No. 9682, pp. 2182–2184.

Bingham, T. (2000). *The Rule of the Law*. London: Allen Lane.

Birckmayer, J. D., and Weiss, C. H. (2000). "Theory-based evaluation in practice: What do we learn?" *Evaluation Review*, Vol. 24, Issue 4, pp. 407–431.

Bloch, P., Toft, U., Reinbach, H. C., Clausen, L. T., Mikkelsen, B. E., Poulsen, K., and Jensen, B. B. (2014). Revitalizing the setting approach: Supersettings for sustainable impact in community health promotion. *International Journal of Behavioral Nutrition and Physical Activity*, Vol. 11, p. 118.

Blum, R., and Dick, B. (2013). "Strengthening global programs and policies for youth based on the emerging science". *Journal of Adolescent Health*, Vol. 52, Issue 2, Supp. 2, pp. S1–S3.

Blum, R. W., McNeely, C. A., and Rinehart, P. M. (2002). *Improving the Odds: The Untapped Power of Schools to Improve the Health of Teens*. Minneapolis: Center for Adolescent Health and Development, University of Minnesota.

Bond, L., Daube, M., and Chikritzhs, T. (2010). "Selling addictions: Similarities in approaches between big tobacco and big booze". *Australia Medical Journal*, Vol. 3, Issue 6, pp. 325–332.

Boonekamp, G. M. M., Colomer, C., Tomás, A., and Nuñez, A. (1999). "Healthy Cities evaluation: The co-ordinators perspective". *Health Promotion International*, Vol. 14, Issue 2, pp. 103–110.

Brotons, C., Björkelund, C., Bulc, M., Ciurana, R., Godycki-Cwirko, M., Jurgova, E., Kloppe, P., Lionis, C., Mierzecki, A., Piñeiro, R., Pullerits, L., Sammut, M. R., Sheehan, M., Tataradze, R., Thireos, E. A., Vuchak, J., and the EUROPREV Network. (2005). "Prevention and health promotion in clinical practice: The views of general practitioners in Europe". *Preventive Medicine*, Vol. 40, Issue 5, pp. 595–601.

Brownell, K. D., Kersh, R., Ludwig, D. S., Post, R. C., Puhl, R. M., Schwartz, M. B., and Willett, W. C. (2010). "Personal responsibility and obesity: A constructive approach to a controversial issue". *Health Affairs*, Vol. 29, No. 3, pp. 379–387.

Brug, J., te Velde, S., De Bourdeaudhuij, I., and Kemers, S. (2010). "Evidence of the influence of home and family environment". In: Waters, E., Swinburn, B. A., Seidell, J. C., and Uauy, R. (Eds.), *Preventing Childhood Obesity: Evidence Policy and Practice* (p. 64–70). Oxford, UK: Wiley-Blackwell.

Buck, D., Baylis, A., Dougall, D., and Robertson, R. (2018). A *Vision of Population Health: Towards a Healthier Future*. London, UK: Kings Fund.

Bui, D. S., Lodge, C. J., Burgess, J. A., Lowe, A. J., Perret, J., Bui, M. Q., Lodge, C. J., Burgess, J. A., Lowe, A. J., Perret, J., Bui, M. Q., Bowatte, G., Gurrin, L., Johns, D. P., Thompson, B. R., Hamilton, G. S., Frith, P. A., James, A. L., Thomas, P. S., Jarvis, D., Svanes, C., Russell, M., Morrison, S. C., Feather, I., Allen, K. J., Wood-Baker, R., Hopper, J., Giles, G. G., Abramson, M. J., Walters, E. H., Matheson, M. C., and Dharmage, S. C. (2018). "Childhood predictors of lung function trajectories and future COPD risk: A prospective cohort study from the first to the sixth decade of life". *Lancet Respiratory Medicine*, Vol. 6, Issue 7, pp. 535–544.

Burton, S. (1999). "Evaluation of healthy city projects: Stakeholder analysis of two projects in Bangladesh". *Environment and Urbanisation*, Vol. 11, Issue 1, pp. 41–52.

Bustreo, F., and Chestnov, O. (2013). "Emerging issues in adolescent health and the positions and priorities of the World Health Organisation". *Journal of Adolescent Health*, Vol. 52, Issue 2, Supp. 2, pp. S4.

Capello, R. (2000). "The city-network paradigm: Measuring urban network externalities". *Urban Studies*, Vol. 37, Issue 11, pp. 1925–1945.

Carmichael, L., Prestwood, E., Marsh, R., Ige, J., Williams, B., Pilkington, P., Eaton, E., and Michalec, A. (2020). "Healthy buildings for a healthy city: Is the public health evidence base informing current building policies?" *Science of the Total Environment*, Vol. 719, No. 137146.

Carter, O. B. (2006). "The weight issue of Australian television food advertising and childhood obesity". *Health Promotion Journal of Australia*, Vol. 17, Issue 1, pp. 5–11.

Catalano, R. F., Haggerty, K. P., Oesterle, S., Fleming, C. B., and Hawkins, J. D. (2004). "The importance of bonding to school for healthy development: Findings from the Social Development Research Group". *Journal of School Health*, Vol. 74, Issue 7, pp. 252–261.

Catford, J. (1993). "Auditing health promotion: What are the vital signs of quality?" *Health Promotion International*, Vol. 8, Issue 2, pp. 67–68.

Central Intelligence Agency [CIA]. (2015). *Distribution of Family Income — Gini Index* [online]. Available at: www.cia.gov/the-world-factbook/field/gini-index-coefficient-distribution-of-family-income/.

Centre for Health Education and Health Promotion [CHEHP]. (2012). *Health Promoting School Performance Indicators*. CHEHP, The Chinese University of Hong Kong, Hong Kong. Available at: www.cuhk.edu.hk/med/hep/consultancy/indicator.pdf, accessed 15 November 2019.

Chen, M. S. (1988). "Wellness in the workplace: Beyond the point of no return". *Health Values*, Vol. 12, pp. 16–22.

Chen, F. L., and Lee, A. (2016). "Health-promoting educational settings in Taiwan: Development and evaluation of the Health-Promoting School Accreditation System". *Global Health Promotion*, Vol. 23, Supp. 1, pp. 18–25.

Chow, Y. H. (2018). *Kwai Tsing Health System: Enhancement of Community Health Care*. Hong Kong: Kwai Tsing Safe Community and Healthy City Association.

Chu, C. M., and Forrester, C. A. (1992). *Workplace Health Promotion in Queensland*. Brisbane: Queensland Health.

Chu, C., Breucker, G., Harris, N., Stitzel, A., Gan, X., Gu, X., and Dwyer, S. (2000). "Health-promoting workplaces: International settings development". *Health Promotion International*, Vol. 15, Issue 2, pp. 155–167.

Cohen, D. A. (2010). "Evidence on the food environment and obesity". In: Waters, E., Swinburn, B. A., Seidell, J. C., and Uauy, R. (Eds.), *Preventing Childhood Obesity: Evidence, Policy and Practice* (pp. 113–119). Oxford, UK: Wiley-Blackwell.

Cole, H., Shokry, G., Connolly, J. J. T., Pérez-del-Pulgar, C., Alonso, J., and Anguelovski, I. (2017). "Can Healthy Cities be made really healthy". *Lancet Public Health*, Vol. 2, Issue 9, pp. 394–395.

Collins, J. J., Baase, C. M., Sharda, C. E., Ozminkowski, R. J., Nicholson, S., Billotti, G. M., Turpin, R. S., Olson, M., and Berger, M. L. (2005). "The assessment of chronic health conditions on work performance, absence, and total economic impact for employers". *Journal of Occupational and Environmental Medicine*, Vol. 47, Issue 6, pp. 547–557.

Commission on Social Determinants of Health [CSDH]. (2008). *CSDH Final Report: Closing the Gap in a Generation: Health Equity through Action on the Social Determinants of Health*. Geneva: World Health Organisation.

Corburn, J. (2017). "Equitable and healthy city planning: Towards healthy urban governance in the century of the city". In: de Leeuw, E., Simos, J. (Eds.) (2017). *Healthy Cities: The Theory, Policy, and Practice of Value-Based Urban Planning* (pp. 31–41). New York: Springer.

Crown, J. (2003). "Analysis of health determinants for Healthy Cities programmes". In: Takano, T. (Ed.), *Healthy Cities and Urban Policy Research* (pp. 59–75). London: Routledge.

Cullen, K., Baranowski, T., Owens, E., Marsh, T., Rittenberry, L., and de Moor, C. (2003). "Availability, accessibility, and preferences for fruit, 100% fruit juice, and vegetables influence children's dietary behaviour". *Health Education and Behavior*, Vol. 30, Issue 5, pp. 615–626.

Curriculum Development Council and the Hong Kong Examination Authority. (2007a). *Liberal Studies, Curriculum and Assessment Guide (Secondary 4–6)* (updated in 2015) [online]. Available at: http://334.edb.hkedcity.net/doc/chi/curriculum2015/LS_CAGuide_e_2015.pdf.

Curriculum Development Council and the Hong Kong Examination Authority. (2007b). *Health Management and Social Care, Curriculum and Assessment Guide (Secondary 4–6)* (updated in 2015) [online]. Available at: http://334.edb.hkedcity.net/doc/chi/curriculum2015/HMSC_CA_Guide_e_2015.pdf.

Davey, P. (2010). *Logan Public Health Plan 2003–2008: Evaluation Report.* Queensland: Griffith University Centre for Environment and Population Health and Logan Health Council.

Day, M. E., Strange, K. S., McKay, H. A., and Naylor, P. J. (2008). "Action schools! BC — Healthy eating: Effects of a whole-school model to modifying eating behaviours of elementary school children". *Canadian Journal of Public Health*, Vol. 99, No. 4, pp. 328–331.

Delaney, F. G. (1994). "Muddling through the middle ground: Theoretical concerns in intersectoral collaboration and health promotion". *Health Promotion International*, Vol. 9, Issue 3, pp. 217–225.

de Leeuw, E. (1993). "Health policy, epidemiology and power: The interest web". *Health Promotion International*, Vol. 8, Issue 1, pp. 49–52.

de Leeuw, E. (1999). "Healthy Cities: Urban social entrepreneurship for health". *Health Promotion International*, Vol. 14, Issue 3, pp. 261–270.

de Leeuw, E. (2000). "Community as a setting for health promotion". In: Poland, B. D., Green, L. W., and Rootman I. (Eds.), *Settings for Health Promotion: Linking Theory and Practice* (pp. 287–300). Thousand Oaks, CA: SAGE Publications.

de Leeuw, E. (2009). "Mixing urban health research methods for best fit". *Journal of Urban Health*, Vol. 87, Issue 1, pp. 1–4.

de Leeuw, E. (2011). "Do healthy cities work? A logic of method for assessing impact and outcome of healthy cities". *Journal of Urban Health*, Vol. 89, Issue 2, pp. 217–231.

de Leeuw, E. (2017a). "Healthy Cities are back! (They were never gone)". *Health Promotion International*, Vol. 32, Issue 4, pp. 606–609.

de Leeuw, E. (2017b). "Cities and health from the neolithic to the anthropocene". In: De Leeuw, E., and Simos, J. (Eds.), *Healthy Cities: The Theory, Policy, and Practice of Value-Based Urban Planning* (pp. 3–30). New York: Springer.

de Leeuw, E. (2017c). "From urban projects to healthy city policies". In: de Leeuw, E., and Simos, J. (Eds.), *Healthy Cities: The Theory, Policy, and Practice of Value-Based Urban Planning* (pp. 407–437). New York: Springer.

de Leeuw, E., and Skovgaard, T. (2005). "Utility-driven evidence for healthy cities: Problems with evidence generation and application". *Social Science and Medicine*, Vol. 61, Issue 6, pp. 1331–1341.

de Leeuw, E., and Simos, J. (Eds). (2017). *Healthy Cities: The Theory, Policy, and Practice of Value-Based Urban Planning*. New York: Springer.

de Leeuw, E., Green, G., Dyakova, M., Spanswick, L., and Palmer, N. (2015). "European Healthy Cities evaluation: Conceptual framework and methodology". *Health Promotion International*, Vol. 30, Supp. 1, pp. i8–i17.

Denaxas, S. C., Asselbergs, F. W., and Moore, J. H. (2016). "The tip of the iceberg: Challenges of accessing hospital electronic health record data for biological data mining". *BioData Mining*, Vol. 9, Art. No. 29.

Denzin, N. K. (1978). *The Research Act: A Theoretical Introduction to Sociological Methods*. New York: McGraw Hill.

Denzin, N. K. (2009). *The Research Act: A Theoretical Introduction to Sociological Methods* (3rd edition). Englewood Cliffs, NJ: Prentice Hall.

Denzin, N. K. (2012). "Triangulation 2.0". *Journal of Mixed Methods Research*, Vol. 6, Issue 2, pp. 80–88.

Denzin, N. K., and Lincoln, Y. S. (Eds.). (2011). *The SAGE Handbook of Qualitative Research* (4th edition). Thousand Oaks, CA: SAGE Publications.

Denzin, N. K., and Lincoln, Y. S. (Eds.). (2018). *The SAGE Handbook of Qualitative Research* (5th edition). Los Angeles, CA: SAGE Publications.

Department of Health [DH], United Kingdom (2004). *Choosing Health: Making Healthy Choices Easier*. HM Government, UK: The Stationary Office.

Diez Roux, A. V. (2001). "Investigating neighbourhood and area effects on health". *American Journal of Public Health*, Vol. 91, No. 11, pp. 1783–1789.

Dixon, J., Omwega, A. M., Friel, S., Burns, C., Donati, K., and Carlisle, R. (2007). "The health equity dimension of urban food systems". *Journal of Urban Health*, Vol. 84, Issue 3, pp. 118–129.

Donchin, M., Shemesh, A. A., Horowitz, P., and Daoud, N. (2006). "Implementation of the healthy cities' principles and strategies: An evaluation of the Israel healthy cities network". *Health Promotion International*, Vol. 21, Issue 4, pp. 266–273.

Dooris, M. (2004). "Joining up settings for health: A valuable investment for strategic partnerships?" *Critical Public Health*, Vol. 14, Issue 1, pp. 49–61.

Dooris, M. (2006). "Healthy settings: Challenges to generating evidence of effectiveness". *Health Promotion International*, Vol. 21, Issue 1, pp. 55–65.

Dooris, M. (2009). "Holistic and sustainable health improvement: The contribution of the settings-based approach to health promotion". *Perspectives in Public Health*, Vol. 129, Issue 1, pp. 29–36.

Dooris, M., Poland, B., Kolbe, L., de Leeuw, E., McCall, D., and Wharf-Higgins, J. (2007). "Healthy settings: Building evidence for the effectiveness of whole-system health promotion-challenges and future directions". In: McQueen, D., and Jones, C. (Eds.), *Global Perspectives on Health Promotion Effectiveness* (pp. 327–352). New York: Springer.

Dooris, M., Wills, J., and Newton, J. (2014). "Theorizing healthy settings: A critical discussion with reference to Healthy Universities". *Scandinavian Journal of Public Health*, Vol. 42, Supp. 15, pp. 7–16.

Douglas, F., Van Teijlingen, E., Torrance, N., Fearn, P., Kerr, A., and Meloni, S. (2006). "Promoting physical activity in primary care settings: Health visitors' and practice nurses' view and experiences". *Journal of Advanced Nursing*, Vol. 55, Issue 2, pp. 159–168.

Doyle, Y. G., Tsouros, A. D., Cryer, P. C., Hedley, S., and Russell-Hodgson, C. (1999). "Practical lessons in using indicators of determinants of health across 47 European cities". *Health Promotion International*, Vol. 14, Issue 4, pp. 289–299.

Duhl, L. (1986). "The healthy city: Its function and its future". *Health Promotion International*, Vol. 1, Issue 1, pp. 55–60.

Duhl, L. (1996). "An ecohistory of health: The role of 'healthy cities'". *American Journal of Health Promotion*, Vol. 10, Issue 4, pp. 258–261.

Economist Intelligence Unit (written by Becca Lipman and edited by Elizabeth Sukkar). (2019). *Enabling People to Manage Their Health and Well-being: Policy Approach to Self-care*. London: Economist Intelligence Unit.

Elsey, H., Agyepong, I., Huque, R., Quayyem, Z., Baral, S., Ebenso, B., Kharel, C., Shawon, R. A., Onwujekwe, O., Uzochukwu, B., Nonvignon, J., Aryeetey, G. C., Kane, S., Ensor, T., and Mirzoev, T. (2019) "Rethinking health systems in the context of urbanisation: Challenges from four rapidly urbanising low-income and middle-income countries". *BMJ Global Health*, Vol. 4, Issue 3, e001501.

Epstein, L., and Ogden, J. (2005). "A qualitative study of GPs' views of treating obesity". *British Journal of General Practice*, Vol. 55, Issue 519, pp. 750–754.

Eriksson, C. (2000). "Learning and knowledge-production for public health: A review of approaches to evidence-based public health". *Scandinavian Journal of Public Health*, Vol. 28, Issue 4, pp. 298–308.

Farmer, T., Robinson, K., Elliott, S. J., and Eyles, J. (2006). "Developing and implementing a triangulation protocol for qualitative health research". *Qualitative Health Research*, Vol. 16, Issue 3, pp. 377–394.

Federal Institute for Occupational Safety and Health (Ed.) (1996). *European Network Workplace Health Promotion*. 1st Meeting of the Member States. Reports of the work-shop on 21 June 1995 in Dortmund. Conference Report Tb 72. Bremerhaven, Wirtschaftsverlag NW.

Feinstein, L., Sabates, R., Sorhaindo, A., Rogers, I., Herrick, D., Northstone, K., and Emmett, P. (2008). "Dietary patterns related to attainment in school: The importance of early eating patterns". *Journal of Epidemiology and Community Health*, Vol. 62, Issue 8, pp. 734–739.

Frank, L. D., Engelke, P. O., and Schmid, T. L. (2003). *Health and Community Design: The Impact of the Built Environment on Physical Activity*. London: Island Press.

Frieden, T. R. (2015). "The future of public health". *New England Journal of Medicine*, Vol. 373, No. 18, pp. 1748–1754.

Fusch, P., Fusch, G. E., and Ness, L. R. (2018). "Denzin's paradigm shift: Revisiting triangulation in qualitative research". *Journal of Social Change*, Vol. 10, Issue 1, pp. 19–31.

Galea, S., and Vlahov, D. (2005). *Handbook of Urban Health: Populations, Methods, and Practice*. New York: Springer.

GBD 2013 Risk Factors Collaborators. (2015). "Global, regional, and national comparative risk assessment of 79 behavioural, environmental and occupational, and metabolic risks or clusters of risks in 188 countries, 1990–2013: A systematic analysis for the Global Burden of Disease Study 2013". *Lancet*, Vol. 386, Issue 10010, pp. 2287–2323.

GBD 2016 Alcohol Collaborators. (2018). "Alcohol use and burden for 195 countries and territories, 1990–2016: A systematic analysis for the Global Burden of Disease Study 2016". *Lancet*, Vol. 392, No. 10152, pp. 1015–1035.

Ghebreyesus, T. A. (2018). "Acting on NCDs: Counting the cost". *Lancet*, Vol. 391, No. 10134, pp. 1973–1974.

Gifford, S. (1996). "Qualitative research: The soft option?" *Health Promotion Journal of Australia*, Vol. 6, Issue 1, pp. 58–61.

Giles-Corti, B., Badland, H. M., Mavoa, S., Turrell, G., Bull, F., Boruff, B., Pettit, C., Bauman, A. E., Hooper, P., Villanueva, K., Astell-Burt, T., Feng, X., Learnihan, V., Davey, R., Grenfell, R., and Thackway, S. (2014). "Reconnecting urban planning with health: A protocol for the development and validation of national liveability indicators associated with noncommunicable disease risk behaviours and health outcomes". *Public Health Research and Practice*, Vol. 25, Issue 1, e2511405.

Gose, M., Plachta-Danielzik, S., Willié, B., Johannsen, M., Landsberg, B., and Müller, M. J. (2013). "Longitudinal influences of neighbourhood built and social environment on children's weight status". *International Journal of Environmental Research and Public Health*, Vol. 10, Issue 10, pp. 5083–5096.

Gostin, L. O. (2014a). "Global health justice: Toward a transformative agenda for health equity". In: Gostin, L. O. (Ed.), *The Global Health Law* (pp. 13–31). Cambridge, MA: Harvard University Press.

Gostin, L. O. (2014b). "The Framework Convention on Tobacco Control: The global response to tobacco". In: Gostin, L. O. (Ed.), *The Global Health Law* (pp. 205–242). Cambridge, MA: Harvard University Press.

Gostin, L. O., and Gostin, K. G. (2009). "A broader liberty: JS Mill, paternalism, and the public's health". *Journal of Public Health*, Vol. 123, Issue 3, pp. 214–221.

Gostin, L. O., and Sridhar, D. (2014). "Global health and the law". *New England Journal of Medicine*, Vol. 370, Issue 18, pp. 1732–1740.

Gostin, L. O., and Wiley, L. F. (2016). *Public Health Law: Power, Duty, Restraint* (3rd edition). Berkeley: University of California Press.

Gostin, L. O., Friedman, E. A., Ooms, G., Gebauer, T., Gupta, N., Sridhar, D., Chenguang, W., Røttingen, J. A., and Sanders, D. (2011). "The Joint Action and Learning Initiative: Towards a global agreement on national and global responsibilities for health". *PLoS Medicine*, Vol. 8, Issue 5, p. e1001031.

Gostin, L. O., Monahan, J. T., DeBartolo, M. C., and Horton, R. (2015). "Law's power to safeguard global health: A Lancet-O'Neill Institute, Georgetown University Commission on Global Health and the Law". *Lancet*, Vol. 385, No. 9978, pp. 1603–1604.

Gostin, L. O., Abou-Taleb, H., Roache, S. A, and Alwan, A. (2017). "Legal priorities for prevention of non-communicable diseases: Innovations from WHO's Eastern Mediterranean Region". *Public Health*, Vol. 144, pp. 4–12.

Goumans, M., and Springett, J. (1997). "From projects to policy: 'Healthy Cities' as a mechanism for policy change for health?" *Health Promotion International*, Vol. 12, Issue 4, pp. 311–322.

Grant, M. (2015). "European Healthy City Network Phase V: Patterns emerging for healthy urban planning". *Health Promotion International*, Vol. 30, Supp. 1, pp. i54–i70.

Green, G., Jackisch, J., and Zamaro, G. (2015). "Healthy cities as catalysts for caring and supportive environments". *Health Promotion International*, Vol. 30, Supp. 1, pp. i99–i107.

Green, J. (2000). "The role of theory in evidence-based health promotion practice". *Health Education Research*, Vol. 15, Issue 2, pp. 125–129.

Green, J., and Tones, K. (1999). "Towards a secure evidence base for health promotion". *Journal of Public Health*, Vol. 21, Issue 2, pp. 133–139.

Green, L. A., Fryer, G. E. Jr., Yawn, B. P., Lanier, D., and Dovey, S. M. (2001). "The ecology of medical care revisited". *New England Journal of Medicine*, Vol. 344, Issue 26, pp. 2021–2025.

Green, L. W., and Kreuter, M. W. (2005). *Health Program Planning: An Education and Ecological Approach* (4th edition). New York: McGraw Hill.

Green, L. W., Poland, B. D., and Rootman, I. (2000). "The settings approach to health promotion". In: Poland, B. D., Green, L. W., and Rootman, I. (Eds.), *Settings for Health Promotion: Linking Theory and Practice* (pp. 1–43). Thousands Oaks, CA: SAGE Publications.

Hall, C., Davies, J. K., and Sherriff, N. (2009). "Health in the urban environment: A qualitative review of the Brighton and Hove WHO Healthy City Program". *Journal of Urban Health*, Vol. 87, Issue 1, pp. 8–28.

Hancock, T. (1985). "The mandala of health: A model of the human ecosystem". *Family and Community Health: The Journal of Health Promotion and Maintenance*, Vol. 8, Issue 3, pp. 1–10.

Hancock, T. (1988). "Healthy Toronto: A vision of a healthy city". In: Ashton, J. (Ed.), *Healthy Cities: Concepts and Visions — A Resource for the WHO Healthy Cities Project*. Liverpool: Department of Community Health, University of Liverpool.

Hancock, T. (2001). "People, partnerships and human progress: Building community capital". *Health Promotion International*, Vol. 16, Issue 3, pp. 275–280.

Hancock, T., and Duhl, L. (1998). *Promoting Health in the Urban Context*. WHO Healthy Cities Paper No 1. Copenhagen, Denmark: FADI Publishers.

Hanlon, G., and Pickett, J. (1984). *Public Health: Administration and Practice*. St Louis: Times Mirror/Mosby.

Havas, S. (2009). "The ACCORD Trial and control of blood glucose level in type two diabetes mellitus: Time to challenge conventional wisdom". *Archives of Internal Medicine*, Vol. 169, Issue 2, pp. 150–154.

Hawe, P., Degeling, D., and Hall, J. (1990). *Evaluating Health Promotion: A Health Worker's Guide*. New South Wales, Australia: MacLennan & Petty Pty.

Heale, R., and Forbes, D. (2013). "Understanding triangulation in research". *Evidence-Based Nursing*, Vol. 16, Issue 4, p. 98.

Higgins, C., Lavin, T., and Metcalfe, O. (2008). *Health Impacts of Education: A Review*. Ireland: The Institute of Public Health in Ireland.

Ho, M., Yuen, W. K., Suen, Y. P., Lee, C. K., and Lee, A. (2007). *Enhancing School Improvement through the Health Promoting School Mentorship Scheme: Hong Kong's Experience*. The 19th World Conference on Health Promotion and Health Education. International Union of Health Promotion and Health Education, Vancouver, 10–15 June 2007.

Ho, M., Garnett, S. P., Baur, L., Burrows, T., Stewart, L., Neve, M., and Collins, C. (2012). "Effectiveness of lifestyle interventions in child obesity: Systematic review with meta-analysis". *Pediatrics*, Vol. 130, Issue 6, pp. e1647–e1671.

Hoek, J. (2008). "Public health, regulation and the nanny state fallacy". Partnerships, Proof and Practice: International Nonprofit and Social Marketing Conference 2008 Proceedings, University of Wollongong, 15–16 July 2008. Available at: https://ro.uow.edu.au/insm08/2.

Hong Kong Census and Statistics Department. (2006a). *Hong Kong 2006 Population By-census — Main Tables*. Hong Kong: Census and Statistics Department.

Hong Kong Census and Statistics Department. (2006b). *Hong Kong 2006 Population By-census — Thematic Report: Household Income Distribution in Hong Kong*. Hong Kong: Government Printer.

Hong Kong Government of Special Administrative Region [HKSAR]. (2005). *Director of Audit's Report. Report No. 45.* (Chapter 9, 4.29). Hong Kong: HKSAR.

Hong Kong Project Team on the development of the Hong Kong Chinese Version WHOQOL. (1997). *Hong Kong Chinese Version World Health Organisation Quality of Life Measures, Abbreviated Version.* Hong Kong: Hospital Authority.

Horton, R., and Sargent, J. (2018). "2018 must be the year for action against NCDs". *Lancet*, Vol. 391, Issue 10134, pp. 1971–1973.

Hoyle, T. B., Todd Bartee, R., and Allensworth, D. D. (2010). "Applying the process of health promotion in schools: A commentary". *Journal of School Health*, Vol. 80, Issue 4, pp. 163–166.

Huang, T. T., and Story, M. T. (2010). "A journey just started: Renewing efforts to address childhood obesity". *Obesity (Silver Spring)*, Vol. 18, Supp. 1, pp. S1–S3.

Hunt, P., Yamin, A. E., and Bustreo, F. (2015). "Making the case: What is the evidence of impact of applying human rights-based approaches to health?" *Health and Human Rights Journal*, Vol. 2, Issue 17, pp. 1–9.

Inchley, J., and Currie, C. (2003). *Promoting Healthy Eating in Schools Using a Health Promoting School Approach: Final Report of the ENHPS Healthy Eating Project.* Edinburgh: Child and Adolescent Health Research Unit (CAHRU), University of Edinburgh.

Inchley, J., Todd, J., Bryce, C., and Currie, C. (2001). "Dietary trends among Scottish school children in the 1990s". *Journal of Human Nutrition and Dietetics*, Vol. 14, Issue 3, pp. 207–216.

Inchley, J., Muldoon, J., and Currie, C. (2006). "Becoming a health promoting school: Evaluating the process of effective implementation in Scotland". *Health Promotion International*, Vol. 22, Issue 1, pp. 65–71.

International Union for Health Promotion and Education [IUHPE]. (2000a). *The Evidence of Health Promotion Effectiveness: Shaping Public Health in a New Europe, Part One: Core document.* Brussels: ECSC-EC-EAEC.

International Union for Health Promotion and Education [IUHPE]. (2000b). *The Evidence of Health Promotion Effectiveness: Shaping Public Health in a New Europe, Part Two: Evidence*. Brussels: ECSC-EC-EAEC.

International Union for Health Promotion and Education [IUHEP]. (2009). *Achieving Health Promoting Schools: Guidelines for Promoting Health in Schools*. Paris, France: IUHEP.

Jan, S., Laba, T. L., Essue, B. M., Gheorghe, A., Muhunthan, J., Engelgau, M., Mahal, A., Griffiths, U., McIntyre, D., Meng, Q., Nugent, R., Atun, R. (2018). "Action to address the household economic burden of non-communicable disease". *Lancet*, Vol. 391, Issue 10134, pp. 2047–2058.

Janesick, V. J. (1994). "The dance of qualitative research design: Metaphor, methodolatry and meaning". In: Denzin, N. K., and Lincoln, Y. S. (Eds.), *Handbook of Qualitative Research* (pp. 209–219). London: SAGE Publications.

Jeet, G., Thakur, J. S., Prinja, S., Singh, M., Paika, R., Kunjan, K., and Dhadwal, P. (2018). "Effectiveness of targeting the health promotion settings for non-communicable disease control in low/middle-income countries: Systematic review protocol". *BMJ Open*, Vol. 8, Issue 6, p. e014559.

Jordan, J., Dowswell, T., Harrison, S., Lilford, R. J., and Mort, M. (1998). "Health needs assessment. Whose priorities? Listening to users and the public". *BMJ Clinical Research*, Vol. 316, Issue 7145, pp. 1668–1670.

Joyce, A., Dabrowski, A., Aston, R., and Carey, G. (2017). "Evaluating for impact: What type of data can assist a health promoting school approach?" *Health Promotion International*, Vol. 32, Issue 2, pp. 403–410.

Kahneman, D. (2003). "A perspective on judgement and choice: Mapping bounded rationality". *American Psychologist*, Vol. 58, Issue 9, pp. 697–720.

Kang, E. (2016). "Inter-sectoral collaboration for physical activity in Korean Healthy Cities". *Health Promotion International*, Vol. 31, Issue 3, pp. 551–561.

Kaplan, R. M., Chadwick, M. V., and Schimmel, L. E. (1985). "Social learning intervention to promote metabolic control in type I diabetes mellitus: Pilot experiment results". *Diabetes Care*, Vol. 8, Issue 2, pp. 152–155.

Karlsson, M. L., Bush, H., Aboagye, E., and Jensen, I. (2015). "Validation of a measure of health-related production loss: Construct validity and responsiveness — A cohort study". *BMC Public Health*, Vol. 15, Art. No. 1148.

Khanal, S., Lloyd, B., Rissel, C., Portors, C., Grunseit., A., Indig, D., Ibrahim, I., and McElduff, S. (2016). "Evaluation of the implementation of Get Healthy at Work — A workplace health promotion program in New South Wales, Australia". *Health Promotion Journal of Australia*, Vol. 27, Issue 3, pp. 243.250.

Kickbusch, I. (2005). "The health society: Importance of the new policy proposal by the EU Commission on Health and Consumer Affairs". *Health Promotion International*, Vol. 20, Issue 2, pp. 101–103.

Kickbusch, I., and Gleicher, D. (2012). *Governance for Health in the 21st Century*. Copenhagen: World Health Organization Regional Office for Europe.

Kirdar, U. (1997). *Cities Fit for People*. New York: UNDP.

Kjellstrom, T., and Hinde, S. (2006). "Car culture, transport policy and public health". In: Kawachi, I., and Wamala, S. (Eds.), *Globalization and Health* (pp. 98–121). New York: Oxford University Press.

Kjellstrom, T., Mercado, S., Sattherthwaite, D., McGranahan, G., Friel, S., and Havemann, K., the Knowledge Network on Urban Settings (2007). *Our Cities, Our Health, Our Future: Acting on Social Determinants for Health Equity in Urban Settings. Report to the WHO Commission on Social Determinants of Health from the Knowledge Network on Urban Settings* [online]. WHO Kobe Centre, Kobe, Japan. Available at: www.who.int/social_determinants/resources/knus_report_16jul07.pdf.

Kolbe, L. J. (2005). "A framework for school health programs in the 21st century". *Journal of School Health*, Vol. 75, Issue 6, pp. 226–228.

Lai, A. (2010). *Evidence-based Healthy City Case Study in Hong Kong*. Fourth Global Conference of Alliance for Healthy City, Gangnam-gu, Seoul, Korea, 27–29 October 2010.

Langford, R., Bonell, C. P., Jones, H. E., Pouliou, T., Murphy, S. M., Waters, E., Komro, K. A., Gibbs, L. F., Magnus, D., and Campbell, R. (2014). "The WHO Health Promoting School framework for improving the health and well-being of students and their academic achievement". *Cochrane Database of Systematic Reviews*, Vol. 4, Art. No. CD008958.

Last, J. M. (Ed.) (1985). "Proceedings of a Working Conference on Healthy Public Policy". *Canadian Journal of Public Health*, Vol. 76, Supp. 1, pp. 1–104.

Lee, A. (2002). "Helping schools to promote healthy educational environments as new initiatives for school-based management: The Hong Kong Healthy Schools Award scheme". *Promotion and Education*, Vol. 9, Supp. 1, pp. 29–32.

Lee, A. (2004a). *Bringing Healthy Cities to Greater Heights through the SPIRIT Framework to Strengthen Networking*. Alliance for Healthy Cities Conference and Inaugural General Assembly, Plenary Presentation, 12–14 October 2004, Kuching, Malaysia.

Lee, A. (2004b). "An analysis of the main factors generating educational changes in Hong Kong to implement the concept of Health Promoting Schools and how the schools responding to the changes". *Promotion and Education*, Vol. 11, Issue 2, pp. 79–84.

Lee, A. (2008). *Report on WHO Consultancy to Lao P.D.R under Agreement of Performance of Work to Provide Consultancy Support to ProLead Team to Build Capacity and Sustain the Momentum for Stronger Health Promotion Policies and Programmes*. Hong Kong: Centre for Health Education and Health Promotion, The Chinese University of Hong Kong.

Lee, A. (2009a). *Healthy City as Ecological Model for Health Improvement and Strengthening Social Capital: Hong Kong Healthy City Projects*. Seongbuk International Conference on Healthy Cities [Conference paper]. Korea, 26–27 August 2009.

Lee, A. (2009b). "Hong Kong: Health promoting school". In: Aldinger, C., and Whitman, C. V. (Eds.), *Case Studies in Global School Health Promotion: From Research to Practice* (pp. 297–314). New York: Springer.

Lee, A. (2009c). *Enhancing Community Resilience within Municipal Setting, to Influenza Pandemic Preparedness and Response, by Empowering Communities to Mitigate the Impact of a Pandemic*. Geneva: WHO.

Lee, A. (2009d). "Health promoting schools: Evidence for a holistic approach in promoting health and improvement of health literacy". *Applied Health Economics and Health Policy*, Vol. 7, Issue 1, pp. 11–17.

Lee, A. (2010a). *Process of Evaluation of Healthy City*. Mayors' meeting of Fourth Global Conference of Alliance for Healthy City, Gangnam-gu, Seoul, Korea, 27–29 October 2010.

Lee, A. (2010b). *Evidence-based Healthy City*. Fourth Global Conference of Alliance for Healthy City, Gangnam-gu, Seoul, Korea, 27–29 October 2010.

Lee, A. (2010c). "Trends in Hong Kong and Macao and other Chinese communities". In: O'Dea, J. A., and Eriksen, M. (Eds.), *Childhood Obesity Prevention: International Research, Controversies, and Intervention* (pp. 117–131). New York: Oxford University Press.

Lee, A. (2011a). "Social capital and health". In: Ng, S. H., Cheung, S. Y. L., and Prakash, B. (Eds.), *Social Capital in Hong Kong — Connectivities and Social Enterprise* (Chapter 6). Hong Kong: City University Press.

Lee, A. (2011b). *Manual for School Health Professionals.* Macao SAR: Department of Education and Youth Affairs, Macao SAR Government.

Lee, A. (2014) *Introduction of Workplace Wellness and Its Benefit.* Healthful Company Seminar. 2 December 2014, Hong Kong.

Lee, A. (2015). *Effective Integration with School System: Health Promotion School as Alternate Model of Schooling.* Health and Social Programs within Education Systems: A Global Dialogue/European Discussion. Organised by International School Heath Network, Education Division of UNESCO, Association for Supervision and Curriculum Development (ASCD), Paris, 31 May–2 June 2015.

Lee, A. (2017). *School Health against Triple Burden of Diseases, Part 2: Non-Communicable Disease.* Centre for Health Education and Health Promotion, Hong Kong. Available at: www.cuhk.edu.hk/med/hep/hchsc/School_Health_part2.pdf.

Lee, A. (2018a). *Enhancing Sustainable Development Goals and Health Equity via Healthy Setting Approach.* Invited Plenary Lecture, Global Conference of Alliance for Health Cities organized by Ministry of Health, Sarawak and Kuching City, Malaysia, 17–20 October.

Lee, A. (2018b). *What Do We Know about Prevention and Health Education?* Kick-off Meeting: Contributing to the UN strategy, Building a Global UNITWIN Network. Organised by UNESCO, Clermont-Auvergne University, the Inter-ministerial Mission for Combating Drugs and Addictive Behaviours, the International Union for Health Promotion and Education, the French League against Cancer and Prev 3.0. UNESCO Headquarter, Paris, 26–27 February 2018. Available at: www.cuhk.edu.hk/med/hep/hchsc/UNESCO.pdf.

Lee, A. (2018c). *Well-being and Mental Health with Business/Social Development Opportunities.* Youth Dialogue: Youth Livelihoods and Wellness through South-South. Hong Kong: Government of Hong Kong (Cyberport), UNOSSC, and UNESCO Hong Kong Association, 29 March 2018.

Lee, A. (2019a). *Evaluation of Korean Healthy Cites: SPIRIT Framework Checklist.* International Forum on Healthy Cities, Gangdong-Su, Korea, 25–26 September 2019.

Lee, A (2019b). "Editorial: Family physician and district health system". *The Hong Kong Practitioner*, Vol. 41, No. 3. Available at: www.hkcfp.org.hk/Upload/HK_Practitioner/2019/hkp2019vol41Sep/editorial.html.

Lee, A. (2019c). *Health Promoting School and School Effectiveness*. Centre for Health Education and Health Promotion, The Chinese University of Hong Kong. Available at: www.cuhk.edu.hk/med/hep/hchsc/HPS%20&%20School%20Effectivenes.pdf, accessed 22 November 2019.

Lee, A. (2019d) *Managing Human Resources: Promoting Staff Well-being and Enhancing Productivity*. South-South Entrepreneurship Academy Conference: Building Global Citizenship and Harnessing Entrepreneurial Skills and Mindset through South-South Cooperation, "Technology, Financial Innovation and Entrepreneurship". Organised by the United Nation Office of South-South Co-operation (UNOSSC) and the Centre for Business/Social Sustainability and Innovations (BSSI), School of Business, Gratia Christian College. 3–4 April 2019, Hong Kong.

Lee, A. (2019e). *Setting Approach for Effective Prevention and Heath Promotion*. Centre for Health Education and Health Promotion, Hong Kong, The Chinese University of Hong Kong. Available at: www.cuhk.edu.hk/med/hep/hchsc/Setting_approach_prevention.pdf, last accessed 22 November 2019.

Lee, A. (2020). *Rights to Health: What Type(s) of Health Care?* 60th Annual Health Law and Legal Medicine: The Old, the New, and the Now in conjunction with the 13th Annual Ethical and Legal Aspects of Dentistry Conference, Scottsdale, Arizona, USA, 20–23 February 2020.

Lee, A., and Cheung, M. B. (2017). "School as setting to create a healthy learning environment for teaching and learning using the model of Health Promoting School to foster school-health partnership". *Journal of Professional Capital and Community*, Vol. 2, Issue 4, pp. 200–214.

Lee, A., and Chuh, A. A. T. (2010). "Facing the threat of influenza pandemic: Roles of and implications to general practitioners". *BMC Public Health*, Vol. 10, Art. No. 661.

Lee, A., and de Leeuw, E. (2009). *Municipal Approaches to Community Response and Resilience in the Face of Pandemic Influenza A H1N1*. "Strengthening Community Responses to Pandemics: A Settings Approach", 26 October 2009. Seventh Global Conference on Health Promotion, Nairobi, 26–30 October 2009.

Lee, A., and Gibbs, S. E. (2013). "Neurobiology of food addiction and adolescent obesity prevention in low and middle-income countries". *Journal of Adolescent Health*, Vol. 52, Issue 2, Supp. 2, pp. S39–S42.

Lee, A., and Keung, V. M. W. (2012). "Epidemics of childhood obesity among Chinese children and effectiveness of school-based interventions". *Health Education Monograph Series*, Vol. 29, Issue 1, pp. 37–46.

Lee, A., and Poon, P. K. K. (2020). "District health systems and capacity building". In: Fong, B. Y. F., Law, V. T. S., and Lee, A. (Eds.), *Primary Care Revisited: Interdisciplinary Perspectives for a New Era* (pp. 369–381). Singapore: Springer.

Lee, A., and Wei, R. (2018). *District-level Primary Care in Hong Kong: 'Current Practice and Future Development' in Kwai Tsing*. Community Health Care Conference Organised by Caritas Institute of Higher Education and Open University of Hong Kong, Hong Kong.

Lee, A., Chan, K., Wun, Y. T., Ma, P. L., Li, L., and Siu, P. C. (1995). "A morbidity survey in Hong Kong 1994". *Hong Kong Practitioner*, Vol. 17, Issue 6, pp. 246–255.

Lee, A., Tsang, K. K., Lee, S. H., and To, C. Y. (2000). "'Healthy Schools Program' in Hong Kong: Enhancing positive health behavior for school children and teachers". *Special Joint Issue of Education for Health, and Annals of Behavior Science and Medical Education*, Vol. 13, Issue 3, pp. 399–403.

Lee, A., Cheng, F. F. K., Yuen, H., Ho, M., and Healthy Schools Support Group. (2003a). "How would schools step up public health measure to control spread of SARS?" *Journal of Epidemiology and Community Health*, Vol. 57, Issue 12, pp. 945–949.

Lee, A., Tsang, C., Lee, S. H., and To, C. (2003b). "A comprehensive 'Healthy Schools Programme' to promote school health: The Hong Kong experience in joining the efforts of health and education". *Journal of Epidemiology and Community Health*, Vol. 57, Issue 3, pp. 174–177.

Lee, A., Tsang, C. K. K., and Healthy School Research Support Group. (2004a). "Youth risk behaviour in a Chinese population: A territory-wide youth risk behavioural surveillance in Hong Kong". *Public Health*, Vol. 118, Issue 2, pp. 88–95.

Lee, A., Chow, C. B., Cheng, F. (2004b). *Kwai Tsing Safe and Healthy City: Community Diagnosis*. Centre for Health Education and Health Promotion, The Chinese University of Hong Kong and Kwai Tsing District Council. Available at: www.cuhk.edu.hk/med/hep/research/pdf/reports/Kwai%20Tsing%202004.pdf (in Chinese).

Lee, A., Cheng, F. F. K., St Leger, L. (2005a). "Evaluating health promoting schools in Hong Kong: The development of a framework". *Health Promotion International*, Vol. 20, Issue 2, pp. 177–186.

Lee, A., St Leger, L., and Moon, A. M. (2005b). "Evaluating health promotion in schools meeting the needs for education and health professionals: A case study of developing appropriate indicators and data collection methods in Hong Kong". *Promotion and Education*, Vol. 20, Issue 2, pp. 177–186.

Lee, A., Cheng, F., Fung, Y., St Leger, L. (2006). "Can Health Promoting Schools contribute to the better health and well-being of young people: Hong Kong experience?" *Journal of Epidemiology and Community Health*, Vol. 60, Issue 6, pp. 530–536.

Lee, A., Kiyu, A., Milman, H. M., and Jimenez, J. (2007a). "Improving health and building human capital through an effective primary care system". *Journal of Urban Health*, Vol. 84, Supp. 1, pp. 75–85.

Lee, A., Cheng, F., St Leger, L., and Hong Kong Healthy School Team. (2007b). "The status of Health Promoting Schools in Hong Kong and implications for further development". *Health Promotion International*, Vol. 22, Issue 4, pp. 316–326.

Lee, A., Cheng, F., Yuen, H., Ho, M., Lo, A., and Leung, T. (2007c). "Achieving good standards in health promoting schools: Preliminary analysis one-year after the implementation of the Hong Kong Healthy Schools Award scheme". *Public Health*, Vol. 121, Issue 10, pp. 752–760.

Lee, A., St Leger, L., Cheng, F. F. K., and Hong Kong Healthy School Team. (2007d). "The status of health-promoting schools in Hong Kong and implications for further development". *Health Promotion International*, Vol. 22, Issue 4, pp. 316–326.

Lee, A., Fu, H., and Ji, C. Y. (2007e). "Health promotion activities in China from the Ottawa Charter to the Bangkok Charter: Revolution to evolution". *Promotion and Education*, Vol. XIV, Issue 4, pp. 219–223.

Lee, A., Wong, M. C. S., Keung, V. M. W., Yuen, H. S. K., Cheng, F. F. K., and Mok, J. S. Y. (2008). "Can the concept of Health Promoting Schools help to improve students' health knowledge and practices to combat the challenge of communicable diseases: Case study in Hong Kong?" *BMC Public Health*, Vol. 8, Art. No. 42. Available at: https://doi.org/10.1186/1471-2458-8-42.

Lee, A., Ho, M., and Keung, V. M. W. (2010a). "Healthy school as an ecological model for prevention of childhood obesity". *Research in Sports Medicine*, Vol. 18, Issue 1, pp. 49–61.

Lee, A., Siu, C. F., Leung, K. T., Lau, L. C., Chan, C. C., and Wong, K. K. (2010b). "General practice and social service partnership for better clinical outcomes, patient self-efficacy and lifestyle behaviours of diabetic care: Randomised control trial of a chronic care model". *Postgraduate Medical Journal*, Vol. 87, Issue 1032, pp. 688–693.

Lee, A., Ho, M., and Keung, V. M. W. (2011). "Global epidemics of childhood obesity is hitting a quiet corner in Asia: Case study in Macao". *International Journal of Paediatric Obesity*, Vol. 6, Supp. 3, pp. e252–e256.

Lee, A., Keung, V. M. W., Lo, A. S. C., Kwong, A. C. M., and Armstrong, E. S. (2014a). "Framework for evaluating efficacy in Health Promoting Schools". *Health Education*, Vol. 114, Issue 3, pp. 225–242.

Lee, A., Ho, M., Kwong, A., and Keung, A. (2014b). "Childhood obesity management shifting from health care system to school system: Intervention study of school-based weight management programme". *BMC Public Health*, Vol. 14, No. 1128.

Lee, A., Ho, M., Keung, V. M. W., and Kwong, A. C. M. (2014c). "Childhood obesity management shifting from health care system to school system: Intervention study of school-based weight management programme". *BMC Public Health*, Vol. 14, Art. No. 1128.

Lee, A., Chua, H. W., Chan, M., Leung, P. W. L., Wong, J. W. S., and Chuh, A. A. T. (2015a). "Health disparity still exists in an economically well-developed society in Asia". *PLoS One*, Vol. 10, No. 6, e0130424.

Lee, A., Keung, M. W., Tam, W., and Ho, K. (2015b). *Assessment of Dietary Patten and Nutritional Status in Macao School Children*. Hong Kong: Centre for Health Education and Health Promotion, Jockey Club School of Public Health and Primary Care, The Chinese University of Hong Kong.

Lee, A., Keung, V., Lo, A., and Kwong, A. (2016). "Healthy school environment to tackle youth mental health crisis". *Hong Kong Journal of Paediatrics*, Vol. 21, Issue 2, pp. 134–135.

Lee, A., Cheung, C. K. M., Lo, K., Keung, V. M. W., Mui, L. W. H., and Tam, W. W. S. (2017). "Studying impact of nutrition on growth (SING): A prospective cohort for comparing the health outcomes of young children with the dietary quality score". *BMJ Open*, Vol. 7, Issue 11, e018380.

Lee, A., St Leger, L. H., Ling, K. W. K., Keung, V. M. W., Lo, A. S. C., Kwong, A. C. M., Ma, H. P. S., and Armstrong, E. S. (2018a). "The Hong Kong Healthy Schools Award scheme, school health and student health: An exploratory study". *Health Education Journal*, Vol. 77, Issue 8, pp. 857–871.

Lee, A., Chan, C. H. Y., and Tse, H. H. Y. (2018b). *"Healthy Plan-Net": Advancing Health Literacy to Meet Health Education Needs* [online]. Available at: www.cuhk. edu.hk/med/hep/hchsc/Healthy%20Plan-Net.pdf.

Lee, A., Lo, A. S. C., Keung, M. W., Kwong, C. M., Wong, K. K. (2019). "Effective health promoting school for better health of children and adolescents: Indicators for success". *BMC Public Health*, Vol. 19, Art. No. 1088. Available at: https://doi. org/10.1186/s12889-019-7425-6.

Leyden, K. M. (2003). "Social capital and the built environment: The importance of walkable neighborhoods". *American Journal of Public Health*, Vol. 93, No. 9, pp. 1546–1551.

Lieu, C., Janssen, W. J., Saint, S., and Dhaliwal, G. (2009). "The tip of iceberg". *Journal of Hospital Medicine*, Vol. 16, Issue 4, pp. 317–320.

Lineback, N., and Lineback Gritzner, M. (2014). "Geography in the news: The growth of megacities". *National Geographic*, 17 February 2014.

Lo, Y. Y. C., Lam, C. L. K., Lam, T. P., Lee, A., Lee, R., Chiu, B., Tang, J., Chiu, B., Chao, D., Lam, A., and Chan, K. (2010). "Hong Kong primary care morbidity survey 2007–08". *Hong Kong Practitioner*, Vol. 32, Issue 1, pp. 17–26.

Lock, K., and Hillier, R. (2010). "The prevention of childhood obesity in primary care settings: Evidence and practice". In: Waters, E., Swinburn, B. A., Seidell, J. C., and Uauy, R. (Eds.), *Preventing Childhood Obesity: Evidence, Policy and Practice* (pp. 94–104). Oxford, UK: Wiley-Blackwell.

Lopez, A. D., Shibuya, K., Rao, C., Mathers, C. D., Hansell, A. L., Held, L. S., Schmid, V., and Buist, S. (2006). "Chronic obstructive pulmonary disease: Current burden and future projections". *European Respiratory Journal*, Vol. 27, Issue 2, pp. 397–412.

Lorig, K. (2003). "Self-management education: More than a nice extra". *Medical Care*, Vol. 41, Issue 6, pp. 699–701.

Mackay, S. (2011). "Legislative solutions to unhealthy eating and obesity in Australia". *Public Health*, Vol. 125, Issue 12, pp. 896–904.

Macintyre, S., and Ellaway, A. (2003). "Neighbourhoods and health: An overview". In: Kawachi, I., and Berkman, B. (Eds.), *Neighbourhoods and Health* (pp. 21–42). Oxford: Oxford University Press.

Macnab, A. J., Gagnon, F. A., and Stewart, D. (2014a). "Health promoting schools: Consensus, strategies, and potential". *Health Education*, Vol. 114, Issue 3, pp. 170–185.

Macnab, A. J., Stewart, D., and Gagnon, F. A. (2014b). "Health promoting schools: Initiatives in Africa". *Health education*, Vol. 114, No. 4, pp. 246–259.

Magnusson, R. S. (2008a). "What's law got to do with it? Part 1: A framework for obesity prevention". *Australia and New Zealand Health Policy*, Vol. 5, Art. No. 10.

Magnusson, R. S. (2008b). "What's law got to do with it? Part II: Legal strategies for healthier nutrition and obesity prevention". *Australia and New Zealand Health Policy*, Vol. 5, Art. No. 11.

Magnusson, R. S., Gostin, I. O., and Studdert, D. M. (2011). "Can law improve prevention and treatment of cancer?" *Public Health*, Vol. 125, Issue 12, pp. 813–820.

Mamudu, H. M., Hammond, R., and Glantz, S. A. (2011). "International trade versus public health during the FCTC negotiations, 1999-2003". *Tobacco Control*, Vol. 20, e3.

Marmot, M., and Bell, R. (2012). "Fair society, healthy lives". *Public Health*, Vol. 126, Supp. 1, pp. S4–10.

Marmot, M., Friel, S., Bell, R., Houweling, T. A., Taylor, S., and Commission on Social Determinants of Health. (2008). "Closing the gap in a generation: Health equity through action on the social determinants of health". *Lancet*, Vol. 372, Issue 9650, pp. 1661–1669.

Marmot, M., Goldblatt, P., and Allen, J. (2010). *Fair Society, Healthy Lives: The Marmot Review* [online]. Institute of Health Equity website. Available at: www.instituteofhealthequity.org/resources-reports/fair-society-healthy-lives-the-marmot-review.

McCallum, Z., Wake, M., Gerner, B., Baur, L. A., Gibbons, K., Gold, L., Gunn, J., Harris, C., Naughton, G., Riess, C., Sanci, L., Sheehan, J., Ukoumunne, O. C., and Waters, E. (2007). "Outcome data from the LEAP (Live, Eat and Play) trial: A randomised controlled trial of a primary care intervention for childhood overweight/ mild obesity". *International Journal of Obesity*, Vol. 31, Issue 4, pp. 630–636.

McKeown, T., and Lowe, C. R. (1974). *An Introduction to Social Medicine* (2nd edition). London: Blackwell Scientific Publications.

McKee, M., Haines, A., Ebrahim, S., Lamptey, P., Barreto, M. L., Matheson, D., Walls, H. L., Foliaki, S., Miranda, J. J., Chimeddamba, O., Garcia-Marcos, L., Vineis, P., and Pearce, N. (2014). "Towards a comprehensive global approach to prevention and control of NCDs". *Globalisation and Health*, Vol. 10, Art. No. 74.

McLafferty, S., and Grady, S. (2005). "Immigration and geographic access to prenatal clinics in Brooklyn, NY: A geographic information system analysis". *American Journal of Public Health*, Vol. 95, No. 4, pp. 638–640.

Mendez, M. A., and Popkin, B. M. (2004). "Globalisation, urbanisation and nutritional change in the developing world". *Electronic Journal of Agricultural and Development Economics*, Vol. 1, Issue 2, pp. 220–241.

Mercer, S. W., and Tessier, S. (2001). "A qualitative study of general practitioners' and practice nurses' attitudes to obesity management in primary care". *Health Bulletin*, Vol. 59, Issue 4, pp. 248–253.

Micha, R., Khtibzadeh, S., Shi, P., Fahimi, S., Lim, S., Andrews, K. G., Engell, R. E., Powles, J., Ezzati, M., Mozaffarian, D., and the Global Burden of Diseases Nutrition and Chronic Diseases Expert Group (NutriCoDE). (2014). Global, regional, and national consumption levels of dietary fats and oils in 1990 and 2010: A systematic analysis including 266 country-specific nutrition surveys. *BMJ*, Vol. 348, p. g2272.

Mitchell, G. (2000). "Indicators as tools to guide progress on the sustainable development pathway". In: Lawrence, R. J. (Ed.), *Sustainable Human Settlement: A Challenge for the New Millennium* (pp. 55–104). North Shields, England: Urban International Press.

Monasta, L., Batty, G. D., Cattaneo, A., Lutje, V., Ronfani, L., Van Lenthe, F. J., and Brug, J. (2010). "Early-life determinants of overweight and obesity: A review of systematic reviews". *Obesity Reviews*, Vol. 11, Issue 10, pp. 695–708.

Montano, D., Hoven, H., and Siegrist, J. (2014). "Effects of organisational-level interventions at work on employees' health: A systematic review". *BMC Public Health*, Vol. 14, Art. No. 135.

Moon, A. M., Mullee, M. A., Rogers, L., Thompson, R. L., Speller, V., and Roderick, P. (1999a). "Health-related research and evaluation in schools". *Health Education*, Vol. 1, pp. 27–34.

Moon, A. M., Mullee, M. A., Rogers, L., Thompson, R. L., Speller, V., and Roderick, P. (1999b). "Helping schools to become health-promoting environments: An evaluation of the Wessex Healthy Schools Award". *Health Promotion International*, Vol. 14, Issue 2, pp. 111–122.

Moon, J. Y., Nam, E. W., and Dhakal, S. (2014). "Empowerment for healthy cities and communities in Korea". *Journal of Urban Health*, Vol. 91, No. 5, pp. 886–893.

Moy, F., Sallam, A. A. B., and Wong, M. (2006). "The results of a worksite health promotion programme in Kuala Lumpur, Malaysia". *Health Promotion International*, Vol. 21, Issue 4, pp. 301–310.

Moynihan, S., Jourdan, D., and McNamara, P. M. (2016). "An examination of health promoting schools in Ireland". *Health Education*, Vol. 116, Issue 1, pp. 16–33.

Muijs, D., and Reynolds, D. (2001). *Effective Teaching: Evidence and Practice*. London: Paul Chapman Publishing.

Nakamura, K. (2003). "Indicators for Healthy Cities: Tools for evidence-based urban policy formation". In: Takano, T. (Ed.), *Healthy Cities and Urban Policy Research* (pp. 76–103). London: Routledge.

Nam, E. W., and Engelhardt, K. (2007). "Health promotion capacity mapping: The Korean situation". *Health Promotion International*, Vol. 22, Issue 2, pp. 155–162.

Nam, E. W., Moon, J., and Lee, A. (2010). "Evaluation of Healthy City Project using SPIRIT checklist: Wonju City case". *Korean Journal of Health Education and Promotion*, Vol. 27, No. 5, pp. 15–25.

Nam, E. W., de Leeuw, E., Moon, J. Y., Ikeda, N., Dorjsuren, B., and Park, M. B. (2011). "Sustainable funding of health initiatives in Wonju, Republic of Korea via a tobacco consumption tax". *Health Promotion International*, Vol. 26, Issue 4, pp. 457–464.

National Health Services [NHS] Providers. (2017). *Providers Voices — Public Health: Everyone's Business?* London, UK: Foundation Trust Network. Available at: https://nhsproviders.org/provider-voices-public-health.

National Institute of Health [NIH]. (2021) *National Institute on Alcohol Abuse and Alcoholism: Alcohol's Effects on Health*. Available at: www.niaaa.nih.gov/alcohols-effects-health, accessed 13 April 2021.

National Institute for Health and Clinical Excellence [NICE]. (2006). *CG43 Obesity: Full Guideline, Section 5a-Management of Obesity in Clinical Settings (Children): Evidence Statements and Reviews*. London: NICE.

Naylor, C., and Buck, D. (2018). *The Role of Cities in Improving Health: International Insights*. London, UK: The King's Funds.

Niessen, L. W., Mohan, D., Akuoku, J. K., Mirelman, A. J., Ahmed, S., Koehlmoos, T. P., Trujillo, A., Khan, J., and Peters, D. H. (2018). "Tackling socioeconomic inequalities and non-communicable diseases in low-income and middle-income countries under the Sustainable Development agenda". *Lancet*, Vol. 391, Issue 10134, pp. 2036–2046.

Norheim, O. F., Jha, P., Admasu, K., Godal, T., Hum, R. J., Kruk, M. E., Gómez-Dantés, O., Mathers, C. D., Pan, H., Sepúlveda, J., and Suraweera, W. (2015) "Avoiding 40% of the premature deaths in each country, 2010–30: Review of national mortality trends to help quantify the UN Sustainable Development Goal for health". *Lancet*, Vol. 385, Issue 9964, pp. 239–252.

Norris, S. L., Engelgau, M. M., and Narayan, K. M. (2001). "Effectiveness of self-management training in type two diabetes: A systematic review of randomised controlled trials". *Diabetes Care*, Vol. 24, Issue 3, pp. 561–587.

Nutbeam, D. (1996). "Health outcomes and health promotion-defining success in health promotion". *Health Promotion Journal of Australia*, Vol. 6, Issue 2, pp. 58–60.

Nutbeam, D. (2000). "Health literacy as a public health goal: A challenge for contemporary health education and communication strategies into the 21st century". *Health Promotion International*, Vol. 15, Issue 3, pp. 259–267.

Nutbeam, D. (2008). "The evolving concept of health literacy". *Social Science and Medicine*, Vol. 67, Issue 12, pp. 2072–2078.

Nutbeam, D., Smith, C., Murphy, S. and Catford, J. (1993). "Maintaining evaluation designs in long-term community-based health promotion programmes: Heartbeat Waltes case study". *Journal of Epidemiology and Community Health*, Vol. 47, Issue 2, pp. 127–133.

Ogawa, H. (2002). "Healthy cities programme in the Western Pacific Region". *Promotion and Education*, Supp. 1, pp. 10–12.

Ompad, D. C., Galea, S., Caiaffa, W. T., and Vlahov, D. (2007). "Social determinants of the health of urban populations: methodologic considerations". *Journal of Urban Health*, Vol. 84, Supp. 1, pp. i42–i53.

O'Neill, O. (2005). "The dark side of human rights". *International Affairs*, Vol. 81, Issue 2, pp. 427–439.

O'Neill, M., and Simard, P. (2006). "Choosing indicators to evaluate Healthy Cities projects: A political task?" *Health Promotion International*, Vol. 21, Issue 2, pp. 145–152.

Pacione, M. (2003). "Urban environmental quality and human well-being: A social geographic perspectives". *Landscape and Urban Planning*, Vol. 65, Issue 1–2, pp. 19–30.

Panter, J. R., and Jones, A. (2010). "Attitudes and environment as determinants of active travel in adults: what do and don't we know?" *Journal of Physical Activity and Health*, Vol. 7, Issue 4, pp. 551–561.

Paton, K., Sengupta, S., and Hassan, L. (2005). "Setting, systems and organisation development: The Healthy Living and Working Model". *Health Promotion International*, Vol. 20, Issue 1, pp. 81–89.

Patrick, K., Calfas, K. J., Norman, G. J., Zabinski, M. F., Sallis, J. F., Rupp, J., Covin, J., and Cella, J. (2006). "Randomised control trial of a primary care and home-based intervention for physical activity and nutrition behaviours: PACE+ for adolescents". *Archives of Pediatrics and Adolescent Medicine*, Vol. 160, Issue 2, pp. 128–136.

Patterson, R., McNamara, E., Tainio, M., de Sá, T. H., Smith, A. D., Sharp, S. J., Edwards, P., Woodcock, J., Brage, S., and Wijndaele, K. (2018). "Sedentary behaviour and risk of all-cause, cardiovascular and cancer mortality, and incident type 2 diabetes: A systematic review and dose response meta-analysis". *European Journal of Epidemiology*, Vol. 33, No. 9, pp. 811–829.

Patton, G., Bond, L., Carlin, J. B., Thomas, L., Butler, H., Glover, S., Catalano, R., and Bowes, G. (2006). "Promoting social inclusion in schools: A group-randomised trial of effects on student health risk behaviour and well-being". *American Journal of Public Health*, Vol. 96, Issue 9, pp. 1582–1587.

Pawson, R., and Tilley, N. (1997). *Realistic Evaluation*. Thousand Oaks, CA: SAGE Publications.

Pelikan, J. M., Dietscher, C., Röthlin, F., and Schmied, H. (2010). *Hospitals as Organisational Settings for Health and Health Promotion*. Vienna, Ludwig Boltzmann Institute for Health Promotion Research, Working Paper 5.

Pelletier, K. R. (2001). "A review and analysis of the clinical- and cost-effectiveness studies of comprehensive health promotion and disease management programs at the worksite: 1998–2000 update". *American Journal of Health Promotion*, Vol. 16, Issue 2, pp. 107–116.

Poland, B. D., Green, L. W., and Rootman, I. (2000). "Reflections on settings for health promotion". In: Poland, B. D., Green, L. W., and Rootman, I. (Eds.), *Settings for Health Promotion: Linking Theory and Practice* (pp. 341–351). Thousand Oaks, CA: SAGE Publications.

Polit, K. M. (2005). "The effects of inequality and relative marginality on the well-being of low caste people in central Uttaranchal". *Anthropology and Medicine,* Vol. 12, Issue 3, pp. 225–237.

Potenza, M. N. (2013). "Biological contributions to addictions in adolescents and adults: Prevention, treatment, and policy implication". *Journal of Adolescent Health,* Vol. 52, Issue 2, Supp. 2, pp. S22–S32.

Protheroe, J., Woolf, M. S., and Lee, A. (2011). "Health literacy and health outcomes". In: Begoray, D. L., Gillis, D., and Rowlands, G. (Eds.), *Health Literacy in Context: International Perspectives* (Chapter 4). New York: Nova Science Publishers.

Radio Television Hong Kong [RTHK]. (2016). *Voluntary Health Insurance Not Solving the Root of the Problem for Healthcare Delivery System.* Family Letter to Hong Kong on Voluntary Health Insurance, 10 December 2016 [online]. Available at: http://app3.rthk.hk/special/pau/article.php?aid=2166.

Reubi, D. (2011). "The promise of human rights for global health: A programmed deception? A commentary on Schrecker, Chapman, Labonté and De Vogli (2010), 'Advancing health equity in the global market place: How human rights can help'". *Social Science and Medicine,* Vol. 73, Issue 5, pp. 625–628.

Reilly, J. J., and Kelly, J. (2011). "Long-term impact of overweight and obesity in childhood and adolescence on morbidity and premature mortality in adulthood: Systematic review". *International Journal of Obesity,* Vol. 35, Issue 7, pp. 891–898.

Richardson, B. W. (1876). *Hygeia: A City of Health.* London: Macmillan and Co.

Rogers, E. M. (1995). *Diffusion of Innovations* (4th edition). New York: The Free Press.

Roof, K., and Oleru, N. (2008) "Public health: Seattle and King County's push for the built environment". *Journal of Environmental Health,* Vol. 71, No. 1, pp. 24–27.

Room, R., Schmidt, L., Rehm, J., and Mäkelä, P., (2008). "International regulation of alcohol". *BMJ,* Vol. 337, p. a2364.

Rydin, Y., Bleahu, A., Davies, M., Dávila, J. D., Friel, S., De Grandis, G., Groce, N., Hallal, P. C., Hamilton, I., Howden-Chapman, P., Lai, K. M., Lim, C. J., Martins, J., Osrin, D., Ridley, I., Scott, I., Taylor, M., Wilkinson, P., and Wilson, J. (2012). "Shaping cities for health: Complexity and the planning of urban environments in the 21st century". *Lancet*, Vol. 379, No. 9831, pp. 2079–2108.

Sassi, F., Belloni, A., Mirelman, A. J., Suhrcke, M., Thomas, A., Salti, N., Vellakkal, S., Visaruthvong, C., Popkin, B. M., and Nugent, R. (2018). "Equity impacts of price policies to promote healthy behaviours". *Lancet*, Vol. 391, Issue 10134, pp. 2059–2070.

Schmidt, H., Gostin, L. O., and Emanuel, E. J. (2015). "Public health, universal health coverage and sustainable development goals: Can they co-exist?" *Lancet*, Vol. 386, Issue 9996, pp. 928–930.

Schrecker, T., Chapman, A. R., Labonté, R., and de Vogli, R. (2010). "Advancing equity on the global marketplace: How human rights can help". *Social Science and Medicine*, Vol. 71, Issue 8, pp. 1520–1526.

Scottish Government. (2011). *Health of Scotland's Population — Obesity* [online]. Available at: www.webarchive.org.uk/wayback/archive/20150218140148/http://www.gov.scot/Topics/Statistics/Browse/Health/TrendObesity.

Sidebotham, P. (2017). "Fatal child maltreatment". In: Dixon, L., Perkins, D. F., Hamilton-Giachritsis, C., and Craig, L. A. (Eds.), *Wiley Handbook of What Works in Child Maltreatment: An Evidence-based Approach to Assessment and Intervention in Child Protection* (pp. 48–70). Hoboken, NJ: Wiley-Blackwell.

Sirgy, M. J., Rahtz, D. R., Cicic, M., and Underwood, R. (2000). "A method for assessing residents' satisfaction with community-based services: A quality-of-life perspective". *Social Indicators Research*, Vol. 49, No. 3, pp. 279–316.

Siu, D., Lee, A., Chen, R., Chu, L., and Fung, Y. (2004). *Community Diagnosis on a Local District of Hong Kong: Future Direction for Local Government in Creating a Healthy Living Environment*. The 18th World Conference on Health Promotion and Health Education, International Union for Health Promotion and Education, Melbourne, Australia, 26–30 April 2004.

Smedley, B. D., and Syme, S. L. (2000). *Promoting Health Intervention Strategies from Social and Behavioural Research, Committee on Capitalising on Social Science and Behavioural Research to Improve the Public's Health*. Washington, DC: National Academies Press.

Snow, J. (1849). *On the Mode of Communication of Cholera*. London: John Churchill.

Sørensen, K., Van den Broucke, S., Fullam, J., Doyle, G., Pelikan, J., Slonska, Z., Brand., H., and (HLS-EU) Consortium Health Literacy Project European. (2012). "Health literacy and public health: A systematic review and integration of definitions and models". *BMC Public Health*, Vol. 12, Art. No. 80.

Spear, L. P. (2013). "Adolescent neurodevelopment". *Journal of Adolescent Health*, Vol. 52, Issue 2, Supp. 2, pp. S7–S13.

Stewart, W. F., Ricci, J. A., Chee, E., Morganstein, D., and Lipton, R. (2003). "Lost productive time and cost due to common pain conditions in the US workforce". *Journal of the American Medical Association*, Vol. 290, Issue 18, pp. 2443–2454.

St Leger, L. (2001). "Schools, health literacy and public health: Possibilities and challenges". *Health Promotion International*, Vol. 16, Issue 2, pp. 197–205.

St Leger, L. H. (2005). "Protocols and guidelines for health promoting schools". *Promotion and Education*, Vol. 12, Issue 3-4, pp. 145–147.

St Leger, L. H., and Nutbeam, D. (2000a). "Research in health promoting schools". *Journal of School Health*, Vol. 70, Issue 6, pp. 257–259.

St Leger, L., and Nutbeam, D. (2000b). "A model for mapping linkages between health and education agencies to improve school health". *Journal of School Health*, Vol. 70, Issue 2, pp. 45–50.

St Leger, L., and Young, I. M. (2009). "Creating the document 'Promoting Health in Schools: From Evidence to Action'". *Global Health Promotion*, Vol. 16, Issue 4, pp. 69–71.

St Leger, L., Kolbe, L., Lee, A., McCall, D. S., and Young, I. M. (2007). "School health: Achievements, challenges and priorities". In: McQueen, D. V., and Jones, C. M. (Eds.), *Global Perspective on Health Promotion Effectiveness* (pp. 107–124). New York: Springer.

St Leger, L. H., Young, I., Blanchard, C., Perry, M. (2010). *Promoting Health in Schools: From Evidence to Action*. Paris: International Union for Health Promotion and Education. Available at: https://dashbc.ca/wp-content/uploads/2013/03/Promoting_Health_in_Schools_from_Evidence_to_Action.pdf.

Steckler, A., McLeroy, K. R., Goodman, R. M., Bird, S. T., and McCormick, L. (1992). "Towards integrating qualitative and quantitative methods: An introduction". *Health Education Quarterly*, Vol. 19, Issue 1, pp. 1–8.

Stewart-Brown, S. (2006). *What is the Evidence on School Health Promotion in Improving School Health or Preventing Disease and Specifically What is the Effectiveness of the Health Promoting Schools Approach?* Copenhagen: World Health Organisation.

Stewart-Brown, S., Tennant, A., Tennant, R., Platt, S., Parkinson, J., and Weich, S. (2009). "Internal construct validity of the Warwick-Edinburgh Mental Well-being Scale (WEMWBS): A Rasch analysis using data from the Scottish Health Education Population Survey". *Health and Quality of Life Outcomes*, Vol. 7, Art. No. 15, p. 15.

Stone, L. (2020). "General practice, COVID-19 and living with uncertainty". *Australian Journal of General Practice*, Vol. 49, Supp. 3.

Swinburn, B. A. (2008). "Obesity prevention: The role of policies, laws and regulations". *Australia and New Zealand Health Policy*, Vol. 5, Art. No. 12.

Swinburn, B. A., and de Silva-Sanigorski, A. M. (2010). "Where to from here for preventing childhood obesity: An international perspective". *Obesity (Silver Spring)*, Vol. 8, Supp. 1, pp. S4–S7.

Symons, C. W., Cincelli, B., James, T. C., and Groff, P. (1997). "Bridging student health risks and academic achievement through comprehensive school health programs". *Journal of School Health*, Vol. 67, Issue 6, pp. 220–227.

Takano, T. (2003). "Examples of research activities for Healthy Cities". In: Takano, T. (Ed.), *Healthy Cities and Urban Policy Research* (pp. 172–199). London: Routledge.

Takano, T., Nakamura, K., and Watanabe, M. (2002a). "Urban residential environments and senior citizens' longevity in megacity areas: The importance of walkable green spaces". *Journal of Epidemiology and Community Health*, Vol. 56, Issue 12, pp. 913–918.

Takano, T., Fu, J., Nakamura, K., Uji, K., Fukuda, Y., Watanabe, M., and Nakajima, H. (2002b). "Age-adjusted mortality and its association to variations in urban conditions in Shanghai". *Health Policy*, Vol. 61, Issue 3, pp. 239–253.

Taras, H. (2005a). "Nutrition and student performance at school". *Journal of School Health*, Vol. 75, Issue 6, pp. 199–213.

Taras, H. (2005b). "Physical activity and student performance at school". *Journal of School Health*, Vol. 75, Issue 6, pp. 214–218.

Taras, H., and Potts-Datema, W. (2005). "Obesity and student performance at school". *Journal of School Health*, Vol. 75, Issue 8, pp. 291–295.

Tasioulas, J., and Vayena, E. (2015). "Getting human rights right in global health policy". *Lancet*, Vol. 385, Issue 9978, pp. e42–e44.

Taylor, M. (2012). *Cities, Health and Well-being: Urban Age Conference Report 16–17 November 2011, Hong Kong.* London: LSE Cities: London School of Economic and Political Science. Available at: https://lsecities.net/wp-content/uploads/2012/06/Cities-Health-and-Well-being-Conference-Report_June-2012.pdf.

Thompson, S. R., Watson, M. C., and Tilford, S. (2018). "The Ottawa Charter 30 years on: Still an important standard for health promotion". *International Journal of Health Promotion and Education*, Vol. 56, Issue 2, pp. 73–84.

Timperio, A., Salmon, J., and Ball, K. (2004). "Evidence-based strategies to promote physical activity among children, adolescents and young adults: Review and update". *Journal of Science and Medicine in Sport*, Vol. 7, Issue 1, Supp. 1, pp. 20–29.

Tones, K. (1997). "Beyond the randomised controlled trial: A case for 'judicial review'". *Health Education Research*, Vol. 12, Issue 2, p. 161.

Tones, K. (1998). "Effectiveness in health promotion: Indicators and evidence of success". In: Weston, R., and Scott, D. (Eds.), *Evaluating Health Promotion* (pp. 49–74). Cheltenham: Stanley Thornes.

Tones, K., and Green, J. (2004). *Health Promotion: Planning and Strategies.* London: SAGE Publications.

Tones, K., and Tilford, S. (2001). *Health Education: Effectiveness, Efficiency and Equity* (2nd edition). London: Nelson Thornes.

Topiwala, A., Allan, C. L., Valkanova, V., Zsoldos, E., Filippini, N., Sexton, C., Mahmood, A., Fooks, P., Singh-Manoux, A., Mackay, C. E., Kivimäki, M., and Ebmeier, K. P. (2017). "Moderate alcohol consumption as risk factor for adverse brain outcomes and cognitive decline: Longitudinal cohort study". *BMJ*, Vol. 357, p. j2353.

Tsouros, A. D. (1991). "Review of progress 1987 to 1990". In: *World Health Organization Health Cities Project: A Project Becomes a Movement.* Milan: Sorgress.

Tsouros, A. (1993). *World Health Organisation Healthy Cities Project: A Project Becomes a Movement.* Milan: Sorgress.

Tsouros, A. (2000). "Why urban health cannot be ignored: The way forward". *Reviews on Environmental Health*, Vol. 15, Issue 1–2, pp. 267–271.

Tsouros, A. (2013). "City leadership for health and well-being: Back to the future". *Journal of Urban Health*, Vol. 90, Supp. 1, pp. 4–13.

Tsouros, A. D. (2015). "Twenty-seven years of the WHO European Healthy Cities movement: A sustainable movement for change and innovation at the local level". *Health Promotion International*, Vol. 30, Supp. 1, pp. 3–7.

Tsouros, A., and Draper, R. A. (1993). "The Healthy Cities Project: New developments and research needs". In: Davies, J. K., and Kelly, M. P. (Eds.), *Healthy Cities: Research and Practice* (pp. 25–33). New York: Routledge.

Tulchinsky, T. H., and Varavikova, E. A. (2014). "Preface". In: Tulchinsky, T. H., and Varavikova, E. A. (Eds.) *The New Public Health* (3rd edition) (pp. xxi–xxiii). San Diego, CA: Academic Press.

UN Habitat III. (2016). *A New Urban Agenda. Quito Declaration on Sustainable Cities and Human Settlements for All*. Quito: UN Habitat. Available at: http://habitat3.org/the-new-urban-agenda/.

United Nations [UN]. (2015). *Transforming Our World: The 2030 Agenda for Sustainable Development* [online]. Available at: https://sustainabledevelopment.un.org/post2015/transformingourworld/publication.

Vagerö, D. (2007). "Health inequalities across the globe demand new global politics". *Scandinavian Journal of Public Health*, Vol. 35, pp. 113–115.

Van der Horst, K., Kremers, S., Ferreira, I., Singh, A., Oenema, A., and Brug, J. (2007). "Perceived parenting styles and practices and the consumption of sugar-sweetened beverages by adolescents". *Health Education Research*, Vol. 22, Issue 2, pp. 295–304.

Van Kamp, I., Leidelmeijer, K., Marsman, G., and De Hollander, A. (2003). "Urban environmental quality and human well-being — Towards a conceptual framework and demarcation of concepts: A literature study". *Landscape and Urban Planning*, Vol. 65, Issues 1–2, pp. 5–18.

Ventura, A. K., and Birch, L. L. (2008). "Does parenting affect children's eating and weight status?" *International Journal of Behavioral Nutrition and Physical Activity*, Vol. 5, Art. No. 15.

Verstraeten, R., Roberfroid, D., Lachat, C., Leroy, J. L., Holdsworth, M., Maes, L., and Kolsteren P. W. (2012). "Effectiveness of preventive school-based obesity interventions in low- and middle-income countries: A systematic review". *American Journal of Clinical Nutrition*, Vol. 96, Issue 2, pp. 415–438.

Veugelers, P. J., and Fitzgerald, A. L. (2005). "Effectiveness of school programs in preventing childhood obesity: A multi-level comparison". *American Journal of Public Health*, Vol. 95, No. 3, pp. 432–435.

Vlahov, D., Freudenberg, N., Proietti, F., Ompad, D., Quinn, A., Nandi, V., and Galea, S. (2007). "Urban as a determinant of health". *Journal of Urban Health*, Vol. 84, Supp. 1, pp. i16–i26.

Waage, J., Yap, C., Bell, S., Levy, C., Mace, G., Pegram, T., Unterhalter, E., Dasandi, N., Hudson, D., Kock, R., Mayhew, S., Marx, C., and Poole, N. (2015). "Governing the UN Sustainable Development Goals: Interactions, infrastructures, and institutions". *Lancet Global Health*, Vol. 3, Issue 5, pp. e251–e252.

Wake, M. A., and McCallum, Z. (2004). "Secondary prevention of overweight in primary school children: What place for general practice?" *Medical Journal of Australia*, Vol. 181, Issue 2, p. 82–84.

Walker, O., Strong, M., Atchinson, R., Saunders, J., and Abbott, J. (2007). "A qualitative study of primary care clinicians' views of treating childhood obesity". *BMC Family Practice*, Vol. 8, Art. No. 50.

Wang, G., Walker, S. O., Hong, X., Bartell, T. R., and Wang, X. (2013). "Epigenetics and early life origins of chronic noncommunicable diseases". *Journal of Adolescent Health*, Vol. 52, Issue 2, Supp. 2, pp. S14–S21.

Warwick, I., Mooney, A., and Oliver, C. (2009). *National Healthy Schools Programme: Developing the Evidence Base*. London: Thomas Coram Research Unit, Institute of Education, University of London, UK.

Webster, P., and McCarthy, M. (1997). *Healthy Cities Indicators*. World Health Organisation.

Webster, P., and Sanderson, D. (2012). "Healthy cities indicators: A suitable instrument to measure health?" *Journal of Urban Health*, Vol. 90, Supp. 1, pp. S52–S61.

Welch, K. A. (2017). "Alcohol consumption and brain health". *BMJ*, Vol. 357, p. j2645.

Werna, E., and Harpham, T. (1996). "The implementation of the Healthy Cities Project in developing countries: Lessons from Chittagong". *Habitat International*, Vol. 20, Issue 2, pp. 221–228.

Whitelaw, S., Baxendale, A., Bryce, C., MacHardy, L., Young, I., and Witney, E. (2001). "Settings based health promotion: A review". *Health Promotion International*, Vol. 16, Issue 4, pp. 339–353.

WHOQOL Group. (1994) "The development of the World Health Organization Quality of Life Assessment Instrument (the WHOQOL)". In: Orley, J., and Kuyken, W. (Eds.) *Quality of Life Assessment: International Perspectives* (pp. 41–57) New York: Springer-Verlag.

Wilding, H., Gould, R., Taylor, J., Sabouraud, A., Saraux-Salaün, P., Papathanasopoulou, D., de Blasio, A., Nagy, Z., and Simos, J. (2017) "Healthy Cities in Europe: Structured, unique, and thoughtful". In: de Leeuw, E., and Simos, J. (Eds.), *Healthy Cities: The Theory, Policy, and Practice of Value-Based Urban Planning* (pp. 241–292). New York: Springer.

Winslow, C. E. A. (1920). "The untilled fields of public health". *Science*, Vol. 51, Issue 1306, pp. 23–33.

Wong, S. Y. S., Wong, W. C. W., Jaakkimainen, L., Bondy, S., Tsang, K. K., and Lee, A. (2005). "Primary care physicians in Hong Kong and Canada: How did their practices differ during the SARS epidemic?" *Family Practice*, Vol. 22, Issue 4, pp. 361–366.

Wong, M. C. S., Lee, A., Sun, J., Stewart, D., Cheng, F. F. K., Kan, W., and Ho, M. (2009). "A comparative study on resilience level between WHO health promoting schools and other schools among a Chinese population". *Health Promotion International*, Vol. 24, Issue 2, pp. 149–155.

World Bank. (2015). *The DATA Report 2015: Putting the Poorest First* [online]. Available at: www.one.org/international/policy/data-report-2015/.

World Health Organisation (WHO). (1986). *Ottawa Charter for Health Promotion.* Geneva: WHO.

World Health Organisation [WHO]. (1988). *Adelaide Recommendations on Healthy Public Policy.* Geneva: WHO. Available at: www.who.int/healthpromotion/conferences/previous/adelaide/en/.

World Health Organisation [WHO]. (1991). *Sundsvall Statement on Supportive Environments for Health.* Geneva: WHO. Available at: www.who.int/healthpromotion/conferences/previous/sundsvall/en/.

World Health Organisation [WHO]. (1995). *Global Strategies on Occupational Health for All: The Way to Health at Work.* Geneva: World Health Organisation.

World Health Organisation [WHO]. (1996). *Health-promoting Schools Series 5: Regional Guidelines. Development of Health-promoting Schools — A Framework for Action.* Manila: WHO Regional Office for the Western Pacific. Available at: https://apps.who.int/iris/handle/10665/206847.

World Health Organisation [WHO]. (1997a). *The Jakarta Declaration on Leading Health Promotion into the 21st Century*. Geneva: WHO. Available at: www.who.int/ healthpromotion/conferences/previous/jakarta/declaration/en/.

World Health Organisation [WHO]. (1997b). "Promoting health through schools. Report of a WHO expert committee on comprehensive school health education and promotion". *WHO Technical Report Series*, 47th Report, Report No. 870, pp. 1–93.

World Health Organisation [WHO]. (1997c). *WHO's Global Healthy Work Approach*. Division of Health Promotion, Education & Communication and Office of Occupational Health, Geneva.

World Health Organisation [WHO]. (1997d). *Twenty Steps for Developing a Healthy Cities Project* (3rd edition). Copenhagen: WHO Regional Office for Europe. Available at: https://apps.who.int/iris/handle/10665/107961.

World Health Organisation [WHO]. (1997e). *WHO Healthy Cities Project Phase III: 1998–2002 The Requirements and Designation Process for WHO Project Cities*. Cophengagen: WHO.

World Health Organisation [WHO]. (1998). *City Health Profiles: A Review of Progress*. Copenhagen: WHO Regional Office for Europe.

World Health Organisation [WHO]. (1999). "Programming for adolescent health and development: Report of a WHO/UNFPA/UNICEF Study Group on programming for adolescent health". *WHO Technical Report Series*, Report No. 886. Available at: https://apps.who.int/iris/handle/10665/42149.

World Health Organisation [WHO]. (2000). *Mexico Ministerial Statement for the Promotion of Health: From Ideas to Action*. Geneva: WHO. Available at: www.who.int/healthpromotion/milestones_ch5_20090916_en.pdf.

World Health Organisation [WHO]. (2002). *What is the Healthy Cities Approach?* Copenhagen: WHO Regional Office for Europe.

World Health Organisation [WHO]. (2003). *Phase IV (2003–2007) of the WHO Healthy Cities Network in Europe: Goals and Requirements* [online]. Available at: www.euro.who.int/__data/assets/pdf_file/0004/101110/E81924.pdf.

World Health Organisation [WHO]. (2005). *Bangkok Charter for Health Promotion in Globalised World*. Geneva: WHO. Available at: www.who.int/healthpromotion/ conferences/6gchp/bangkok_charter/en/.

World Health Organisation [WHO]. (2008). *World Health Statistics 2008*. Geneva: World Health Organisation.

World Health Organisation [WHO]. (2009a). *Nairobi Call To Action For Closing the Implementation Gap in Health Promotion*. Geneva: WHO. Available at: www.javeriana.edu.co/documents/245769/3050919/Nairobi_Call_for_Action.pdf/f4cd4466-5d14-4ec1-9344-456670b0dd89.

World Health Organisation [WHO]. (2009b). *Zagreb Declaration for Healthy Cities: Health and Health Equity in All Local Policies* [online]. Available at: www.euro.who.int/__data/assets/pdf_file/0015/101076/E92343.pdf.

World Health Organisation [WHO]. (2009c). *Phase V (2009–2013) of the WHO European Healthy Cities Network: Goals and Requirements*. Copenhagen: WHO Regional Office for Europe.

World Health Organisation [WHO]. (2009d). *City and Public Health Crises: A Report of International Consultation*, 29–30 October 2008. Lyon, France: WHO.

World Health Organisation [WHO]. (2009e). *Health Promoting School: A Framework for Action* [online]. Geneva: WHO.

World Health Organisation [WHO]. (2009f). *Pandemic Influenza Preparedness and Response: A WHO Guidance Document* [online]. Available at: https://apps.who.int/iris/handle/10665/44123.

World Health Organisation [WHO]. (2011). *Global Status Report on Non-communicable Disease 2010* [online]. Available at: www.who.int/nmh/publications/ncd_report2010/en/.

World Health Organisation [WHO]. (2013a). *Healthy Promotion, Healthy Settings*. Geneva: WHO. Available at: www.who.int/healthpromotion/healthy-settings/en/.

World Health Organisation [WHO]. (2013b). *Phase VI (2014–2018) of the WHO European Healthy Cities Network: Goals and Requirements* [online]. Available at: www.euro.who.int/__data/assets/pdf_file/0017/244403/Phase-VI-20142018-of-the-WHO-European-Healthy-Cities-Network-goals-and-requirements-Eng.pdf.

World Health Organisation [WHO]. (2016). *Shanghai Declaration on Promoting Health in the 2030 Agenda for Sustainable Development. (9th Global Conference on Health Promotion*. Geneva: WHO. Available at: www.who.int/healthpromotion/conferences/9gchp/shanghai-declaration/en/.

World Health Organisation [WHO]. (2017). "Shanghai consensus on healthy cities 2016". *Health Promotion International*, Vol. 32, Issue 4, pp. 603–605.

World Health Organisation [WHO]. (2018). *Healthier and Happy Cities for All: A Transformative Approach for Safe, Inclusive, sustainable and Resilient Societies.* Copenhagen: Copenhagen Consensus of Mayors, 13 February 2018.

World Health Organisation [WHO]/European Regional Office. (2018). *Belfast Charter for Healthy Cities: Operationalizing the Copenhagen Consensus of Mayors: Healthier and Happier Cities for All.* WHO European Healthy Cities Network International Healthy Cities Conference, Belfast, United Kingdom of Great Britain and Northern Ireland, 1–4 October 2018. Copenhagen: WHO Office for Europe Region. Available at: www.euro.who.int/__data/assets/pdf_file/0008/384614/belfast-charter-healthy-cities.pdf?ua=1.

World Health Organisation [WHO] Framework Convention on Tobacco Control [FCTC]. (2003). *WHO Framework Convention on Tobacco Control.* Geneva: World Health Organisation. Available at: www.who.int/fctc/text_download/en/.

World Health Organisation [WHO]/Western Pacific Region [WPRO]. (2011). *Healthy Urbanisation: Regional Framework for Scaling Up and Expanding Healthy Cities in the Western Pacific: 2011–2015.* Manila: WHO Regional Office for the Western Pacific. Available at: https://apps.who.int/iris/handle/10665/207613.

World Health Organisation [WHO] and UN-Habitat. (2016). *Global Report on Urban Health: Equitable Healthier Cities for Sustainable Development.* Geneva: WHO. Available at: https://apps.who.int/iris/handle/10665/204715.

Yamaguchi, A. (2014). "Effects of social capital on general health status". *Global Journal of Health Sciences*, Vol. 6, No. 3, pp. 45–54.

Yamin, A. E., and Lander, F. (2015). "Implementing a circle of accountability: A proposed framework for judiciaries and other actors in enforcing health-related rights". *Journal of Human Rights*, Vol. 14, Issue 3, pp. 312–331.

Yeh, A. G. O. (2011). *High-density Living in Hong Kong.* Cities, Health and Well-being: Hong Kong Urban Age Conference 16–17 November 2011. Organised by London School of Economics and The Alfred Herrhausen Society, in partnership with University of Hong Kong.

Yoo, W. S., Kim, K. Y., and Koh, K. W. (2007). "Introduction of health impact assessment and Healthy Cities as a tool for tackling health inequality". *Journal of Preventive Medicine Public Health*, Vol. 40, Issue 6, pp. 439–446.

Young, I. (2005). "Health promotion in schools: A historical perspective". *Promotion and Education*, Vol. 12, Issue 3–4, pp. 112–117.

Yung, T. K. C., Lee, A., Ho, M. M., Keung, V. M. W., and Lee, J. C. K. (2010). "Maternal influences on fruit and vegetable consumption of school children: Case study in Hong Kong". *Maternal and Child Nutrition*, Vol. 6, Issue 2, pp. 190–198.

Acknowledgements

I must first express my sincere thanks to my respectable mentors who have provided me guidance and support throughout my career. Rev Father Harold Naylor SJ (1931–2018) was my high school teacher, and he not only educated me on academic subjects but in life. He and many other dedicated Jesuit priests have nurtured a number of young people, many from grass roots communities with limited or no resources. A number of their students have gone on to become leaders in different professions, public services, and industries. I feel privileged to be one of these beneficiaries. Father Naylor was one of the co-founders of the Hong Kong Conservancy Association and his passion for safeguarding environmental resources enlightened me to consider health in a broader perspective. I was also fortunate to be supported by Professor Anthony Hedley (1941–2014), who played a role in my attachment to the Department of Community Medicine at the University of Hong Kong in the late 1980s and early 1990s when I was a practising general practitioner. Professor Hedley, together with other colleagues in the department, taught me the principles and concepts of public health, and helped me establish the foundation of public health knowledge I would put into practice later in my career. When I started my full time academic career, I had the opportunity to work under Professor Shiu-hung Lee (1932–2012). Professor Lee served as the Director of Health in the Hong Kong Government before his retirement and tenure at the Chinese University of Hong Kong in 1994. He established the first School of Public Health in Hong Kong and guided me during the development of the Healthy Cities and Health-promoting Schools programmes in Hong Kong. Without his continuous support and mentorship, the Healthy Settings Approach would have remained stagnant. I owe my deepest gratitude and thanks to my three mentors, and I wish they could have witnessed the publication of this book.

I also owe my thanks to all my colleagues, past and present, at the Centre for Health Education and Health Promotion (CHEHP) of the Chinese University of Hong Kong. They are my dearest comrades and have shown unfailing support throughout our journey in developing the Healthy Settings Approach. Without them, this book will not appear. I am also very thankful to the support of professionals and scholars in medicine and health, social services, education and public services to add values to the Healthy Settings Approach. I am delighted that many of these colleagues were my former students. I am also grateful to the other series editors and contributing authors for their help in making the dream of publishing this book come true. I must also thank the Thomas Bun-leung Lo Memorial Fund of the Hong Kong Health Education and Health Promotion Foundation for their support of the CHEHP during the preparation of this book. During publication, I also received expert editorial advice and assistance from the City University of Hong Kong Press, in particular, Mr Edmund Chan, Ms Chris Chan, and Dr Abby Leigh Manthey. Last, but certainly not least, I would like to express my deepest appreciation to those implementing the Healthy Settings Approach in Hong Kong and around the world. It is through such diligent efforts towards sustainable development that we will make our world a better place to live.

About the Series Editors and Contributors

Albert Lee, Series Editor-in-Chief

Professor Albert Lee is Clinical Professor of Public Health and Primary Care and Founding Director of the Centre for Health Education and Health Promotion (CHEHP) at The Chinese University of Hong Kong (CUHK). He is also Fellow and Associate Dean of General Education of Wu Yee Sun College, CUHK. He has served as Honorary/Adjunct/Visiting Professor in the following: Faculty of Education, University of Hong Kong; Department of Applied Health Science, Indiana University, USA; Centre for Population and Environmental Health, Griffiths University, Australia; Centre for Health Research, Brighton University, United Kingdom; and Department of Family Medicine, University Sains Malaysia. He is the key founding member of the Alliance for Healthy Cities (AFHC) and is a founding member of the AFHC Steering Committee (2003–2010 and 2014–present). He is currently the President of The Hong Kong Health Education and Health Promotion Foundation. His contributions in health development are recognised by his appointment as a World Health Organisation advisor, election as Honorary Fellow of the United Kingdom Faculty of Public Health (the highest accolade of the Faculty), membership in the United States National Academy of Medicine, Chief Executive Commendation for Community Services in the 2004 Honours list of the Hong Kong Government, and Award for Pioneer in Healthy Cities for Research by the AFHC in 2014.

Robin M. B. Cheung, Series Editor

Robin Cheung is an Adjunct Associate Professor at the Centre for Health Education and Health Promotion (CHEHP) and Honorary Professional Consultant to the Department of Educational Administration and Policy, School of Education, Chinese University of Hong Kong (CUHK). He is a retired principal of Tsung Tsin College, an award-winning Health-promoting School. Robin is also a former Master's Course Instructor in the Department of Education Policy and Leadership, Education University of Hong Kong.

Vera M. W. Keung, Series Editor

Vera Keung is a Health Promotion Officer at the Centre for Health Education and Health Promotion (CHEHP), Chinese University of Hong Kong (CUHK). She received her Bachelor's Degree in Food and Nutritional Sciences at CUHK in 1999. She then pursued further postgraduate study with a Master of Philosophy from the same school in 2004, supervised by Professor Albert Lee. Over the past 20 years, Vera has been working closely with professionals affiliated with the CHEHP and has been involved in various Health-promoting School projects, including the Hong Kong Healthy Schools Award Scheme since 2001 and the Healthy Schools (Pre-school) Award Scheme since 2005. She has taken the coordinating role and promotes health education and health promotion actions in local schools by providing professional support, training and written guidelines, and teaching materials to school teachers. She has also been involved in numerous surveys and research initiated by the CHEHP on children and adolescents' health behaviours and evaluation of Health-promoting Schools. Since 2019, Vera has taken the leading role in a healthy life planning project and has been working closely with a group of secondary school teachers to map out strategies and develop quality health education programmes to promote a healthy lifestyle in adolescents and to sustain the positive effects of the Health-promoting School model leading to further implementation in the city.

Amy C. M. Kwong, Series Editor

Amy Kwong is a registered physiotherapist and worked at the Centre for Health Education and Health Promotion (CHEHP) at the Chinese University of Hong Kong (CUHK) from December 2006 until August 2019. She joined the newly established Kwai Tsing District Health Centre, the first government-funded District

Health Centre that was part of the primary health care initiatives outlined in the Hong Kong Chief Executive's Policy Speech in 2017, where she is in charge of the Rehabilitation Team. She is still affiliated with the CHEHP on an honorary basis. Amy received her Bachelor's Degree in Physiotherapy at The Hong Kong Polytechnic University in 2001 and Master's Degree in Exercise Science at CUHK in 2010. Prior to joining the CHEHP, she worked as a physiotherapist, serving patients in both public hospitals and private clinics. Realising the importance of health promotion in disease prevention, she has a strong interest in and passion for health education and health promotion through the Healthy Settings Approach. Using her substantial experience in school health promotion, especially physical activity promotion, Amy has worked with schools to organise health promotion services and training for teachers and student leaders. Beyond the school setting, she has also been invited to give health talks to non-governmental organisations and private companies with different target audiences, including office workers, parents, and the elderly. She is currently working on a project to develop an online health education video resource platform for promoting positive values and better health of children and youth.

Amelia S. C. Lo, Series Editor

Amelia Lo is Health Promotion Officer in charge of the Centre for Health Education and Health Promotion (CHEHP) at the Chinese University of Hong Kong (CUHK). She has been involved in the Health-promoting School (HPS) Movement for over two decades and worked closely with professionals affiliated with the CHEHP to develop the HPS Performance Indicator and International Benchmarking System. She expanded her responsibilities to oversee HPS evaluation starting in 2009. She has extensive experience in advising schools to successfully build a healthy and safe school environment and has been involved in conducting HPS capacity building workshops for educators and health professionals. Recently, Amelia has taken the leading role in the GoSmart.Net Project, working with the team to produce credible health video clips and resources to cultivate positive values and healthy behaviours among students and to enhance teachers' competence in health education. She also leads a Healthy Kids Programme to promote a healthy lifestyle among primary school students through the engagement and empowerment of parents and teachers. Her research interests are HPSs, emotional well-being, and child and adolescent health. Amelia obtained her Bachelor's Degree in Human Biology at University of Toronto, Canada; Master's Degree in

Health and Hospital Management at Birmingham University, United Kingdom; Diploma in Epidemiology and Applied Statistics, and Professional Diploma in Health Promotion and Education at CUHK. She is currently pursuing her Doctoral Degree in Health Science at Hong Kong Polytechnic University. Amelia has been the Vice President of the Hong Kong Health Education and Health Promotion Foundation since 2017.

Other contributors to this volume

Christine Campbell

Dr. Christine Campbell is a reader in Cancer and Primary Care at the Usher Institute, University of Edinburgh, United Kingdom. She leads a programme of research into socio-demographic and ethnic disparities in cancer outcomes, the role of primary care in screening provisions and symptomatic diagnosis, policy initiatives in promoting early cancer diagnosis, and implementation of "screen and treat" cervical screening in Malawi. She supervises undergraduate and postgraduate students at the University of Edinburgh. Current doctoral projects in her team address the burden of multi-morbidity in low- and middle-income countries as well as evaluation of cervical cancer screening approaches in low-resource settings. She was involved in the United Kingdom's Primary Care Clinical Studies Group from 2005–2017, including serving as Chair of the Screening subgroup for three years. She sits on the Advisory Panel of the Scottish Cancer Prevention Network, as well as on the Executive Group of the Cancer and Primary Care Research International Network (Ca-PRI) and the Executive Group of the International Cancer Screening Network (ICSN). She is also a member of the Scottish Parliament Cross Party Group on Cancer.

Ceci H. Y. Chan

Ceci Chan is a public health practitioner and has been engaged in the primary healthcare sector since 2015. She was involved in several research-based community health education and promotion projects, school health promotion projects, and non-communicable disease prevention for the general public at the Centre for Health Education and Health Promotion (CHEHP), Chinese University of Hong Kong (CUHK) after completing her Bachelor of Science in Community Health

Practice. She obtained her Master's Degree in Public Health, with a concentration in Health Systems Policy and Management, during which she investigated users' perceived self-efficacy towards a community initiative programme. She joined the first government-funded District Health Centre in 2019 to facilitate the public to learn and adopt new health-seeking behaviours. Her interests span all interdisciplinary areas of primary healthcare, with a particular interest in self-management of health and the roles and functions of the healthcare system.

Calvin K. M. Cheung

Calvin Cheung is a Health Promotion Officer and registered dietitian at the Centre for Health Education and Health Promotion (CHEHP), Chinese University of Hong Kong (CUHK). He is also an accredited practicing dietitian in Australia and a full member of the Dietitians Association of Australia as well as the Hong Kong Nutrition Association. Calvin is currently the project leader in charge of organising and implementing a nutritional growth cohort study called the Studying Impact of Nutrition on Growth (SING) Project, which investigates the impact of nutrition on growth in early childhood. With a passion for promoting health, Calvin has also been invited to give nutritional talks and workshops in different settings, including schools, non-governmental organisations, private companies, and governmental department, and to different audiences, including students, full-time workers, parents, and the elderly. Calvin is a graduate of CUHK and majored in Food and Nutritional Science. He also holds a Master's Degree in Nutrition and Dietetics from The University of Sydney. He furthered his studies and recently received his Diploma in Practical Chinese Medicine (Chinese Medicine Nutritional Studies) from HKU Space.

Yick-hay Chow

Mr Chow Yick-hay is the Chairman of Kwai Tsing Safe Community and Health City Association. He is also a member of the North Lantau Hospital Governing Committee and a member of the Municipal Services Appeals Board. Mr Chow served as a Member of the Regional Council (1989–1999) and has served as the Council's Vice Chairman. He also served as member of the Kwai Tsing District Council (1988–2019), acting as its Chairman from 2000 to 2007 and Vice Chairman from 2016 to 2019.

Queenie H. Y. Li

Queenie Li was a research assistant at the Centre for Health Education and Health Promotion (CHEHP), Chinese University of Hong Kong (CUHK) from 2014 to 2019. Queenie received her secondary and tertiary education in the United Kingdom. She is interested in nutrition, especially that of toddlers and children. She is enthusiastic about promoting nutrition to the public. She enjoys taking part in nutritional discussions with and for primary school students and believes it is important to educate children about health at a young age. She was one of the key team members working on the Studying Impact of Nutrition on Growth (SING) Project, a nutrition cohort study.

Hedy H. Y. Tse

Hedy Tse was a research assistant at the Centre for Health Education and Health Promotion (CHEHP), Chinese University of Hong Kong (CUHK), from 2017 to 2020. Hedy obtained her Bachelor's Degree at CUHK in 2017. She strives to improve the health of teenagers through the use of innovative ideas and multimedia channels and is currently a team member of the GoSmart.Net Project, which is involved in the development of online video platforms to promote health among teenagers. She is also passionate about promoting health in developing countries and spent her university life in Mainland China working with various healthcare professionals. She would like to strengthen hers skills in the health promotion field and enhance her efforts in promoting healthy living in different ethnicities.

David Weller

Professor David Weller is the James Mackenzie Professor of General Practice and Programme Co-Director (Master of Family Medicine) at the Usher Institute, University of Edinburgh, United Kingdom. He graduated from the University of Adelaide in 1982 and undertook PhD studies in Adelaide and Nottingham. After serving in academic posts in Australia, he moved to the United Kingdom in 2000 to take up a position at the University of Edinburgh. He has been involved in cancer research in both Australia and the United Kingdom and led the evaluation of the UK Pilot of Colorectal Cancer Screening. His group in Edinburgh run a research programme investigating the roles of primary care in all aspects of cancer control. David sits on various national and international research and government committees on cancer and works as a General Practitioner in central Edinburgh.

Tony K. C. Yung

Dr. Tony Yung is a lecturer at the Jockey Club School of Public Health and Primary Care, Chinese University of Hong Kong (CUHK). He is responsible for teaching and research related to the nutritional aspect of public health. He obtained his Doctor of Philosophy from the same school, with a thesis topic on food avoidance behaviour amongst cancer patients. He attained his Master's Degree in Nutrition and Dietetics from the University of Sydney and registered as an accredited practicing dietitian in Australia. He is also a sports dietitian and accredited nutritionist.

Index

primary healthcare xix, xx, xxi, xxiii, xxiv, xxv, xxvi, xxvii, 32, 34, 47, 53, 76, 132, 133–134, 135, 140, 142, 143, 144, 145, 146, 147, 160–161, 169, 172, 175; see also health-promoting healthcare organisations; see also health-promoting hospitals

Princess Margaret Hospital (PMH) 134, 135–136, 138, 140–141, 143

public health xix–xx, xxvi, xxvii, xxxi, xxxiii, 4–5, 7, 11, 13, 18, 20, 25–26, 27, 29, 30, 33, 38, 39–40, 42, 46, 59, 64, 65, 66, 77, 78, 82, 104, 114, 123, 132, 145, 148, 157–158, 160, 161, 170, 171, 176, 180

Q

Quality Education Fund 94, 95

quality of life xxxiv, 14, 21, 33, 41, 47, 59, 67–68, 71–76, 77, 78, 79, 89, 108, 117, 128, 135

R

randomised controlled trial (RCT) 17–18, 87–88, 111

right to health see human rights

S

Sai Kung District, Hong Kong 33, 59–60, 61

SARS 94, 95, 109, 133, 143–144; see also infection/infectious diseases

school(s), general xx, xxiii, xxvi, xxvii, xxxiv, 2, 3, 19, 47, 53, 55, 60, 61, 64, 131, 139, 140, 147, 148, 150, 163, 179, 180, 181

connectedness see social connectedness

health and health initiatives/services 83, 84–86, 87–88, 89, 90, 97, 100, 107, 109, 111, 113, 114, 116, 117, 148, 149; see also Comprehensive School Health Programme; see also health-promoting schools; see also school(s): role in preventing obesity in children

health profile, screening 39, 88, 90–91, 94, 96

principals, school heads 61, 90, 110, 115, 150, 152, 168

role in preventing obesity in children 148, 151, 152–154, 156, 159–160, 161, 167–168, 169; see also obesity

role in tobacco control 172

student(s) 2, 19, 61, 68, 73, 74, 81–97, 99–117, 139, 149, 157, 168, 75; see also adolescent; see also child, children; see also parents

teacher(s) 36, 61, 83, 88, 90, 97, 102, 106, 109, 110, 115, 116, 149, 151, 154; see also teaching

see also education

see also evaluation: of schools

see also health-promoting schools

see also Hong Kong Healthy School Award

see also learning

see also training

Scotland study xxxiii, 147–161; see also Edinburgh, Scotland

sedentary 67, 106, 123, 159, 160, 166, 180; see also lifestyle(s)